The Campus History Series

Penn State Abington and the Ogontz School

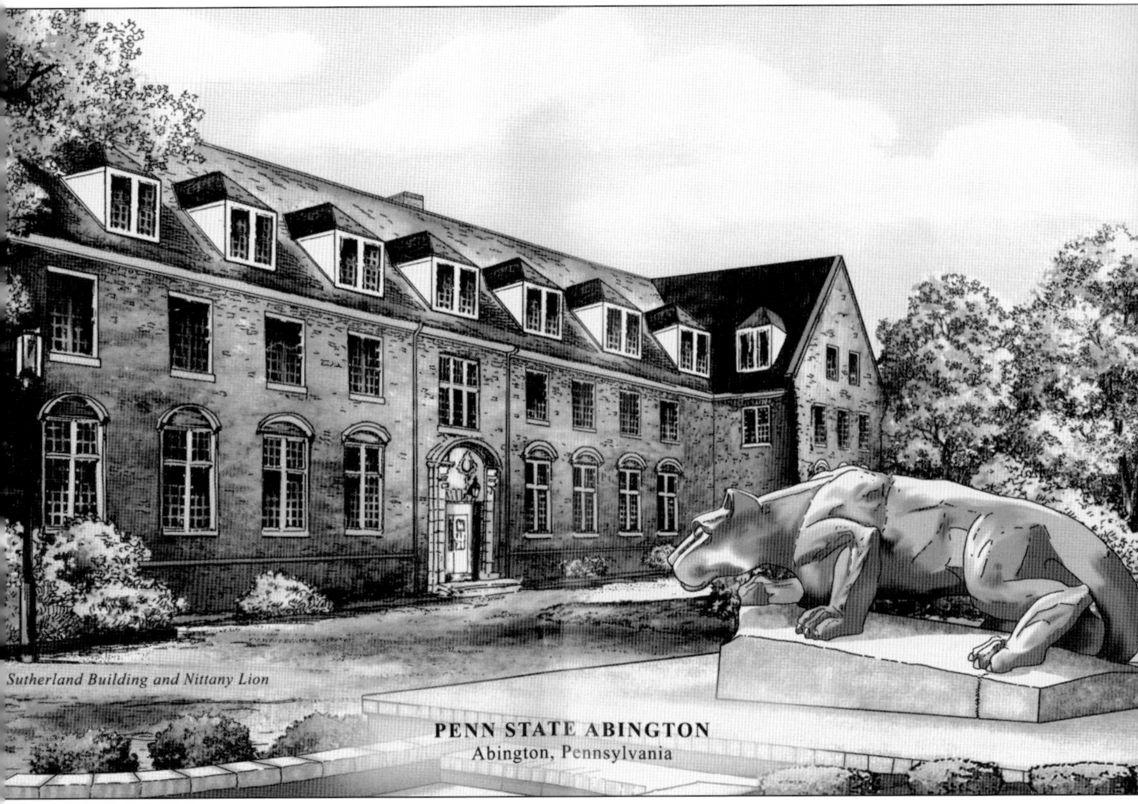

This undated sketch shows the Penn State Abington Nittany Lion, a replica of the original Nittany Lion at University Park, overlooking the main entrance to Sutherland, the main building on campus and the first to be erected (in 1916–1917) at the college's present location. (The Ogontz School Archives, date unknown, Penn State University, Abington College Library.)

On the Front Cover: Taken in the 1950s at the main entrance to the iconic Sutherland Building, this image is proof positive that the boys have arrived. No longer the Ogontz School for Young Ladies, the newly christened Penn State Ogontz Campus became, in 1950, a coeducational two-year college. The beloved bust of Chief Ogontz appears in the archway above the door. (The Old York Road Historical Society.)

Cover Background: Principal Frances E. Bennett (center, in dark dress) teaches her history class in the upper study parlor at the Ogontz School in Elkins Park. (The Ogontz School Archives, date unknown, Penn State University, Abington College Library.)

The Campus History Series

Penn State Abington and the Ogontz School

Frank D. Quattrone

Foreword by Dr. Karen Wiley Sandler, Chancellor Emerita

ARCADIA PUBLISHING

ISBN 978-1-4671-1742-5

Published by Arcadia Publishing
Charleston, South Carolina

Printed in the United States of America

Library of Congress Control Number: 2016936298

For all general information, please contact Arcadia Publishing:
Telephone 843-853-2070
Fax 843-853-0044
E-mail sales@arcadiapublishing.com
For customer service and orders:
Toll-Free 1-888-313-2665

Visit us on the Internet at www.arcadiapublishing.com

To my wonderful family and friends for their unfailing love and support and to the fine students, faculty, and staff at Penn State Abington, who make me proud to be counted among them

Contents

FOREWORD

An exclusive finishing school for young ladies whose families hope they "marry well," and a diverse, inclusive small college within a major research university; what could these two institutions possibly have in common?

A great deal, it turns out.

Education, when done right, is full of surprises, discoveries, and unforeseen twists in a road that first appears deceptively straight. The Ogontz School for Young Ladies and Penn State Abington (née Penn State Ogontz) shared an ambitious openness to doing education right.

Abby Sutherland, owner and headmistress of the Ogontz School from 1912 to 1950, continued the military drill introduced by her predecessor into the curriculum. Military drill? Much later, graduates often described how much they had hated the drills. However, they came to appreciate how transformative those drills had been for their confidence, their character, and their poise.

Penn State's campus system also pioneered a new educational concept. Providing Penn State's curriculum with consistency and high standards in every corner of the state redefined the university's land grant mission. Penn State Ogontz, later Abington, has a history of welcoming those students who sought educational choice, preferred an intimate college environment and chose an urban lifestyle, or those who were late bloomers whose blooms were frequently spectacular. Penn State Abington is a place that nurtures such students, trains them rigorously, and moves them into the "real world," fully prepared to embrace the surprises that come from education done right.

In 1950, when Abby Sutherland gave the Ogontz School to Penn State, she offered a challenge to those who would succeed her: "Guard here the spirit of the best in your dreams of education." Education (or lack of it) has been used progressively and repressively over our nation's history. When deployed in the spirit of progress, education done well has produced and will continue to produce people who shape the future of our society beneficially. This book is dedicated to all who have participated in the grand venture of providing "the best" in our "dreams of education." May that venture flourish in the next 100 years of education at Penn State Abington!

—Dr. Karen Wiley Sandler
Chancellor Emerita

ACKNOWLEDGMENTS

This amazing journey through 165 years of the college's history began when Chuck Marsh, director of university relations, enthusiastically greenlighted the project. He has encouraged me at every milepost, along with my departmental colleagues Judy Reale, Rachael Ortwein, Maria Narodetsky, Jim Hopf, and Regina Broscius (who provided valuable proofreading) and Lydia Kokolskyj, Jill Mensch, and Elizabeth Janczіewski in Alumni and Development.

I thank Jim Mooney, Andrew Windle, and Chai Lo in Computer Network Services and librarians Linda Kinter and Christina Riehman-Murphy for help with the scanning process. Special thanks to head librarian Dolores Fidishun, staff assistant Hudson Saffell, and especially to archivist Lillian Hansberry, who never tired of my countless questions as she guided me through our archives.

I also appreciate the insights provided by faculty colleagues Dr. Leonard Mustazza, Dr. Ellen Knodt, Dr. Judith Newman, Dr. Ross Brinkert, and Dr. Thomas R. Smith, who generously consented to read the manuscript and provided exceptional assistance with the final draft.

For permission to use images not available in our archives, I thank Valerie Gillispie at Duke University, Jennifer Kallend and Barbara Benedett at Curtis Institute of Music, and Elizabeth Odle at the Nashville Public Library.

Always ready to help at the Old York Road Historical Society were Pres. David B. Rowland and staffers Betty Smith, Leslie, Mary, and Jack. Help was also given by Heidi Abbey of Penn State Harrisburg, photographer Dan Johnson, former Penn State Abington writer-in-residence Rachel Simon, and historian supreme Terrie Smith.

My editors at Arcadia Publishing—Erin Vosgien at the outset and Caitrin Cunningham through the challenging final weeks—provided much needed support and guidance.

Special thanks to former students and good friends Joe Darrah and Mike Berman, now editors in their own right, for their patient research and brainstorming as we pored through the hundreds of documents and photographs needed for a successful pictorial history.

I owe much to chancellor emerita Dr. Karen Wiley Sandler for her graciousness, patience, support, and friendship through this arduous process.

But most of all, my heart goes out to my dear wife and best friend Eve for putting up with my mercurial moods through deadlines, always buoying me up with her warm smile, sincere pride, unflagging support, and love.

INTRODUCTION

Penn State Abington and the Ogontz School will trace the circuitous journey that led from the Chestnut Street Female Seminary, a private girls' school in Philadelphia established in 1850, to Penn State Abington, one of the most diverse and highly regarded of the 19 Penn State University campuses.

Along the way, the book will show the influence of celebrated Civil War financier Jay Cooke, whose elegant five-story Elkins Park mansion, called Ogontz, became the new home of the successful finishing school, then known as the Ogontz School for Young Ladies.

Over the course of 100 years, the school was directed brilliantly by just five principals, whose tenures sometimes overlapped. They were Mary Bonney, Harriet Dillaye, Frances Bennett, Sylvia Eastman, and Eastman's protégée, Abby A. Sutherland. It was Sutherland's strong leadership and vision that led to the school's purchasing a handsome tract of land in Rydal, in the rolling hills of Abington Township, in 1916. She built a new campus there that includes the iconic Sutherland Building. Resembling an English manor house, it was designed, like several other campus buildings, by the inspired African American architect Julian Abele, the senior designer for the world-famous Philadelphia architectural firm of Horace Trumbauer.

Sutherland changed the nature of the Ogontz School in Rydal from that of a traditional finishing school, albeit regarded as one of the nation's best, to that of a school more closely resembling an academic institution, offering courses at the elementary, high school, and junior college levels. All the while, from the days of Sylvia Eastman's proprietorship to the closing of the Ogontz School in 1950, the controversial, daring, and ultimately successful military drill drew the attention of national publications like the *Ladies' Home Journal* as well as world leaders and prospective students across the globe.

During her more than 40 years as an instructor and principal of the Ogontz School, Abby Sutherland influenced the lives of countless young ladies, preparing them for the challenges of the world. But by 1950, it was clear that the demand for teaching social graces to women had diminished significantly, so Sutherland held a huge celebration at the end of the spring semester and formally donated the school to the Pennsylvania State College (which later became Penn State University).

Among the celebrated students who applied themselves to the school's demanding standards was Amelia Earhart, who attended the Ogontz School for three semesters in 1916 and 1917 before disappearing into the wild blue yonder and history. The book will visit other noteworthy students and graduates, including Mary Curtis, founder and longtime director of the Curtis Institute of Music; Cornelia Fort, the aviatrix who was the first person to witness the Japanese sneak attack on Pearl Harbor; well-known figures in the literary and performing arts such as Queena Mario, Molly Costain, and Rod Nordland; and noted entrepreneurs such as meteorologist Dr. Joel Myers, who founded AccuWeather while still a graduate student at Penn State University.

The children of affluent and acclaimed national figures attended the Ogontz School, including the daughters and granddaughters of Jay Cooke; Carolyn Grosvenor, the granddaughter of Alexander Graham Bell; Molly Costain, the daughter of best-selling novelist Thomas B. Costain; and Mary Curtis (mentioned previously), the only child of Philadelphia publishing magnate Cyrus H.K. Curtis.

Some well-known teachers also spent productive years at the Ogontz School and Penn State Ogontz, including Oliver Freud, Dr. Sigmund Freud's son, who taught algebra part-time in the late 1950s; Martha Graham, who taught dance at Ogontz for a time; Mrs. Edgar Lee Masters, wife of the famous American poet Edgar Lee Masters (best known for *Spoon River Anthology*). She taught composition at Ogontz Junior College and later became dean of women at Penn State Ogontz. She never revealed her own first name. And there was student Nancy McFeely, valedictorian of the class of 1923, who brought a son into the world named Fred Rogers, star of *Mister Rogers' Neighborhood* on public television for nearly 40 years. Mrs. Edgar Allan Poe—ironically, of no relation to the famous American author; she was Marie Hoopes as a student and president of the class of 1902—became a leader in various Philadelphia and Baltimore charities.

In its new incarnation as Penn State Ogontz from 1950 through the end of the 20th century, the school grew rapidly, offering programs in a variety of disciplines, including business, science, and the liberal arts. In 1997, Penn State Abington became a full-fledged baccalaureate institution, not just a two-year college offering students a great education before they transferred to University Park or another college. The quiet, steady leadership of chancellor Dr. Karen Wiley Sandler, who retired at the end of the 2015–2016 academic year, attracted diverse students from across the commonwealth and 16 states, as well as 29 countries around the world. The college's global studies program offers study abroad opportunities in England, Norway, Italy, Spain, Japan, China, Israel, Central America, and other countries and regions and welcomes students from Germany, England, Japan, and other nations to special academic programs at the college.

When Penn State Ogontz opened in 1950, the 225 students began with a modest number of academic programs in addition to cooperative merchandising and executive secretarial courses. At the time, 100 girls boarded at Sutherland Hall, and 25 boys lived in Rydal Hall. By the early 1960s, the dormitory spaces had vanished with the burgeoning enrollment, and the college had become a commuter campus. Today, with an enrollment nearing 4,000, students can begin and complete their degrees in 18 majors at the campus and start more than 160 majors at Penn State Abington before they complete them at University Park. Dr. Sandler has also presided over the college's upgraded athletic status and its bold plan to erect its first stand-alone dormitory by 2017.

Student life—from elaborate theatrical productions and exotic May Day celebrations to sophisticated art exhibitions in the 2010s, and from swimming and baseball at the end of the 19th century to athletics today—will also be featured. Because of its emphasis on programs championing diversity, Penn State Abington is also the first college in the country to be recognized by the Anti-Defamation League in its No Place for Hate movement. On January 13, 2016, the Pittsburgh-based *Business Insider* reported that the review website Niche.com ranked Penn State Abington the 23rd safest college in the country.

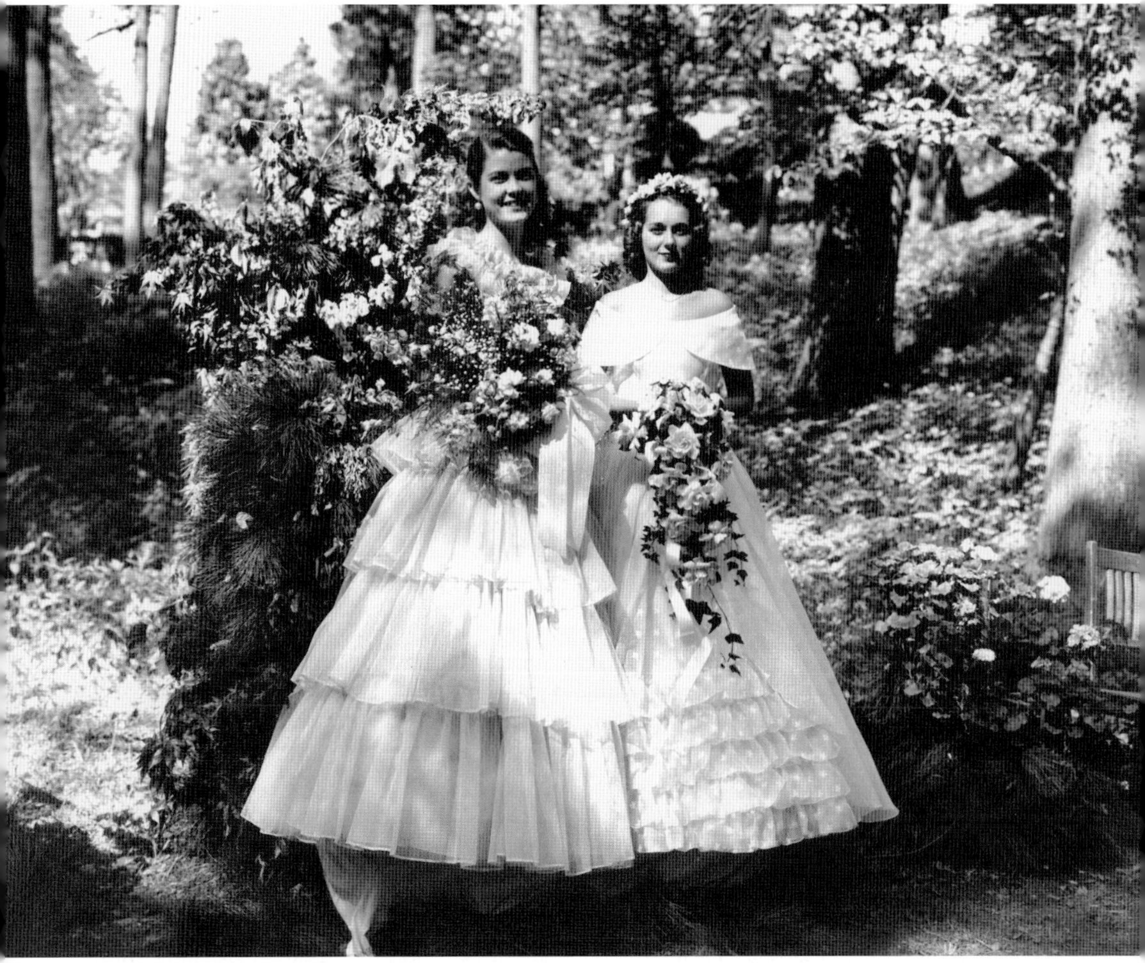

After a mostly unseasonable month, "The sunshine was dazzling and the air like wine," gushed the *Ogontz Mosaic* writer (in the July 1948 issue) as she described the backdrop to the Ogontz School's annual May Day celebration. The May Queen was Sally Heinz (left), accompanied by Maid of Honor Sally Capper. (The Ogontz School Archives, 1948, Penn State University, Abington College Library.)

One

For Ladies Only

By the end of the 19th century, the Ogontz School for Young Ladies had gained renown as one of the top finishing schools in the country. Starting out as the Chestnut Street Female Seminary in 1850, its primary object, according to its first printed catalogue, was "to elicit and strengthen the intellectual powers, refine the taste, and cultivate the heart" of its privileged student body. One of Principal Harriet Dillaye's innovations that assured the school's ability to hire exceptionally fine teachers and staff was a profit-sharing plan for all resident teachers and employees.

The small school at 1615 Chestnut Street in Philadelphia offered a "thorough scientific and literary education" focused on literature, history, foreign languages, and mathematics, as well as music, painting, penciling, and crayon. Tuition was $300 per year, not including "meals carried to pupils in their room," and there were extra fees for laundry, oil painting, and the use of musical instruments. The school could accommodate no more than 20 students. And, like its successor, the Ogontz School, only those students who were recommended by the wealthy and influential could send their daughters there to study.

When the Chestnut Street school outgrew its limited quarters, the move in 1883 to Ogontz, the former estate of Civil War financier Jay Cooke, was more than welcome. The school could now take on as many as 100 students, and the extensive grounds of the Cooke estate afforded the girls plenty of space for walks, wandering, and engaging in the military drill mandated by Sylvia Eastman in the mid-1880s. The drills, intended to instill in the students "an eagerness for athletics," became a distinguishing feature of the school until it closed in 1950.

In the wake of the Industrial Revolution and the rise of a more affluent middle class in the last quarter of the 19th century, the school's usual clientele began to be challenged. Abby Sutherland wrote, "The problem of keeping the group up to the first families grew somewhat difficult as bankers, business men, clergy and teachers in high schools all over the country sought the privilege of putting their friends or acquaintances into the fashionable group."

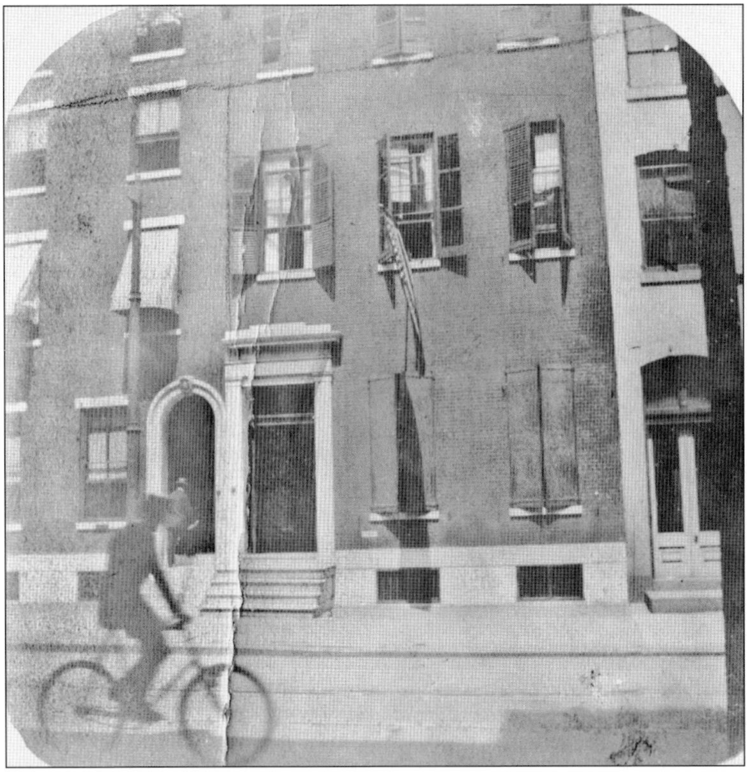

This is the only known photograph of the Chestnut Street Female Seminary, founded in 1850 and located at 1615 Chestnut Street in Philadelphia. An alumna described the building as "a stately commodious four-story brick dwelling with green slat shutters, white marble trimming and broad marble steps in the middle of a row of fine City residences." (The Ogontz School Archives, c. 1850, Penn State University, Abington College Library.)

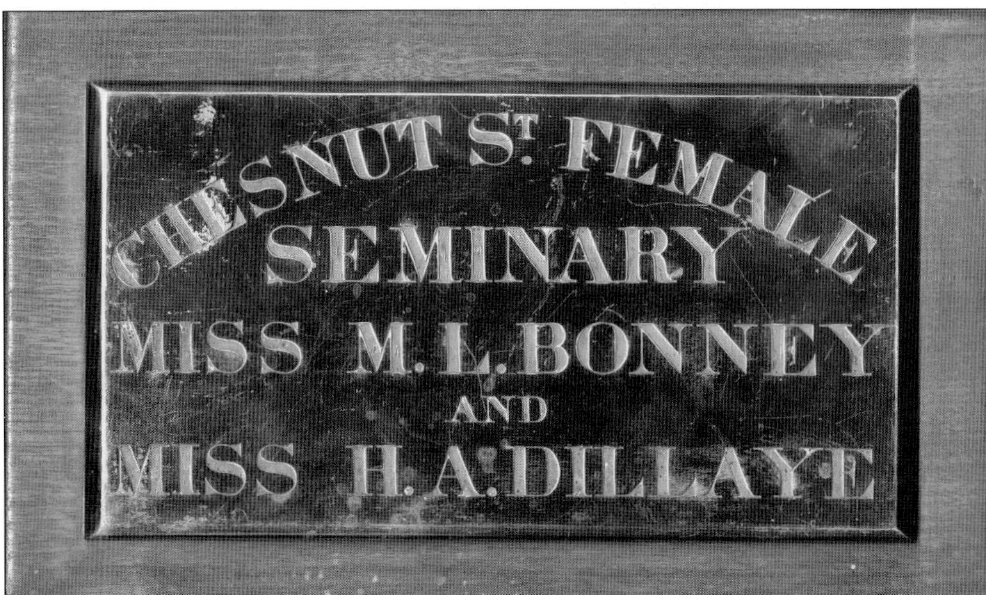

Long before spell-check made it easier to catch errors before they appear in print, this original door plate, salvaged from the Chestnut Street Female Seminary, made it clear that the new students had indeed arrived at their education destination. The sign includes the names of founders Miss M[ary]. L. Bonney and Miss H[arriet]. A. Dillaye. (The Ogontz School Archives, c. 1850, Penn State University, Abington College Library.)

The educators who cofounded the Chestnut Street Female Seminary could not have been more different from each other, yet these graduates of the acclaimed Troy (New York) Female Seminary shared a vision that shaped the school for decades to come. Mary L. Bonney (right), principal from 1850 to 1883, was known for her "quick sympathy, strong will and kind heart," according to [Principal] Abby A. Sutherland. She also fought for the protection of Native American lands and rights. She cofounded the National Indian Association in 1879 and represented the group as its president at the White House in 1880. Her dear friend Harriet Dillaye (below), principal from 1850 to 1890, was an elegant gentlewoman and a Philadelphia Quaker whose customs informed the Ogontz experience. Her annual admonition to her beloved charges was, "Young ladies, aim at the moon and you will hit the church steeple, but if you aim at the church steeple, you will hit the ground." (Right, the Ogontz School Archives, date unknown, Penn State University, Abington College Library; below, the Ogontz School Archives, 1853, Penn State University, Abington College Library.)

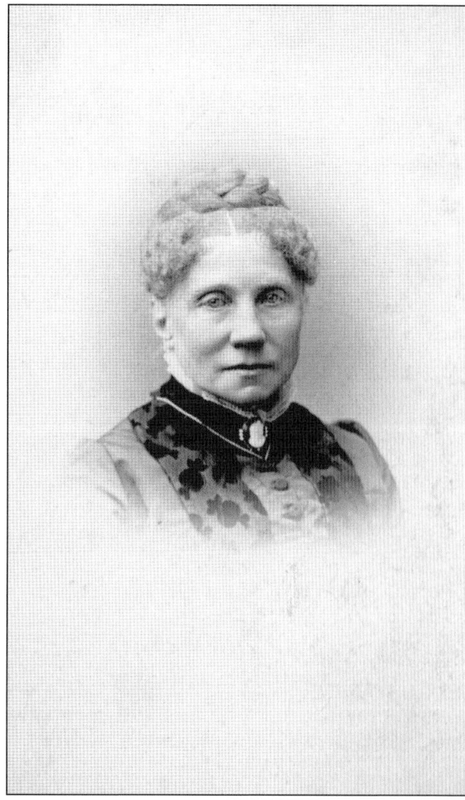

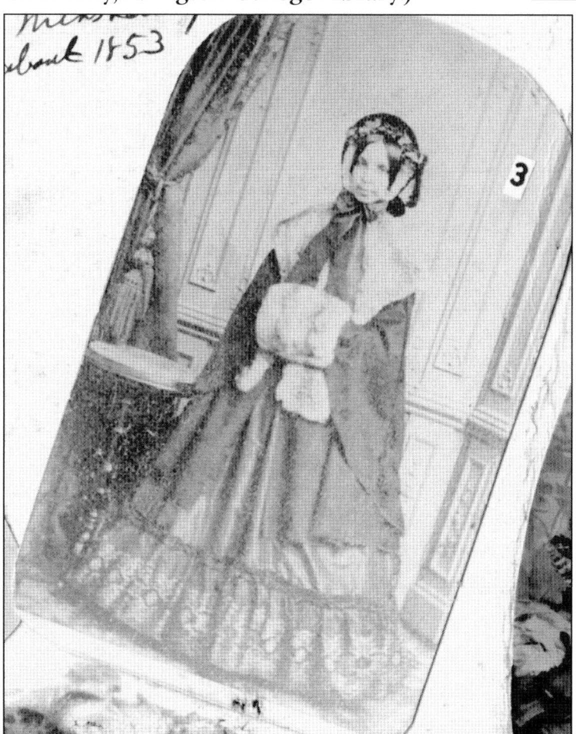

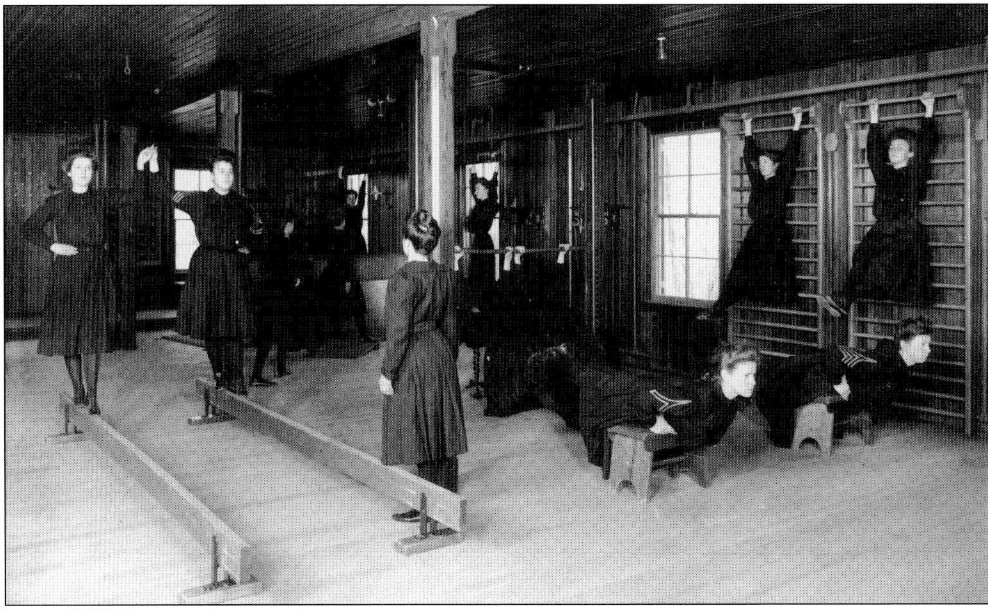

A forerunner of the military drill, calisthenics was an essential component of a day's duties at both the Chestnut Street Female Seminary and the Ogontz School for Young Ladies. Here, the girls can be seen working out in the new gymnasium erected on the Cooke property sometime after 1883. (The Ogontz School Archives, 1910, Penn State University, Abington College Library.)

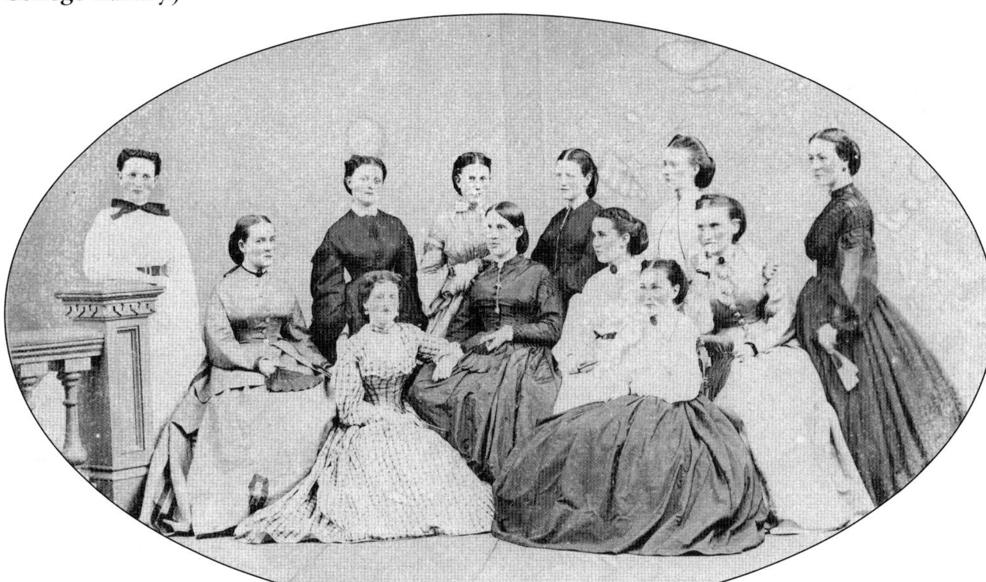

Taken in 1866 and identified as the "First Graduating Class," this image depicts a dozen very serious young ladies. Presumably teenagers no older than 18 or 19, they were the scions of families of influence and wealth. In the early years of the school, classes were listed as junior, middle, and senior. One year higher than senior, "Graduating Class" was added sometime after 1860. (The Ogontz School Archives, 1866, Penn State University, Abington College Library.)

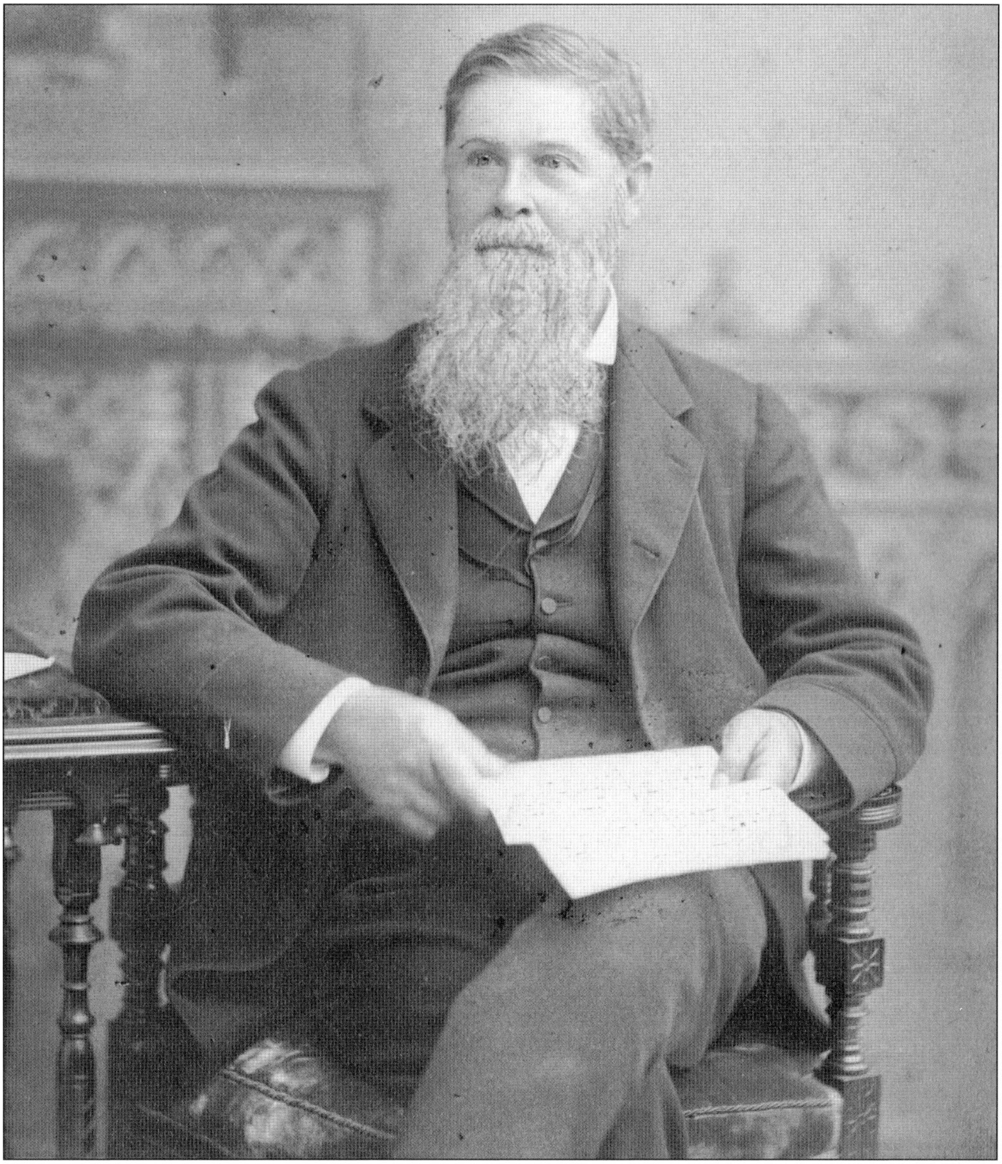

Jay Cooke (1821–1905) was an esteemed Philadelphia banker and patriot whose astute bond issues kept the Union afloat during the Civil War. At the age of 19, he wrote a financial article for the local papers, one of the first of its kind. Hired by R.W. Clark & Company, a prominent bank that was said to control the nation's purse strings, he became the senior member at the age of 40. According to Abby Sutherland, in her book *100 Years of Ogontz*, Cooke responded to an appeal by the government and personally arranged a $50 million loan. Then he procured through other banks an unprecedented $2.5 billion for the war effort. On the eve of General Lee's surrender at Appomattox, Gen. U.S. Grant said of Cooke, "Tell him that it is to his labors more than those of any other man that the people of this country owe the continued life of the nation." Although Cooke suffered severe losses during the Panic of 1873, his stock in the Northern Pacific Railroad, which opened up the West, ultimately proved both lucrative and successful. (The Ogontz School Archives, date unknown, Penn State University, Abington College Library.)

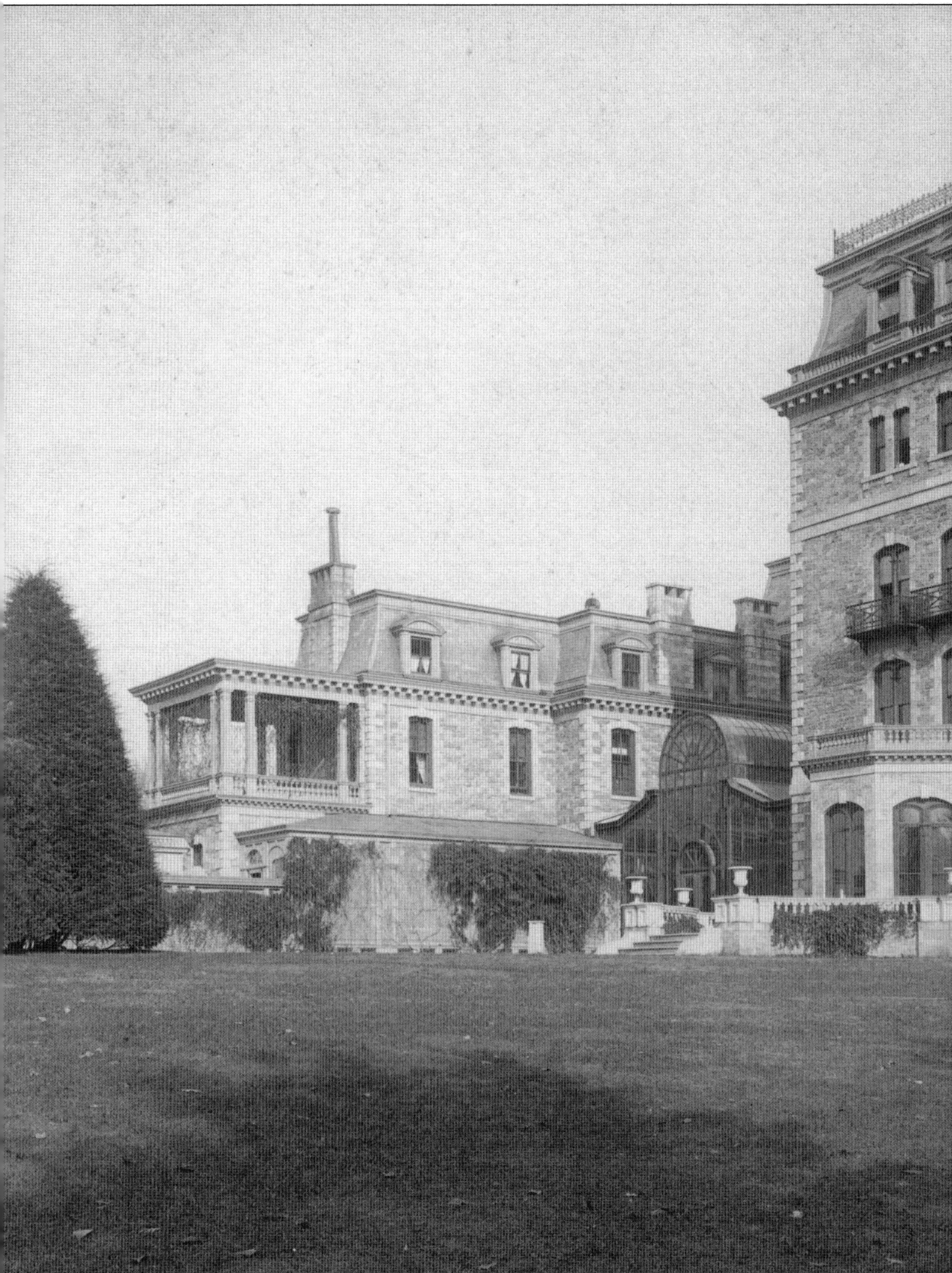

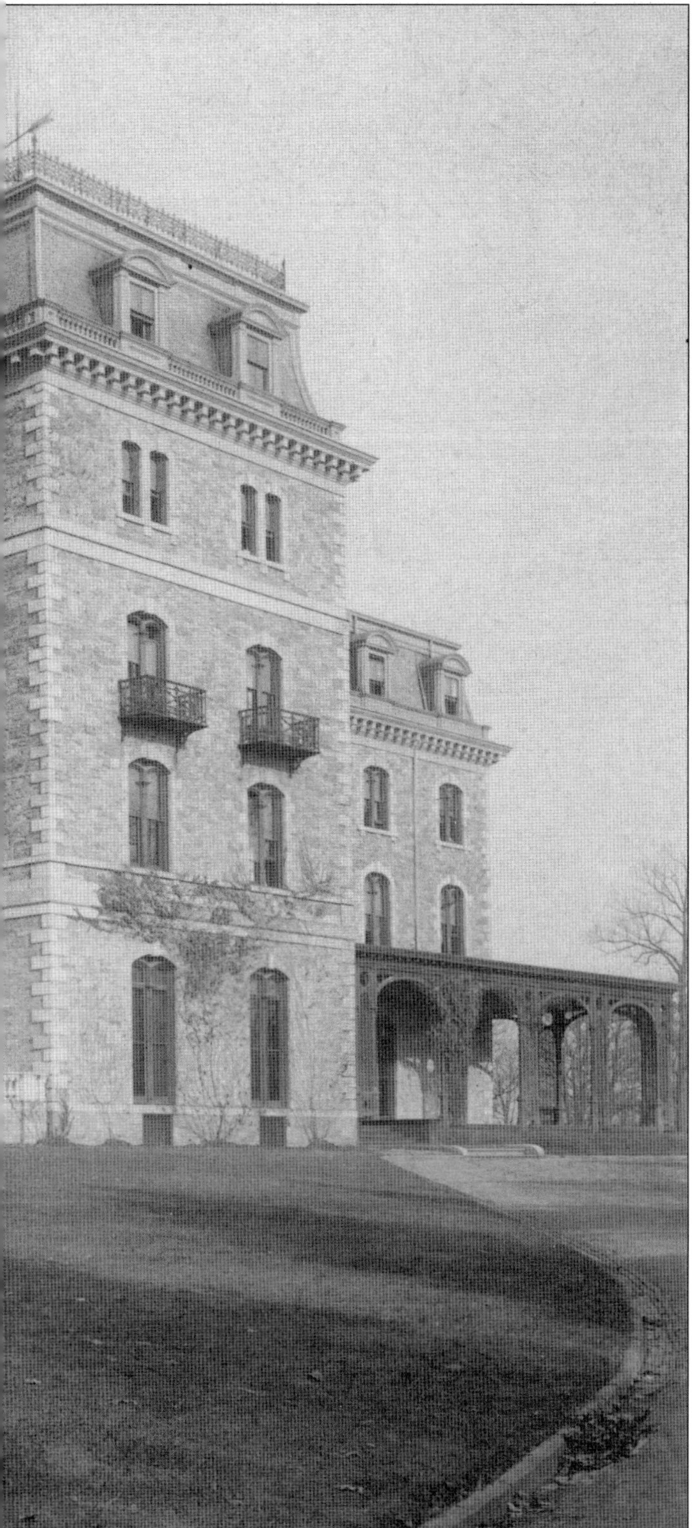

Ogontz, Jay Cooke's stately million-dollar mansion, was built in 1867 near Washington Lane in Elkins Park. Cooke lived there happily for many years, entertaining the likes of US president Ulysses S. Grant, Supreme Court justice Salmon P. Chase, princes and performers from Japan, Native Americans, and more. In 1883, still smarting from financial setbacks during the Panic of 1873 and faced with maintaining a mansion that his large family had outgrown, he offered his estate to the proprietors of the Chestnut Street Female Seminary for an annual rental of $15,000. As the school had also outgrown its tight quarters, it gladly accepted. After Cooke spent $65,000 to replace the walls' frescoes and purchase new furniture, the estate and school were rechristened the Ogontz School for Young Ladies. With its broad verandas, turrets, marble balustrades, and sprawling lawns, Ogontz was the perfect setting for the school, which could now accommodate up to 100 students, as well as faculty, administrative staff, and service attendants. (The Ogontz School Archives, date unknown, Penn State University, Abington College Library.)

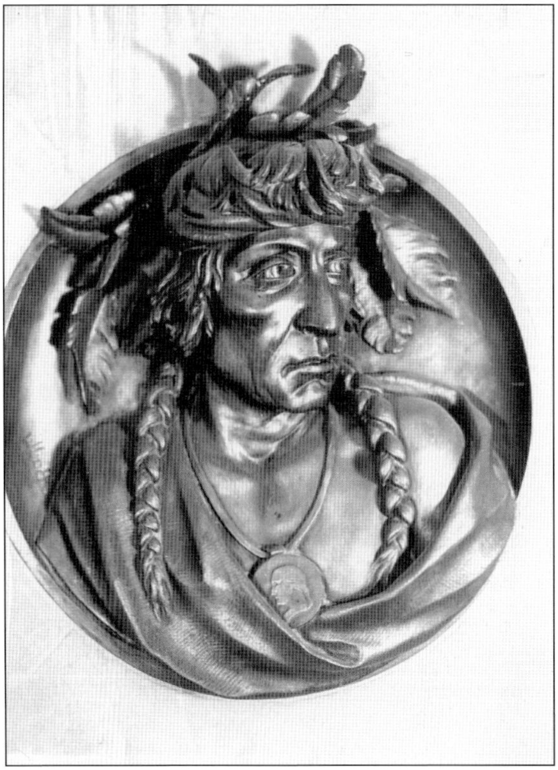

This striking bronze medallion depicts the commanding features of Ottawa, Wyandotte, or Huron Indian Chief Ogontz, a great storyteller who was a frequent visitor to Jay Cooke's boyhood home in Sandusky, Ohio. Beloved by the impressionable young boy, Chief Ogontz has become the symbol of Penn State Abington. Originally placed near the staircase of the main hall at Jay Cooke's mansion, the medallion was eventually relocated above a mantelpiece in Sutherland, the main building of the new campus. Although it can now be seen below the fireplace in the library's archives room in the Woodland Building, a replica of the medallion rests in the archway above the main door to Sutherland, greeting everyone as they enter. (Both, the Ogontz School Archives, dates unknown, Penn State University, Abington College Library.)

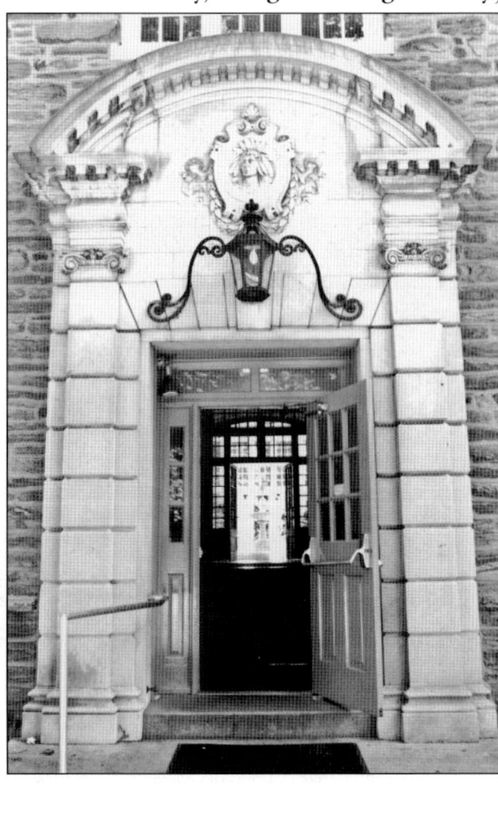

With Sylvia Eastman, the codirector of the newly christened Ogontz School for Young Ladies at Jay Cooke's Elkins Park mansion, Frances E. Bennett (principal from 1860 to 1906) brought a new dimension to the exclusive girls' school. A scholar in William Shakespeare and Samuel Taylor Coleridge and a dynamic teacher of history, Bennett inspired her girls through her own scholarly pursuits, which included the study of literature, art, and music in Germany for a year (1872–1873). One alumna described her as "extraordinary, brilliant, saturnine . . . with her mysterious Buddha-like quality . . . a veritable Dalai Lama." Bennett was later named to the first board of managers at the University of Pennsylvania, whose students later established a scholarship in her honor. She can be seen below (center, in dark dress) teaching her history class in the upper study parlor. (Both, the Ogontz School Archives, dates unknown, Penn State University, Abington College Library.)

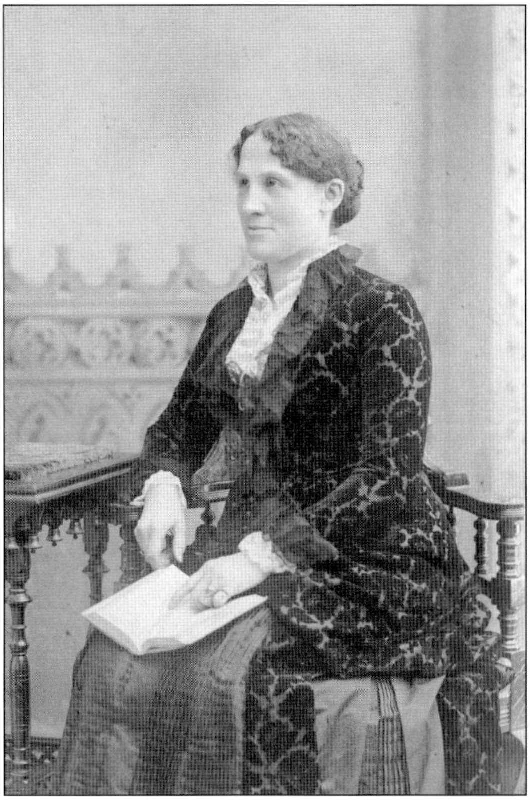

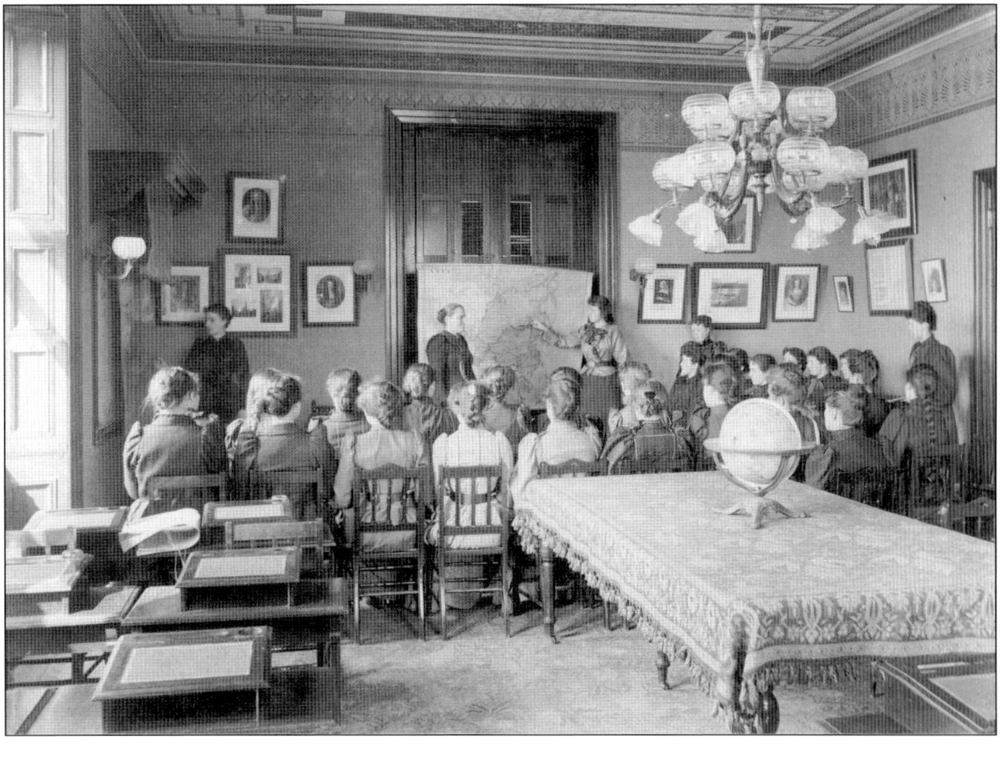

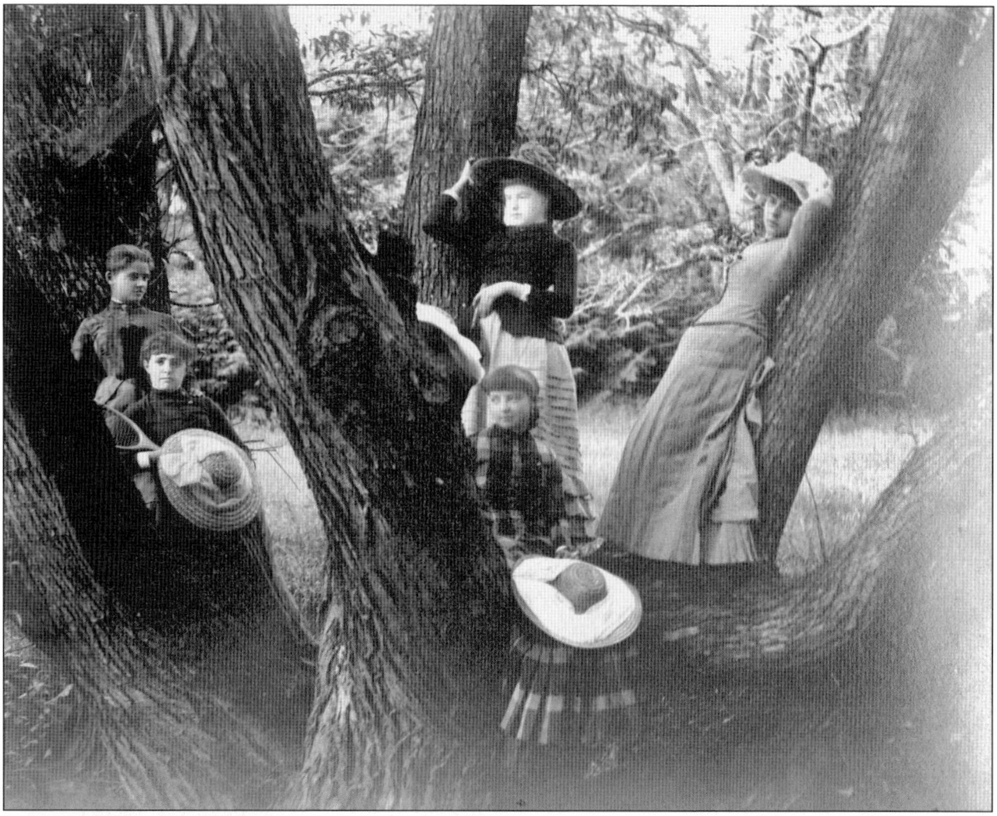

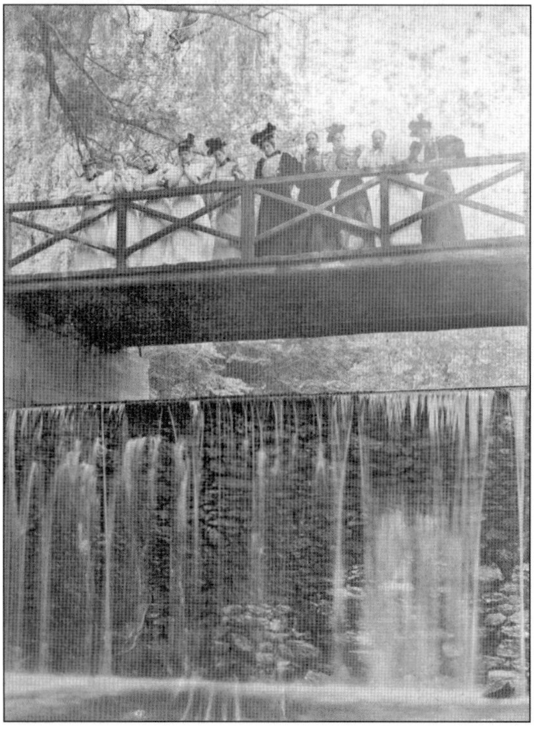

With a brook, a pond, an old mill, greenhouses, and a steep hill inviting sledding in the winter, the grounds of the 40-acre Ogontz estate were idyllic for the young students. The sturdy ancient chestnut trees, eminently suitable for the tree houses the girls loved to build, were popular resting points during the girls' long walks. Seen above are students Hannah "Nan" Gause (top left) and Maude Fuller (bottom left), Belle Irvine (top center) and Cora V. Bailey (bottom center), and Blanche Fuller (right). At left, 10 students, still wearing their long dresses and fashionable bonnets, pause on a wooden bridge during their daily walk to observe the brook's waterfall. (Above, the Ogontz School Archives, 1884, Penn State University, Abington College Library; left, the Ogontz School Archives, date unknown, Penn State University, Abington College Library.)

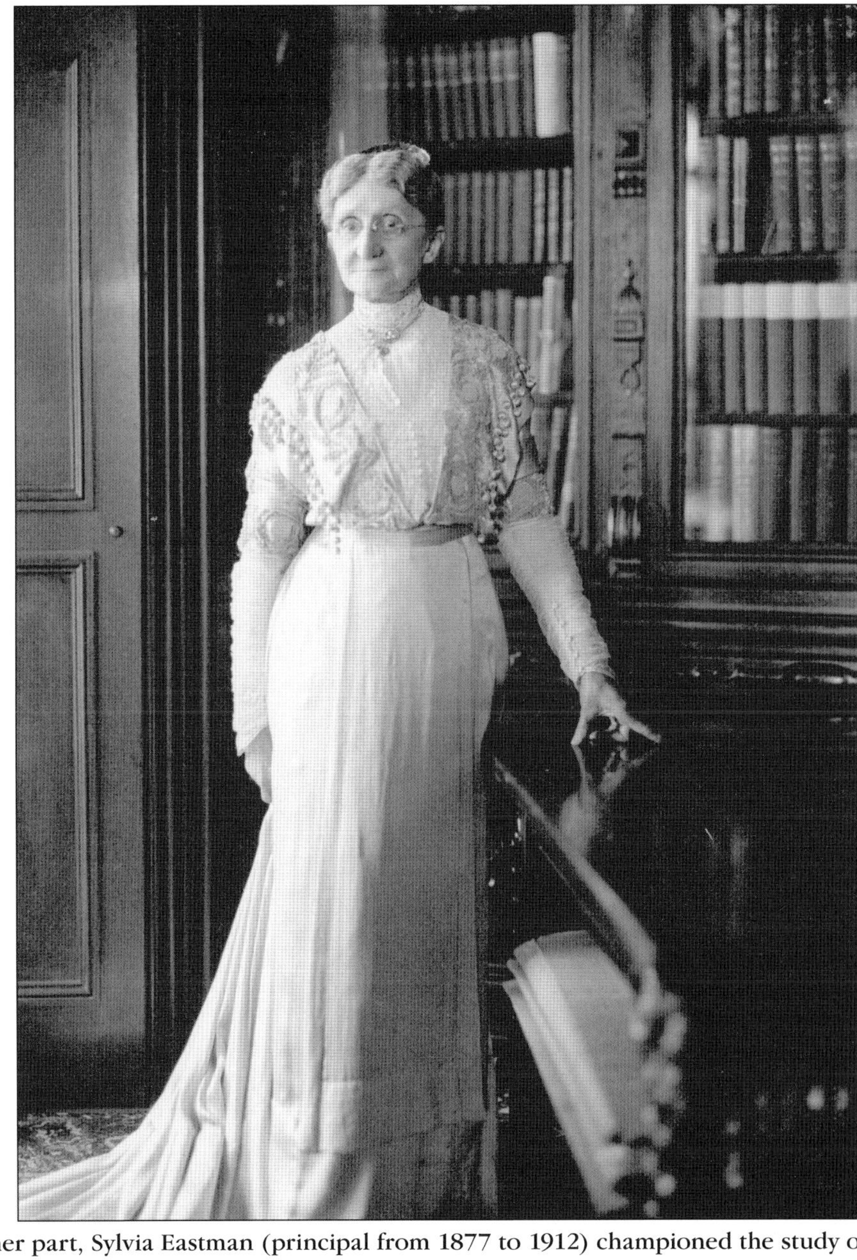

For her part, Sylvia Eastman (principal from 1877 to 1912) championed the study of math, astronomy, and art history at Ogontz and trained her students in good penmanship. She personally supervised the proper order of the girls' dormitory rooms and, most significantly, introduced the innovative and then controversial military drill into the curriculum. A former student wrote, "We went to Miss Eastman as to a wise and understanding and admired Aunt. Her room was feminine and cozy, with shining silver and personal touches." Her protégée, Abby A. Sutherland, wrote of the school's expansion of clientele under Eastman, "The problem of keeping the group up to the first families grew somewhat difficult, as bankers, and business men, clergy and teachers in high schools all over the country sought the privilege of putting their friends or acquaintances into the fashionable group." (The Ogontz School Archives, date unknown, Penn State University, Abington College Library.)

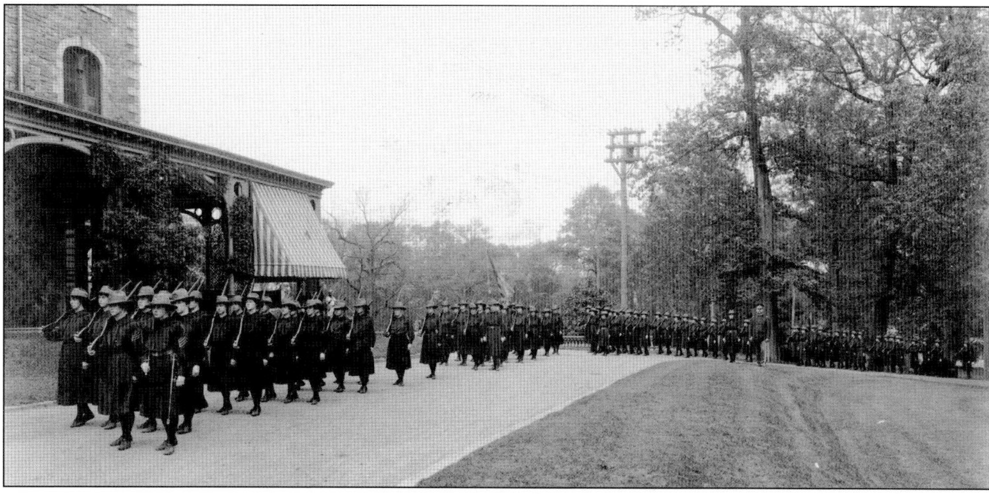

Another of Sylvia Eastman's innovations—adventurous, challenging, and far more rigorous than walking, calisthenics, or any other form of exercise required for the curriculum—was the military drill, arguably the first of its kind for women. Uniformed girls are marching on the expansive driveway at Ogontz. According to Abby A. Sutherland, "Military drill was daring for a young ladies' school in a Quaker environment." (The Ogontz School Archives, 1893, Penn State University, Abington College Library.)

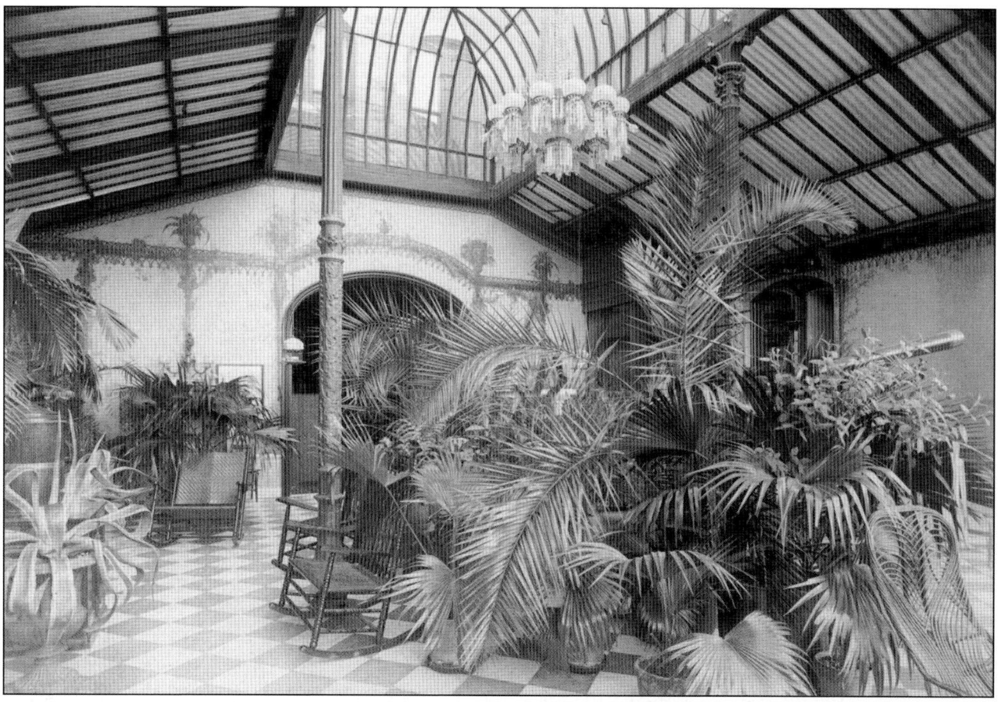

The conservatory at the Cooke mansion was a favorite gathering place for the Ogontz girls. With its lush potted palms and other tropical plants, a sculptured fountain, and a chandelier imported from Austria, it was often the setting for special events, including receptions for returning graduates. One day in 1897, two peacocks made their way in, to the delight (or dismay) of the girls. (The Ogontz School Archives, date unknown, Penn State University, Abington College Library.)

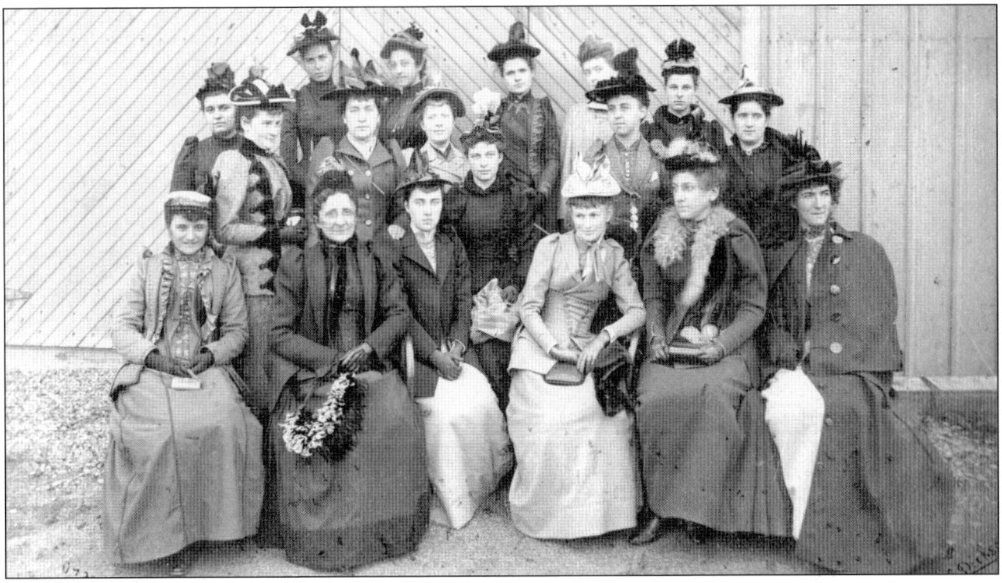

Principal Sylvia Eastman (seated, second from left) has gathered with her students. Although it is not certain, it is reasonable to assume that she is about to chaperone the girls on a Monday, the so-called "Ogontz holiday," when she or one of the school's directors would lead the girls on excursions to Philadelphia, Gettysburg, Valley Forge, Annapolis, or other historic or cultural centers. (The Ogontz School Archives, 1892, Penn State University, Abington College Library.)

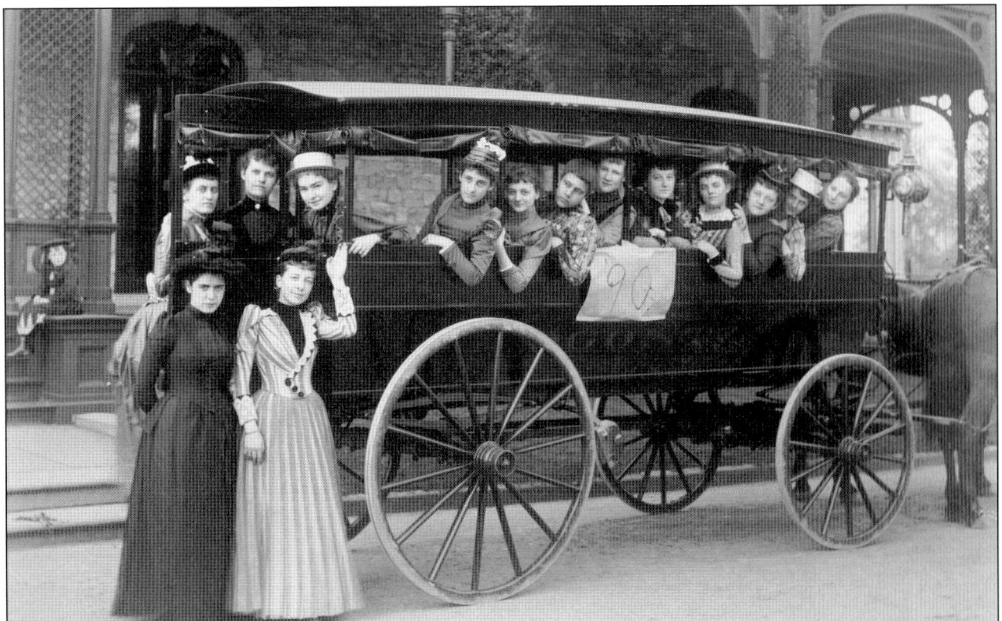

Although their reason for gathering on and around this horse-drawn carriage has never been clearly established, it is likely that the girls of the class of 1890 were about to embark on one of their weekly Monday excursions, which included the Philadelphia Museum of Art, the log cabins and training grounds of Valley Forge, and the battlefields at Gettysburg. (The Ogontz School Archives, 1889, Penn State University, Abington College Library.)

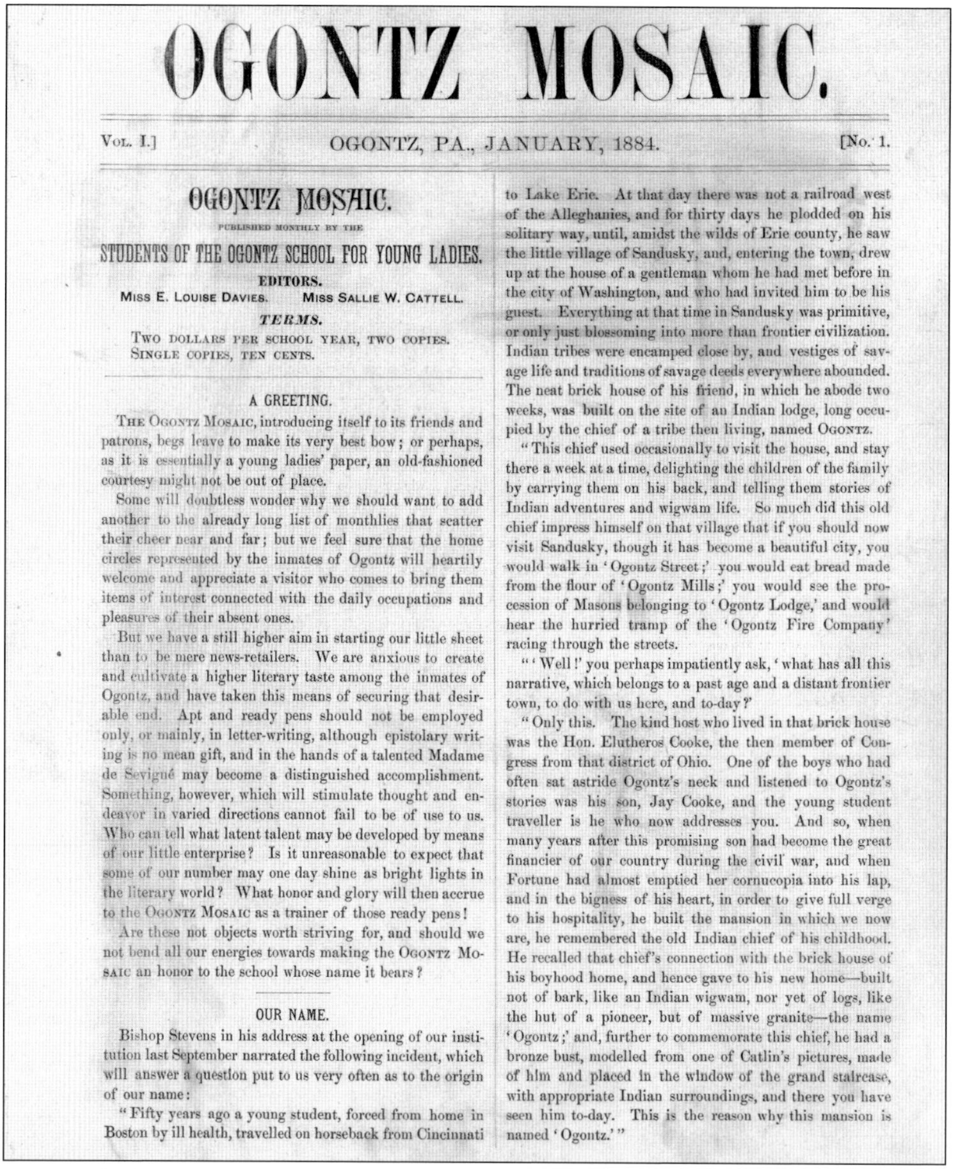

OGONTZ MOSAIC.

VOL. I.] OGONTZ, PA., JANUARY, 1884. [No. 1.

OGONTZ MOSAIC.

PUBLISHED MONTHLY BY THE

STUDENTS OF THE OGONTZ SCHOOL FOR YOUNG LADIES.

EDITORS.

MISS E. LOUISE DAVIES. MISS SALLIE W. CATTELL.

TERMS.

TWO DOLLARS PER SCHOOL YEAR, TWO COPIES.
SINGLE COPIES, TEN CENTS.

A GREETING.

THE OGONTZ MOSAIC, introducing itself to its friends and patrons, begs leave to make its very best bow; or perhaps, as it is essentially a young ladies' paper, an old-fashioned courtesy might not be out of place.

Some will doubtless wonder why we should want to add another to the already long list of monthlies that scatter their cheer near and far; but we feel sure that the home circles represented by the inmates of Ogontz will heartily welcome and appreciate a visitor who comes to bring them items of interest connected with the daily occupations and pleasures of their absent ones.

But we have a still higher aim in starting our little sheet than to be mere news-retailers. We are anxious to create and cultivate a higher literary taste among the inmates of Ogontz, and have taken this means of securing that desirable end. Apt and ready pens should not be employed only, or mainly, in letter-writing, although epistolary writing is no mean gift, and in the hands of a talented Madame de Sevigné may become a distinguished accomplishment. Something, however, which will stimulate thought and endeavor in varied directions cannot fail to be of use to us. Who can tell what latent talent may be developed by means of our little enterprise? Is it unreasonable to expect that some of our number may one day shine as bright lights in the literary world? What honor and glory will then accrue to the OGONTZ MOSAIC as a trainer of those ready pens!

Are these not objects worth striving for, and should we not bend all our energies towards making the OGONTZ MOSAIC an honor to the school whose name it bears?

OUR NAME.

Bishop Stevens in his address at the opening of our institution last September narrated the following incident, which will answer a question put to us very often as to the origin of our name:

"Fifty years ago a young student, forced from home in Boston by ill health, travelled on horseback from Cincinnati to Lake Erie. At that day there was not a railroad west of the Alleghanies, and for thirty days he plodded on his solitary way, until, amidst the wilds of Erie county, he saw the little village of Sandusky, and, entering the town, drew up at the house of a gentleman whom he had met before in the city of Washington, and who had invited him to be his guest. Everything at that time in Sandusky was primitive, or only just blossoming into more than frontier civilization. Indian tribes were encamped close by, and vestiges of savage life and traditions of savage deeds everywhere abounded. The neat brick house of his friend, in which he abode two weeks, was built on the site of an Indian lodge, long occupied by the chief of a tribe then living, named OGONTZ.

"This chief used occasionally to visit the house, and stay there a week at a time, delighting the children of the family by carrying them on his back, and telling them stories of Indian adventures and wigwam life. So much did this old chief impress himself on that village that if you should now visit Sandusky, though it has become a beautiful city, you would walk in 'Ogontz Street;' you would eat bread made from the flour of 'Ogontz Mills;' you would see the procession of Masons belonging to 'Ogontz Lodge,' and would hear the hurried tramp of the 'Ogontz Fire Company' racing through the streets.

"'Well!' you perhaps impatiently ask, 'what has all this narrative, which belongs to a past age and a distant frontier town, to do with us here, and to-day?'

"Only this. The kind host who lived in that brick house was the Hon. Elutheros Cooke, the then member of Congress from that district of Ohio. One of the boys who had often sat astride Ogontz's neck and listened to Ogontz's stories was his son, Jay Cooke, and the young student traveller is he who now addresses you. And so, when many years after this promising son had become the great financier of our country during the civil war, and when Fortune had almost emptied her cornucopia into his lap, and in the bigness of his heart, in order to give full verge to his hospitality, he built the mansion in which we now are, he remembered the old Indian chief of his childhood. He recalled that chief's connection with the brick house of his boyhood home, and hence gave to his new home—built not of bark, like an Indian wigwam, nor yet of logs, like the hut of a pioneer, but of massive granite—the name 'Ogontz;' and, further to commemorate this chief, he had a bronze bust, modelled from one of Catlin's pictures, made of him and placed in the window of the grand staircase, with appropriate Indian surroundings, and there you have seen him to-day. This is the reason why this mansion is named 'Ogontz.'"

It did not take long. Less than a year after the girls had settled into their new home at Ogontz, they were up and writing. Here is the first page of the first volume of *Ogontz Mosaic*, dated January 1884. The award-winning student-run publication was an ambitious project sustained for roughly six issues per annum until Abby A. Sutherland donated the school to Penn State College in 1950. An apt name for the publication, *Ogontz Mosaic* was a pastiche of articles on literature; book reviews; poetry, stories, and plays written in high literary style; and editorials on current events, artistic and ethical issues; and the like. And there was plenty of campus gossip, all written as tastefully as the Victorian era would allow. The first issue recounts how the school received its name. *Mosaic* received the Medal of Excellence of the Exposition Universelle de Paris in 1889. In her book *100 Years of Ogontz* (1958), Sutherland wrote, "The *Mosaic* records how the contemporary consciousness of [thoughtful young women] passed through the scenes which have become history." (The Ogontz School Archives, 1884, Penn State University, Abington College Library.)

With standards worthy of West Point, Sylvia Eastman personally supervised the room order of each student. She felt that keeping their rooms neat and orderly was important training for young ladies who were expected to preside in beautiful homes. Pictured is the Fan Room's study area. Each room accommodated two to five girls. (The Ogontz School Archives, 1910, Penn State University, Abington College Library.)

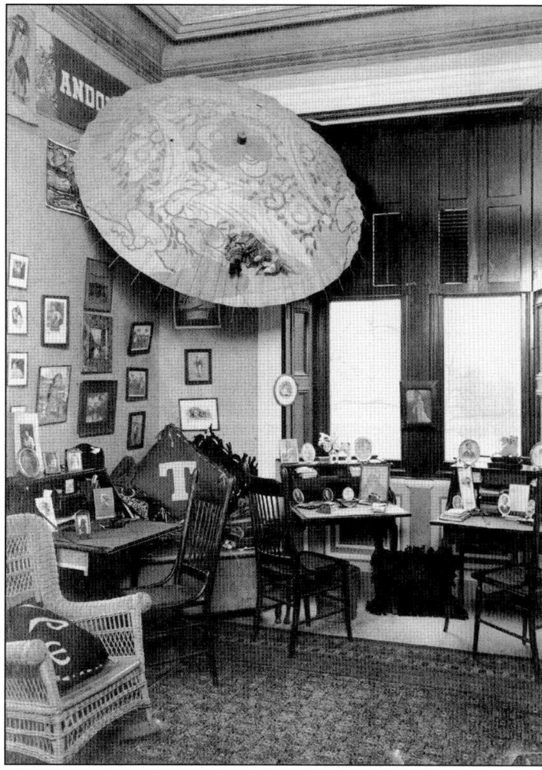

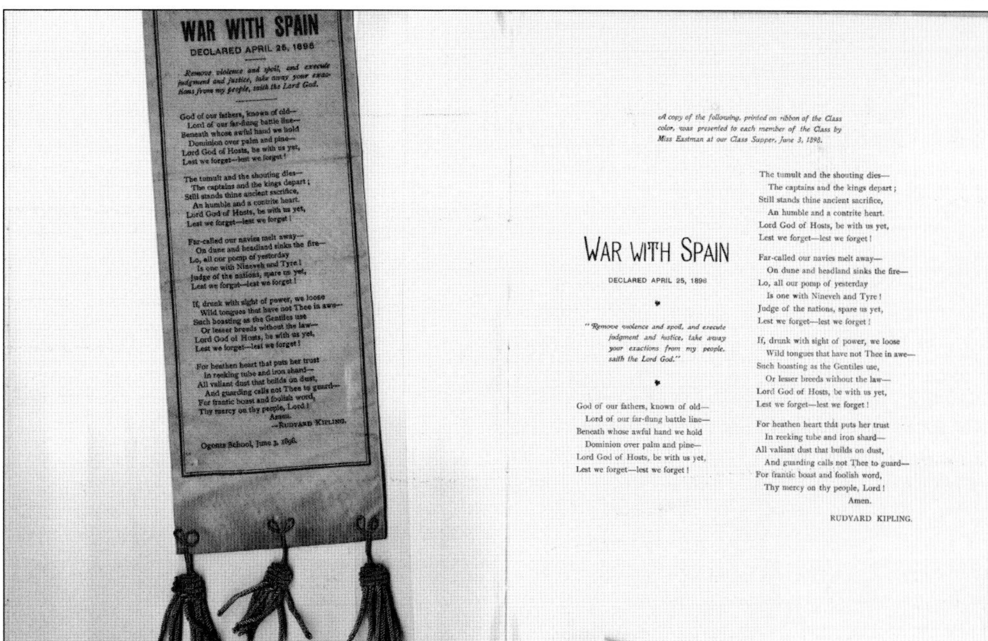

WAR WITH SPAIN

DECLARED APRIL 25, 1898

Remove violence and spoil, and execute judgment and justice, take away your exactions from my people, saith the Lord God.

God of our fathers, known of old—
Lord of our far-flung battle line—
Beneath whose awful hand we hold
Dominion over palm and pine—
Lord God of Hosts, be with us yet,
Lest we forget—lest we forget!

The tumult and the shouting dies—
The captains and the kings depart;
Still stands thine ancient sacrifice,
An humble and a contrite heart.
Lord God of Hosts, be with us yet,
Lest we forget—lest we forget!

Far-called our navies melt away—
On dune and headland sinks the fire—
Lo, all our pomp of yesterday
Is one with Nineveh and Tyre!
Judge of the nations, spare us yet,
Lest we forget—lest we forget!

If, drunk with sight of power, we loose
Wild tongues that have not Thee in awe—
Such boasting as the Gentiles use,
Or lesser breeds without the law—
Lord God of Hosts, be with us yet,
Lest we forget—lest we forget!

For heathen heart that puts her trust
In reeking tube and iron shard—
All valiant dust that builds on dust,
And guarding calls not Thee to guard—
For frantic boast and foolish word,
Thy mercy on thy people, Lord!
Amen.
—RUDYARD KIPLING.

Ogontz School, June 3, 1898.

A copy of the following, printed on ribbon of the Class color, was presented to each member of the Class by Miss Eastman at our Class Supper, June 3, 1898.

WAR WITH SPAIN

DECLARED APRIL 25, 1898

"Remove violence and spoil, and execute judgment and justice, take away your exactions from my people, saith the Lord God."

God of our fathers, known of old—
Lord of our far-flung battle line—
Beneath whose awful hand we hold
Dominion over palm and pine—
Lord God of Hosts, be with us yet,
Lest we forget—lest we forget!

The tumult and the shouting dies—
The captains and the kings depart;
Still stands thine ancient sacrifice,
An humble and a contrite heart.
Lord God of Hosts, be with us yet,
Lest we forget—lest we forget!

Far-called our navies melt away—
On dune and headland sinks the fire—
Lo, all our pomp of yesterday
Is one with Nineveh and Tyre!
Judge of the nations, spare us yet,
Lest we forget—lest we forget!

If, drunk with sight of power, we loose
Wild tongues that have not Thee in awe—
Such boasting as the Gentiles use,
Or lesser breeds without the law—
Lord God of Hosts, be with us yet,
Lest we forget—lest we forget!

For heathen heart that puts her trust
In reeking tube and iron shard—
All valiant dust that builds on dust,
And guarding calls not Thee to guard—
For frantic boast and foolish word,
Thy mercy on thy people, Lord!
Amen.

RUDYARD KIPLING.

To keep in step with current events, at the annual Class Supper on June 3, 1898, Principal Sylvia Eastman presented a ribbon featuring Rudyard Kipling's poem "War with Spain" to each member of the class of 1898. On the right is the book from which the poem was reprinted. (The Ogontz School Archives, 1898, Penn State University, Abington College Library.)

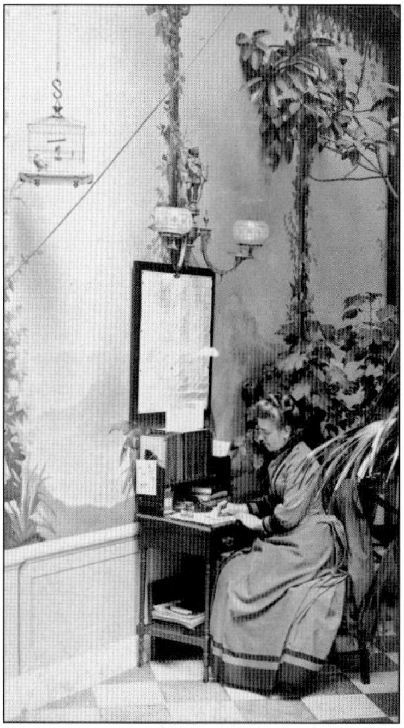

One of the school's popular teachers, seen here writing at her desk, was Lucy A. Putnam, superintendent of the music department. During her well-received lecture on the development of musical instruments on December 12, 1891, she told the students that music originated in an intense desire to give utterance to deep feeling that could not be expressed in words. (The Ogontz School Archives, 1891, Penn State University, Abington College Library.)

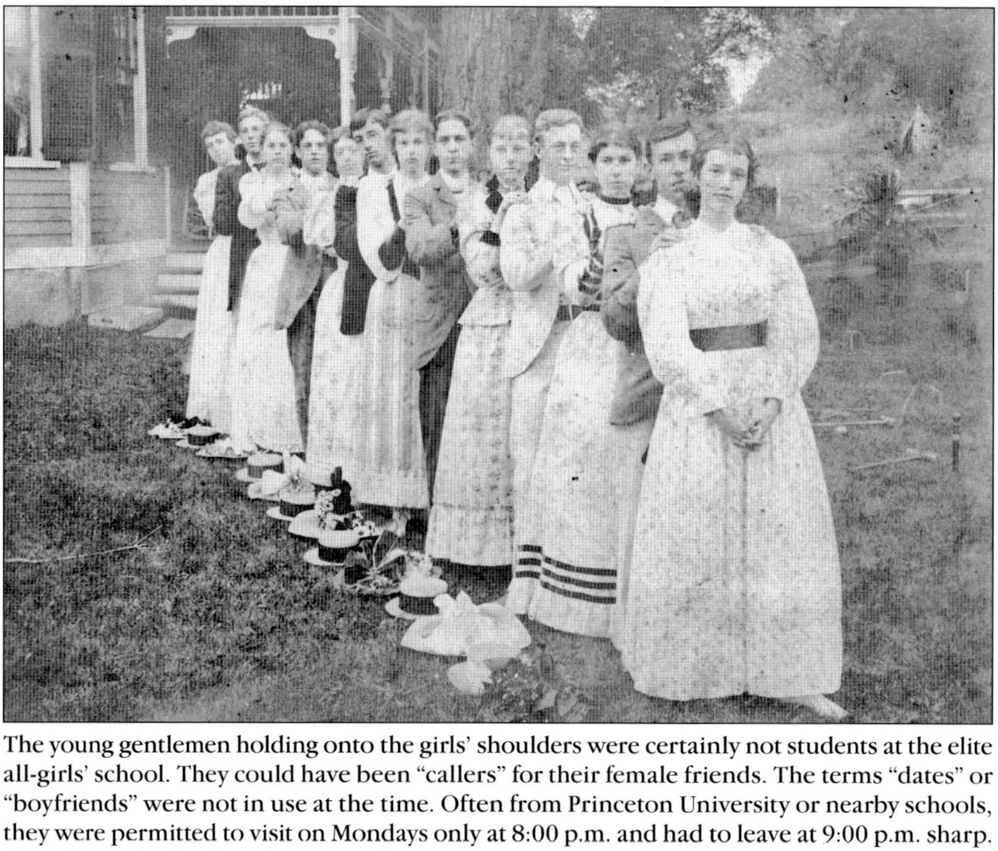

The young gentlemen holding onto the girls' shoulders were certainly not students at the elite all-girls' school. They could have been "callers" for their female friends. The terms "dates" or "boyfriends" were not in use at the time. Often from Princeton University or nearby schools, they were permitted to visit on Mondays only at 8:00 p.m. and had to leave at 9:00 p.m. sharp. (The Ogontz School Archives, 1894, Penn State University, Abington College Library.)

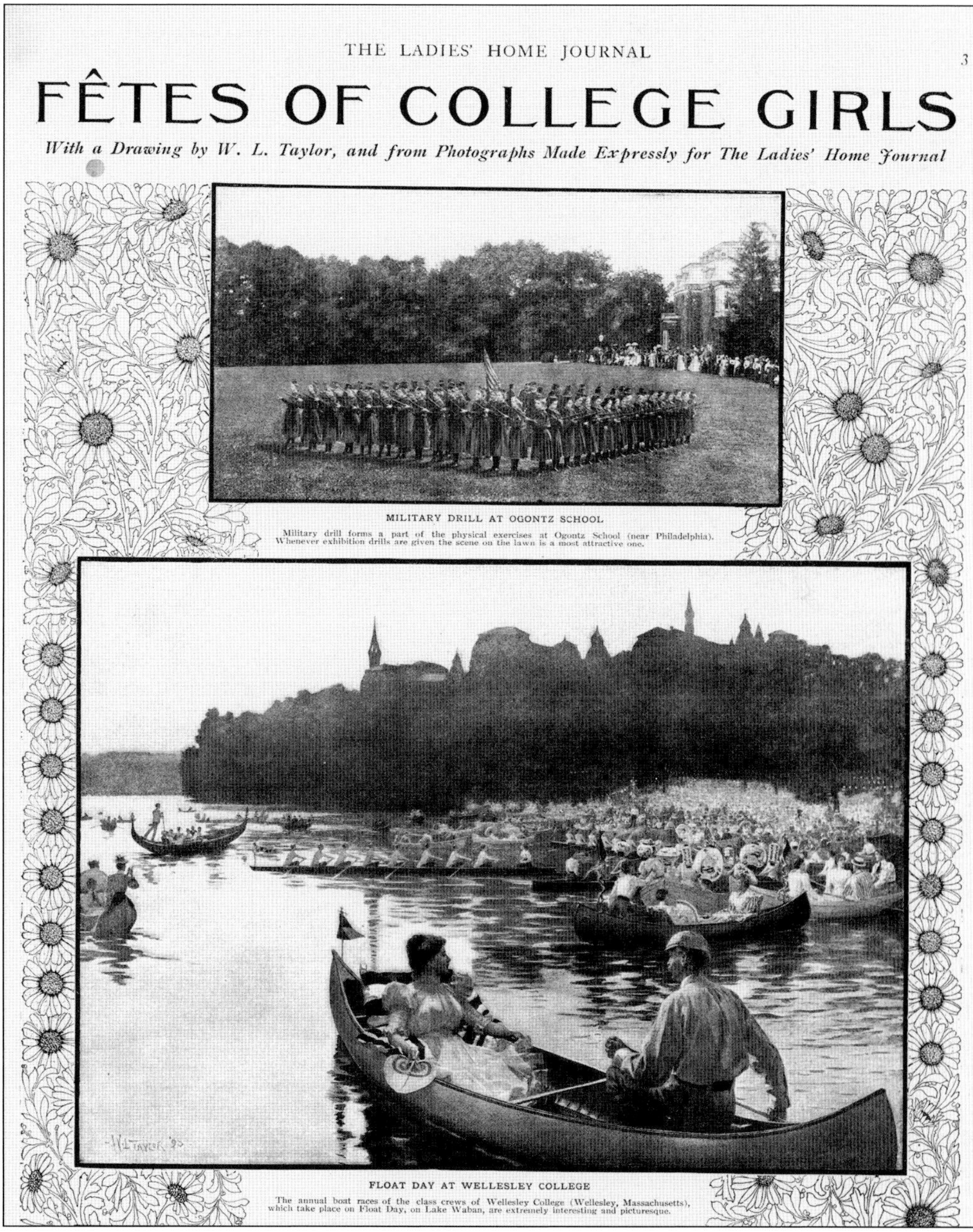

THE LADIES' HOME JOURNAL 3

FÊTES OF COLLEGE GIRLS

With a Drawing by W. L. Taylor, and from Photographs Made Expressly for The Ladies' Home Journal

MILITARY DRILL AT OGONTZ SCHOOL

Military drill forms a part of the physical exercises at Ogontz School (near Philadelphia). Whenever exhibition drills are given the scene on the lawn is a most attractive one.

FLOAT DAY AT WELLESLEY COLLEGE

The annual boat races of the class crews of Wellesley College (Wellesley, Massachusetts), which take place on Float Day, on Lake Waban, are extremely interesting and picturesque.

How well-known had the Ogontz military drill become by the turn of the century? In a graphic spread titled "Fêtes of College Girls" on page 3 of the June 1899 edition of the *Ladies' Home Journal*, a photograph of a drill at Ogontz, made expressly for the popular magazine, appears above an artist's conception of Float Day at Wellesley College (which was also that issue's cover image). Two other fêtes appeared below the Wellesley drawing: Daisy Chain Procession at Vassar College and Ivy Day at Smith College. The parallelism is unmistakable: these were major events at some of the best schools in the country. It might have been a coincidence, but the *Ladies' Home Journal* was published in Philadelphia by Cyrus H.K. Curtis, whose only daughter, Mary Louise Curtis, had attended the Ogontz School just a few years earlier. (The Ogontz School Archives, 1899, Penn State University, Abington College Library.)

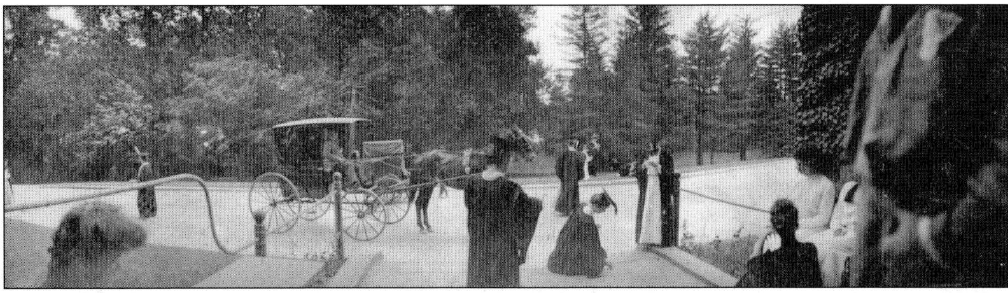

A handwritten note on the sleeve enclosing this image simply notes, "Noon recess Ogontz School 5 21 1903." The photograph shows a horse and buggy in the driveway at the Ogontz estate, with the girls wearing caps and gowns, perhaps after rehearsing for commencement, scheduled to take place a few days later. (The Ogontz School Archives, 1903, Penn State University, Abington College Library.)

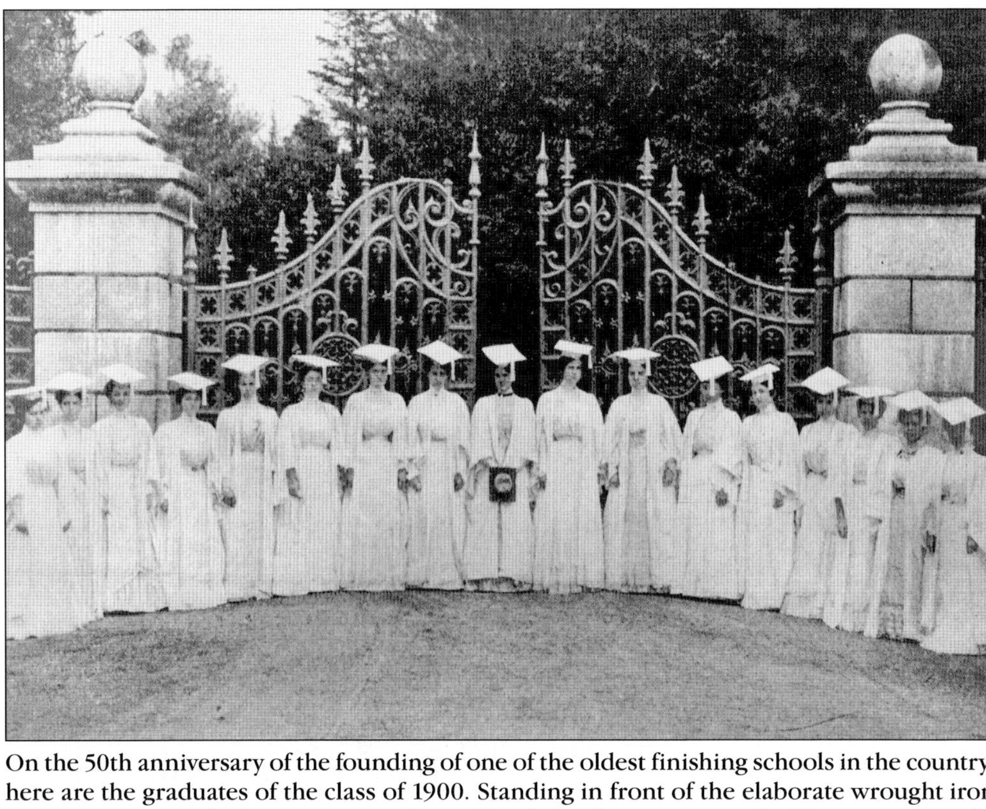

On the 50th anniversary of the founding of one of the oldest finishing schools in the country, here are the graduates of the class of 1900. Standing in front of the elaborate wrought iron entrance gates to the Ogontz estate, dressed in their white gowns and white mortarboards, they are the embodiment of the school's affluent, elite clientele. (The Ogontz School Archives, 1900, Penn State University, Abington College Library.)

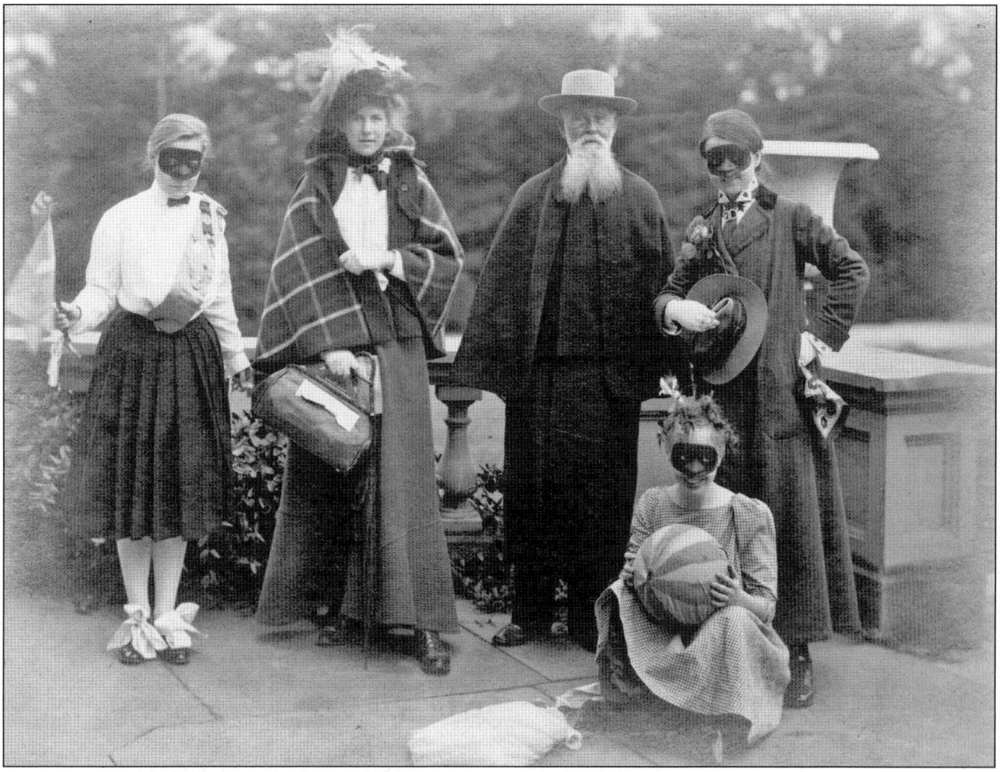

A frequent and beloved visitor to the Ogontz School, Jay Cooke can be seen here wearing his familiar black Gladstone coat, no doubt filled with candies for the girls, in 1901, four years before he died. He is standing on one the mansion's verandas with an unidentified woman and three masked students who presumably performed in the annual minstrel show. (The Ogontz School Archives, 1901, Penn State University, Abington College Library.)

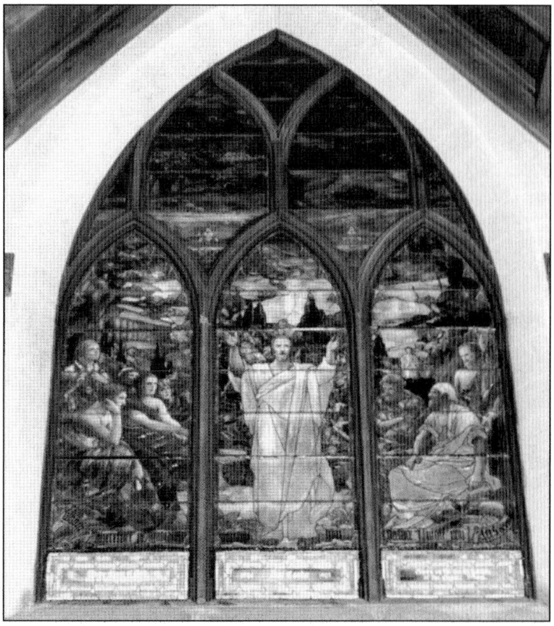

A longtime patron of St. Paul's Episcopal Church in Elkins Park, in whose churchyard he is buried, Jay Cooke was commemorated in this impressive Tiffany window at St. Paul's the year following his death. (Photograph by Thomas Heginbothom; the Ogontz School Archives, 1906, Penn State University, Abington College Library.)

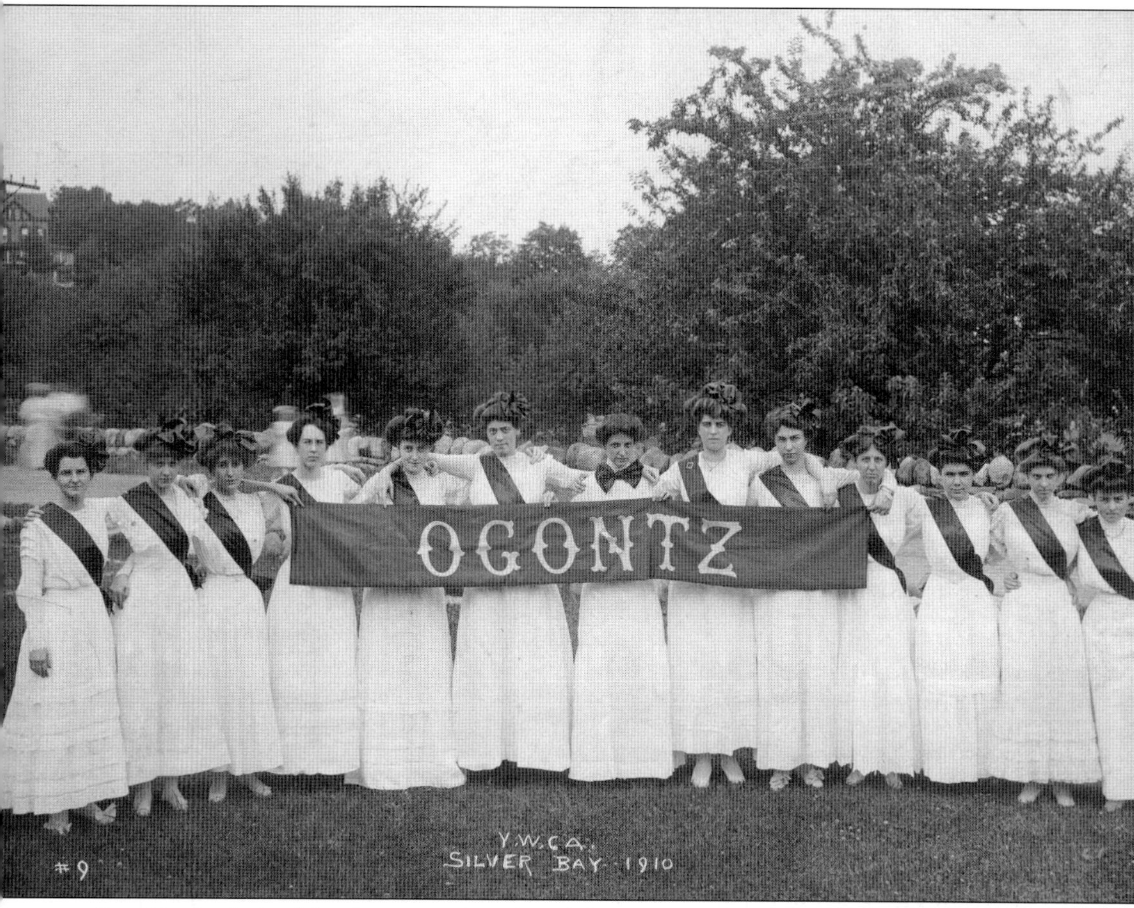

Standing in their white dresses at the edge of the Ogontz estate, holding up a banner reading "Ogontz," are several members of the graduating class of 1910. According to Abby A. Sutherland's "Class Lists" at the end of her book *100 Years of Ogontz*, there were 24 graduates that year, twice as many as those in Ogontz's first graduating class of 1884. These fashionable young ladies, hand-chosen from "families of good American lineage and culture," were destined to become the wives of important men in government, business, finance, and the arts. The graduates shown here arrived from as far off as Minneapolis, Denver, Delray Beach, Florida, and Pasadena, California, and from as near as Princeton, New Jersey, and St. Davids, on suburban Philadelphia's exclusive Main Line. (The Ogontz School Archives, 1910, Penn State University, Abington College Library.)

Two

The Abby Sutherland Years

It was the vision of Abby A. Sutherland (1871–1961) that brought the Ogontz School to Abington in 1916. A product of the excellent public schools of New England, she was initially apprehensive of the wealthy, aristocratic young ladies who comprised the elite student body. But she soon came to realize that working with what she called a "homogeneous group," with intrinsic accrued values of culture, travel, and acquaintance, would be mutually advantageous.

Principal Sylvia Eastman invited Sutherland, a cum laude graduate of Radcliffe College, to teach English and mathematics at Ogontz in 1902. But it soon became clear to Eastman that her new protégée was much more than a teacher. So, in 1909, she offered Sutherland the opportunity to be her understudy. Sutherland would pay Eastman $5,000 a year for four years to assume her invested rights to ownership of the school. Upon Eastman's death in 1912, Sutherland assumed the mantle she would wear so brilliantly for the next four decades. She financed the purchase of the gorgeous property in Abington Township through a bond issue that took her 33 years to pay off.

Although Ogontz was already one of the finest finishing schools in the nation, Sutherland was able to change with the times, introducing a higher-level academic track that would enable students who so chose to transfer to some of the most prestigious colleges in the country. During the Sutherland years, more than 51 percent of the graduates were able to matriculate and succeed at prestigious Ivy League and other great colleges and universities.

As an educator, she also expanded the mission of Ogontz, introducing the Rydal School for elementary grades (chartered in 1924) and the Ogontz Junior College (chartered in 1930), making it possible for a girl to enter the school in elementary school and continue her education through junior college.

But by 1950, faced with a Pennsylvania State Supreme Court ruling that "the Ogontz School was not exempt from paying [back] taxes just because it is an educational institution," she decided to formally donate the school and grounds to the Pennsylvania State College (later the Pennsylvania State University). She only asked that Penn State permit her to live on the premises for the rest of her life. It was easily granted. Thus, the Penn State Ogontz Center was born.

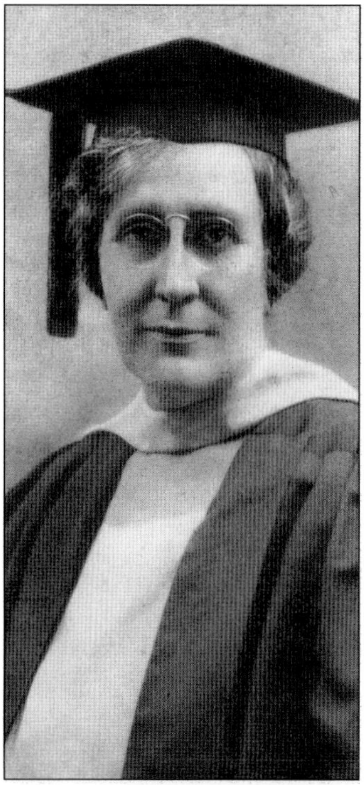

As former Penn State Abington historian Terrie Smith has written, "The driving force behind The Ogontz School for its last four decades was the beloved, occasionally feared, and always formidable Abby A. Sutherland." This lifelong teacher and educator melded the Presbyterian milieu of her upbringing in Nova Scotia and New England with the progressive educational principles she experienced at Radcliffe College, from which she graduated cum laude. Starting out as a teacher of English and mathematics, she eventually became headmistress, president, and owner of the prestigious school. Sutherland recalls that her earliest memory was the desire to teach. At Ogontz, and after 1950 at the Penn State Ogontz Campus, she got her wish. And she never stopped studying. She spent the last decade of her life earning first a master's degree, then a doctorate (at the age of 86), from the University of Pennsylvania. In the photograph below, "1916" marks the spot. Carved into the stone of the Sutherland Building is the year Abby Sutherland purchased the new campus, where education has continued uninterrupted for more than 100 years. (Left, the Ogontz School Archives, date unknown, Penn State University, Abington College Library; below, University Relations Department, Penn State Abington.)

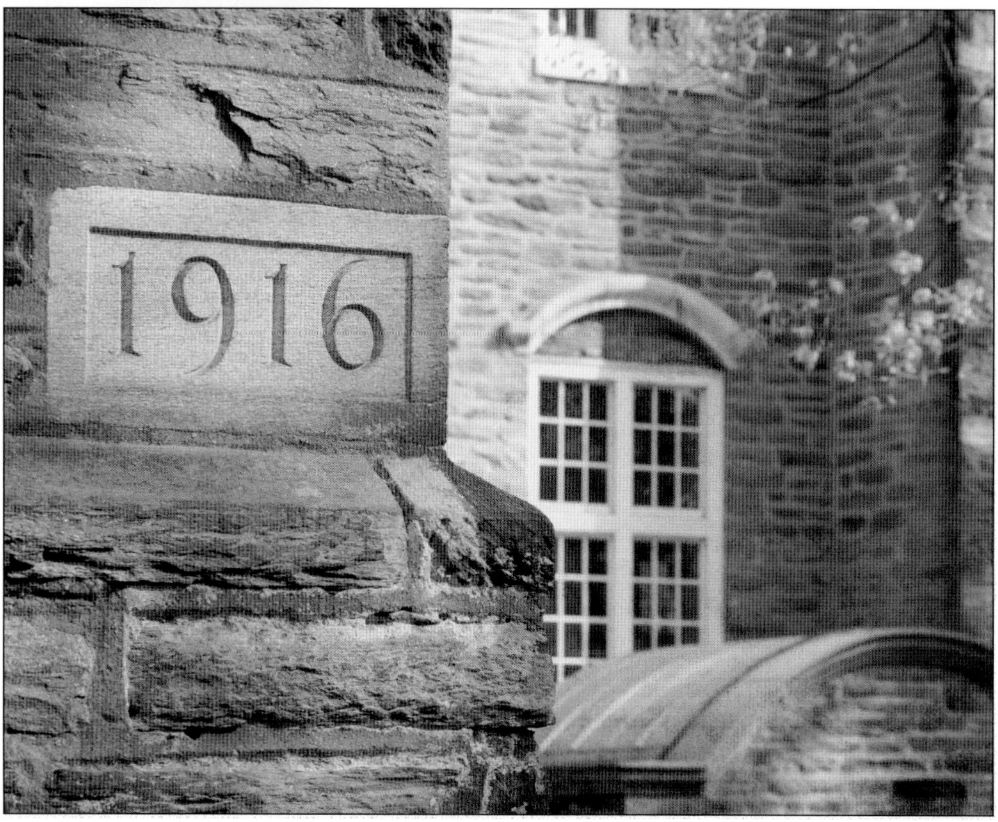

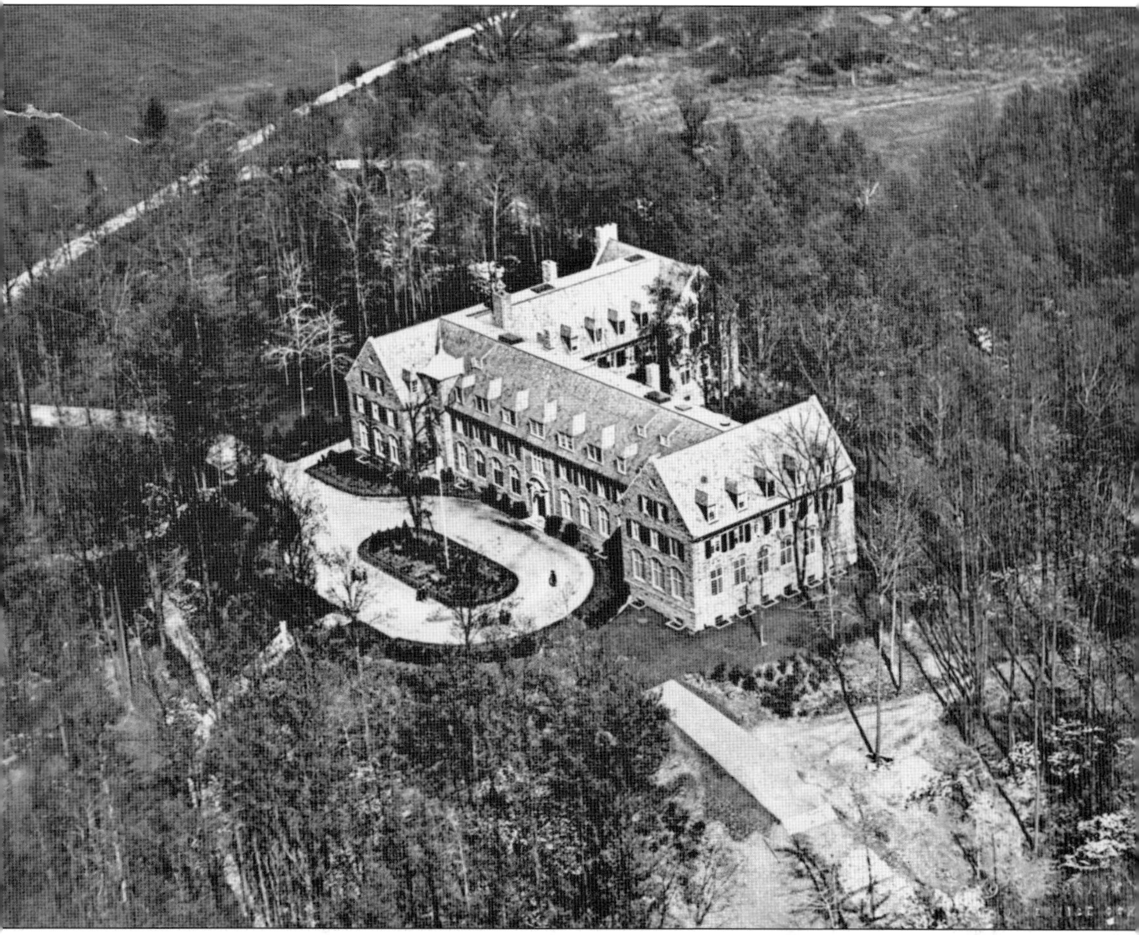

No, this grand edifice did not appear as a subsidiary character on PBS's popular series *Downton Abbey*. But the main building of the new campus, the first to be constructed at the site, was completed in 1917 to emulate the style of an English manor house. Named in honor of the Ogontz School's principal and owner, it remains the chief administrative and classroom building at Penn State Abington. The internationally acclaimed Philadelphia architectural firm of Horace Trumbauer—also responsible for building Gray Towers at Beaver College (now Arcadia University), Widener Library at Harvard University, and later, the Philadelphia Museum of Art and the west campus of Duke University—did Abby Sutherland proud. The building, like all the Trumbauer structures on campus, including Lares, Rydal, and the Conference Center, was built from graystone quarried right on the property. The circle fronting the building initially served as a dirt driveway where chauffeured limousines deposited their privileged young mistresses. (The Ogontz School Archives, 1961, Penn State University, Abington College Library.)

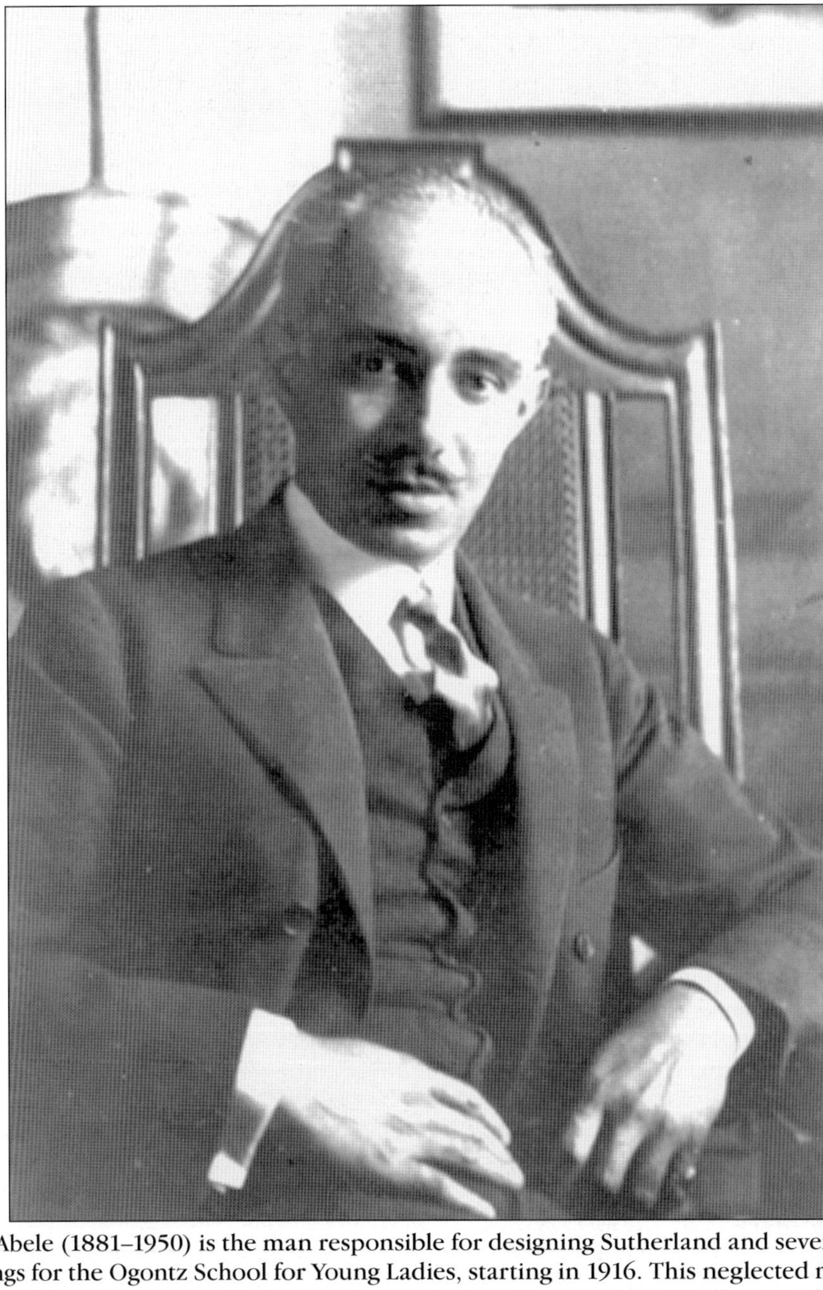

Julian Abele (1881–1950) is the man responsible for designing Sutherland and several other buildings for the Ogontz School for Young Ladies, starting in 1916. This neglected master of public architecture received little recognition during his own time. The first black student to earn a degree in architecture at the University of Pennsylvania (1902), Abele soon became senior designer for the esteemed firm of Horace Trumbauer, which was an unprecedented accomplishment for an African American at the turn of the century. Abele was also the principal designer of the west campus of Duke University (1925–1932). Budgeted at $21 million, it was the largest construction project in the South at the time. Duke has recently championed an effort to bring Abele the acclaim he so deserves. He is credited with having designed more than 400 buildings. (The University Archives in the David M. Rubenstein Rare Book & Manuscript Library, date unknown, Duke University.)

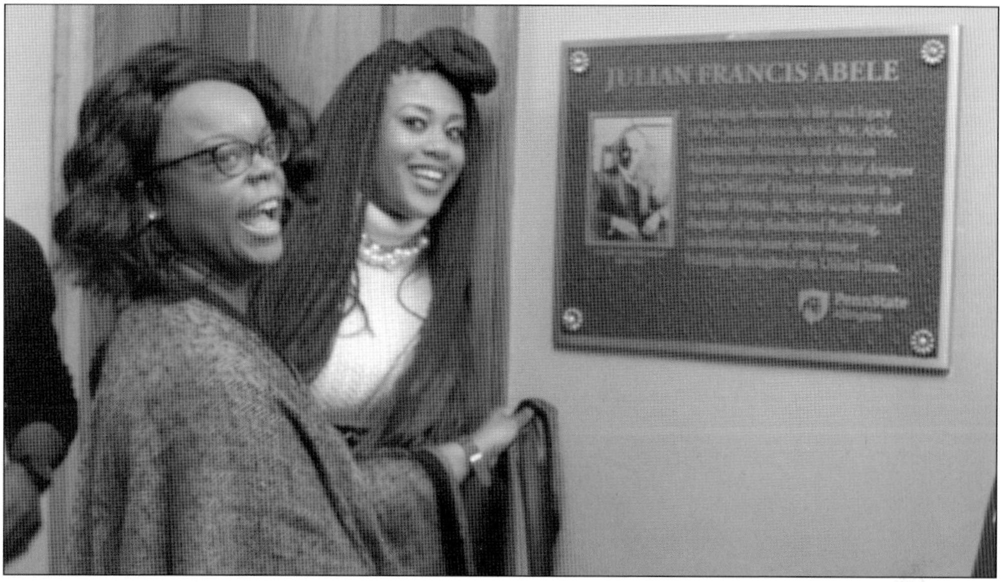

Ashley Auset (left) and Chanel A. Carrero, executive board members of the Penn State Abington Black Student Union, were among the guests at the dedication of a bronze plaque recognizing the achievement of Julian Francis Abele 100 years after he designed the iconic Sutherland Building in 1916. The prominent African American architect was the senior designer for the acclaimed Horace Trumbauer firm. (Photograph by Maria Narodetsky, University Relations Department, Penn State Abington.)

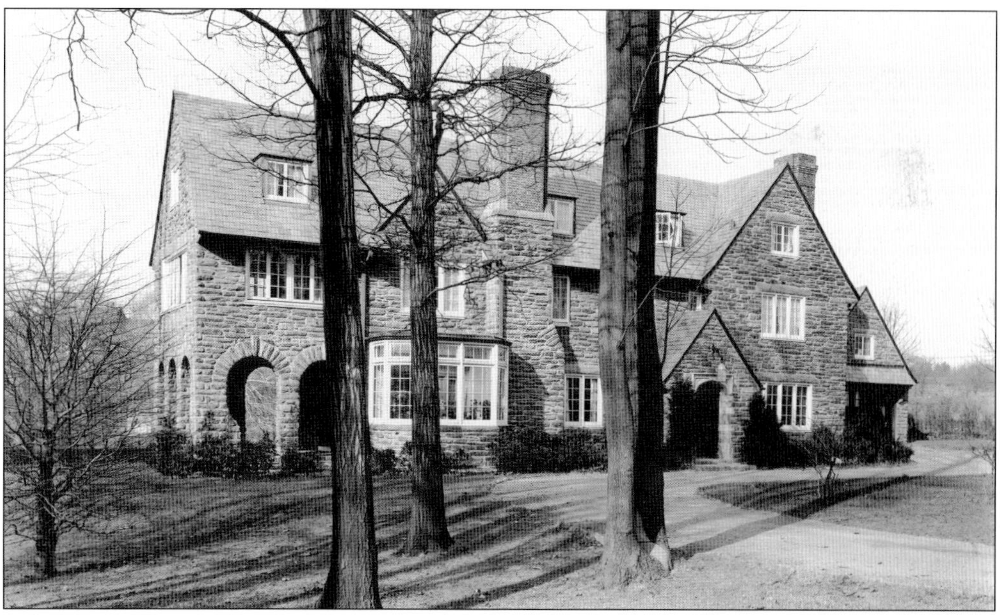

Lares, the Penn State Abington student union building, was Abby Sutherland's personal residence when it was built by Horace Trumbauer in 1923. Seen here long before the renovations and additions of 1967, it was named for Roman demigods who protect the household. Aptly, Lares was also known as the "home economics house" when Ogontz girls resided there for two-week periods to practice domestic sciences. (University Relations Department, Penn State Abington.)

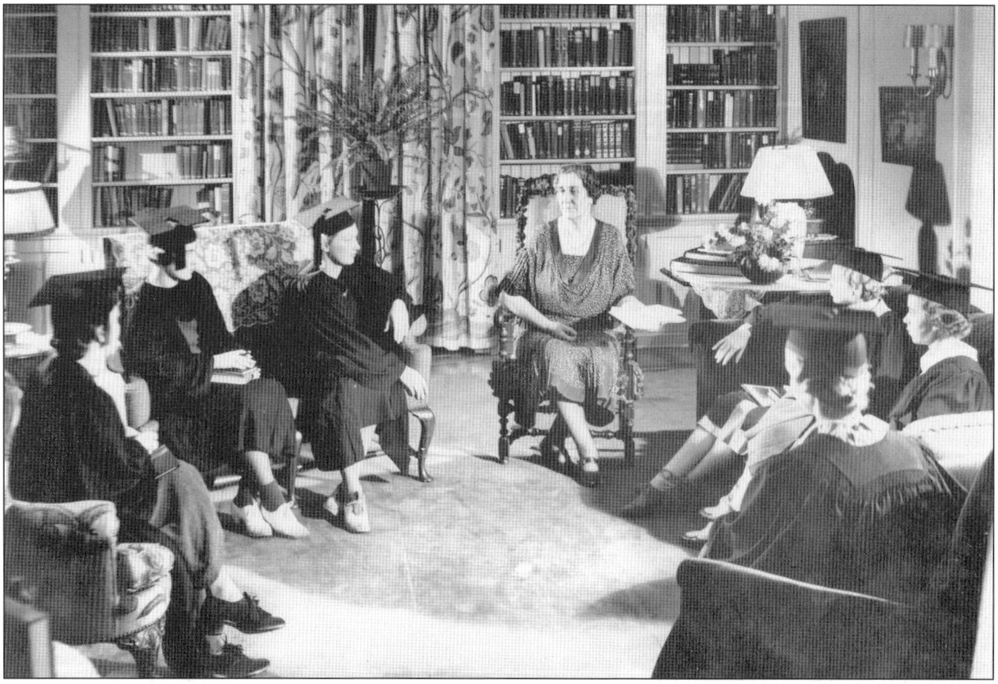

Here, Abby Sutherland is testing her girls, dressed in caps and gowns, on Competitive Day, a serious part of the graduation exercises. Students were expected to speak intelligently on a topic chosen by Sutherland from one of the curriculum's key texts. (The Ogontz School Archives, date unknown, Penn State University, Abington College Library.)

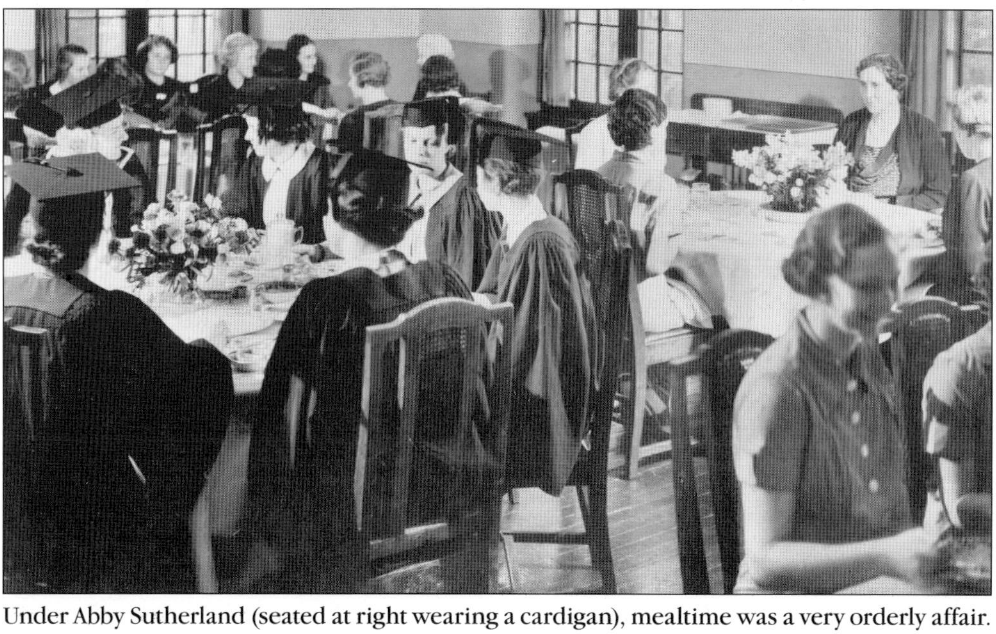

Under Abby Sutherland (seated at right wearing a cardigan), mealtime was a very orderly affair. The seating arrangements were rotated on a regular basis to encourage and improve upon the girls' table manners and conversational skills. She also taught them poise and expected them to curtsy when leaving the table. (The Ogontz School Archives, date unknown, Penn State University, Abington College Library.)

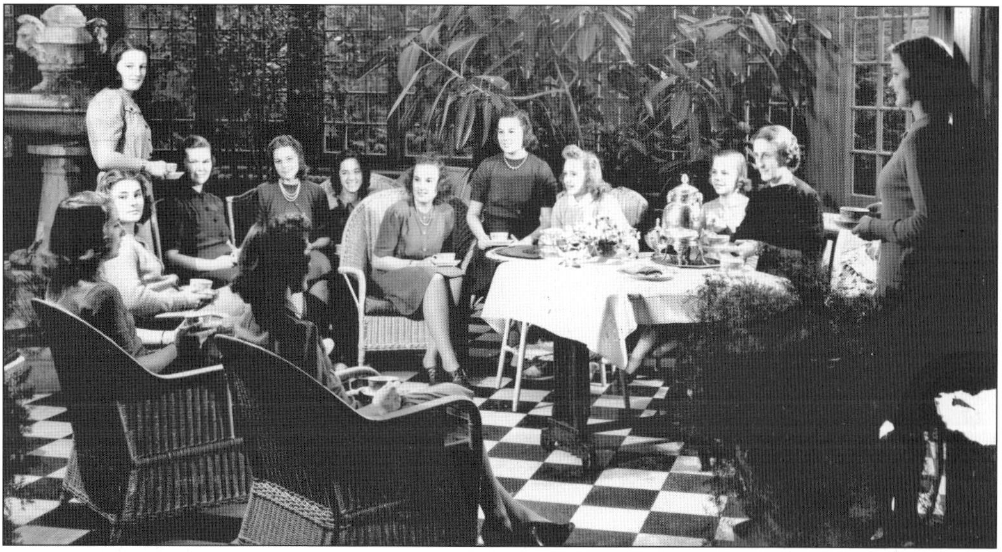

True to her Presbyterian background, Abby Sutherland (seated at table) would frequently sit with her girls for informal talks on serious moral issues. Her book *Talks with Girls*, privately printed at Christmas 1915, opens with her original poem "My Ideal Girl" and contains what amounts to sermons on the subjects of peace, purity, disloyal talk, bad temper, and truth. (The Ogontz School Archives, date unknown, Penn State University, Abington College Library.)

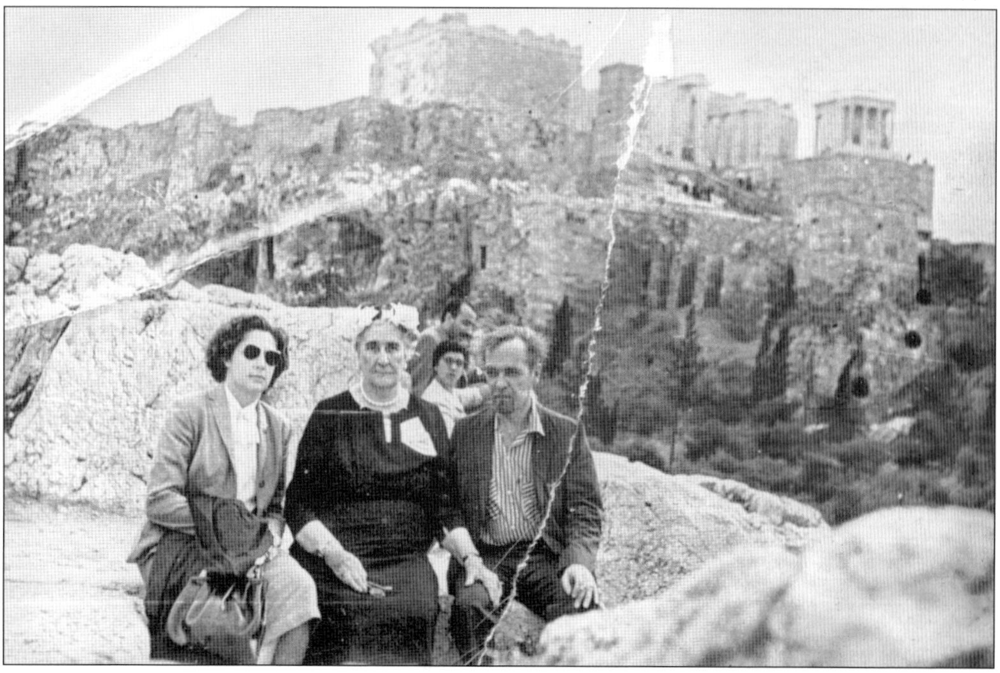

Seated on a rock beneath the Acropolis in Athens, Abby Sutherland is practicing what she preached for years at the Ogontz School. She considered the experience of travel essential to creating a well-rounded young lady. With her are Donald Sutherland (her nephew) and his wife. Her brother, Daniel, the former US representative from the then-territory of Alaska, later lived at Cloverly Hall on campus until he died in 1955. (The Ogontz School Archives, date unknown, Penn State University, Abington College Library.)

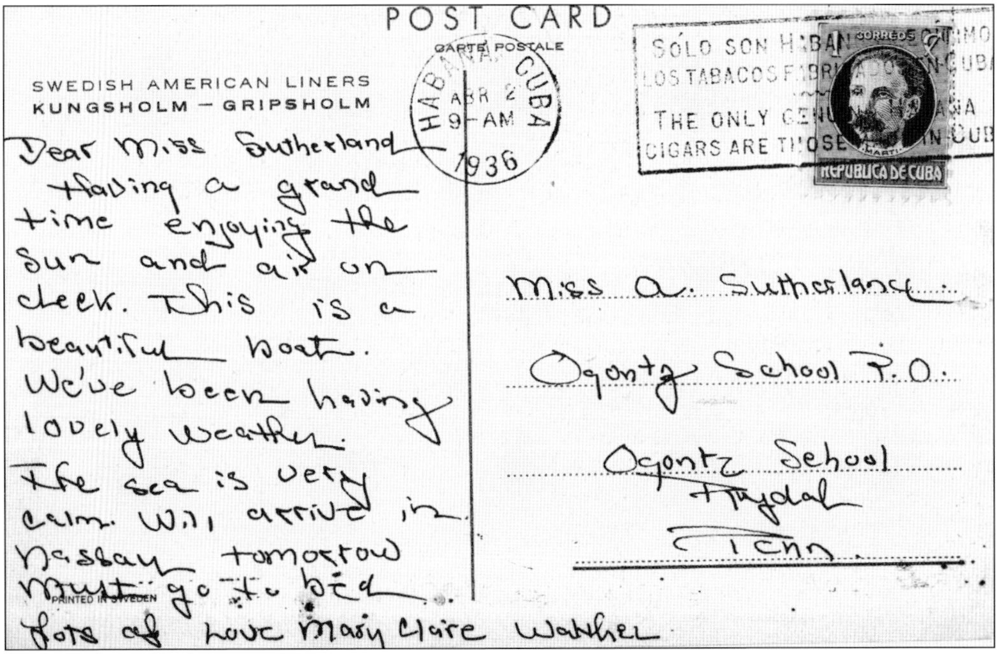
POST CARD
CARTE POSTALE
SWEDISH AMERICAN LINERS
KUNGSHOLM — GRIPSHOLM
HABANA, CUBA ABR 2 9-AM 1936
CORREOS
REPUBLICA DE CUBA

Dear Miss Sutherland
Having a grand time enjoying the sun and air on deck. This is a beautiful boat. We've been having lovely weather. The sea is very calm. Will arrive in Nassau tomorrow. Must go to bed.
Lots of love Mary Claire Walther

Miss A. Sutherland
Ogontz School P.O.
Ogontz School
Rydal
Penn.

PRINTED IN SWEDEN

This affectionate postcard to "Miss A. Sutherland" from her student Mary Clare Walther reveals that her girls indeed took her and her predecessors at Ogontz seriously when they admonished the girls to travel and see the world as part of their overall educational experience. Stamped April 2, 1936, it was sent to Sutherland from "Habana, Cuba." Walther made that trip to Cuba on a Swedish American Liner, ostensibly like the one depicted on the other side of the postcard (below). Posters of various companies offering ocean cruises could be seen on many dormitory walls at Ogontz (see page 108.) (The Ogontz School Archives, 1936, Penn State University, Abington College Library.)

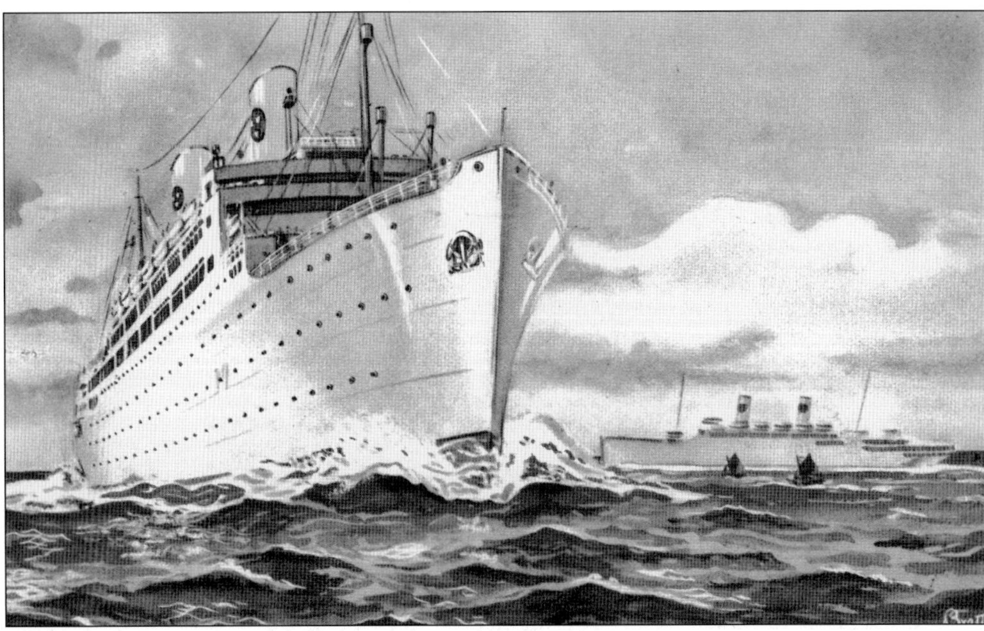

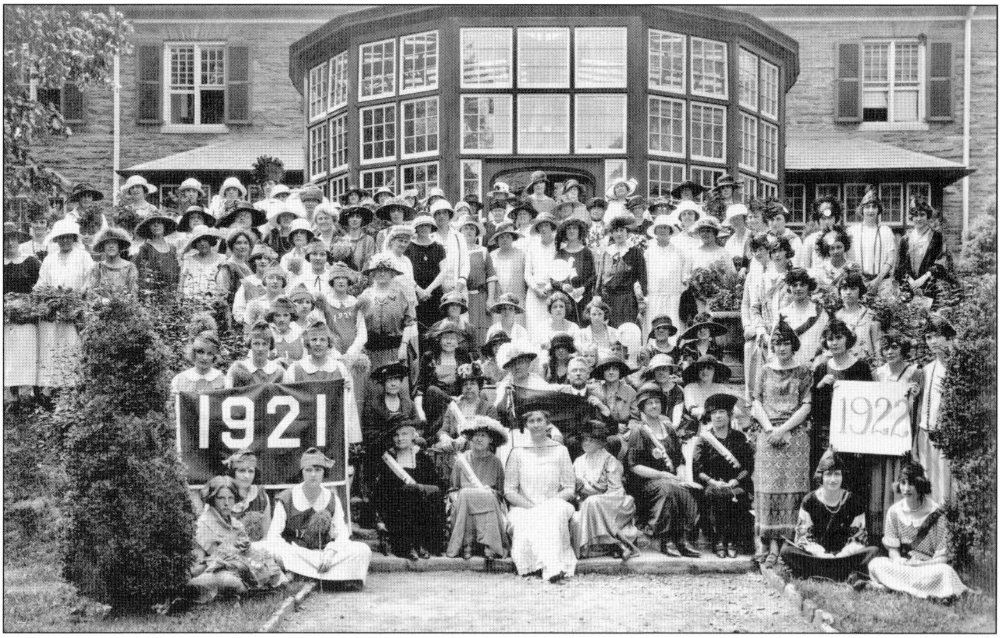

The class reunion of 1923 was an especially glorious event. Celebrating the 40th anniversary of the school's move from 1615 Chestnut Street to Jay Cooke's Ogontz mansion in 1883, it reunited graduates from as far back as the Chestnut Street Female Seminary. Wilma S. Le Van, class of 1905, wrote this recollection in the June 1923 edition of *Ogontz Mosaic*: "MISS SUTHERLAND led the 'old girls' procession, magnificent in her doctor's cap and gown, and looking every inch a Principal. Then came the 1923 Seniors followed by the '1615 girls' and the other years in succession, making a gay and festive line. There were pennants and festoons of every kind; varicolored balloons and hats and muffs and parasols." Eight alumnae who attended that reunion are seated in a semicircle on the grass (below). They are, from left to right, Ruth Robinson Wickwire, Dorothy Liggett, Harriet Horton, Phoebe Weaver, Helen Brooke Lewis Stetson, Zoe Brundred, Marion Marlin Davis, and Lorraine Carstairs Pierce. (Both, the Ogontz School Archives, 1936, Penn State University, Abington College Library.)

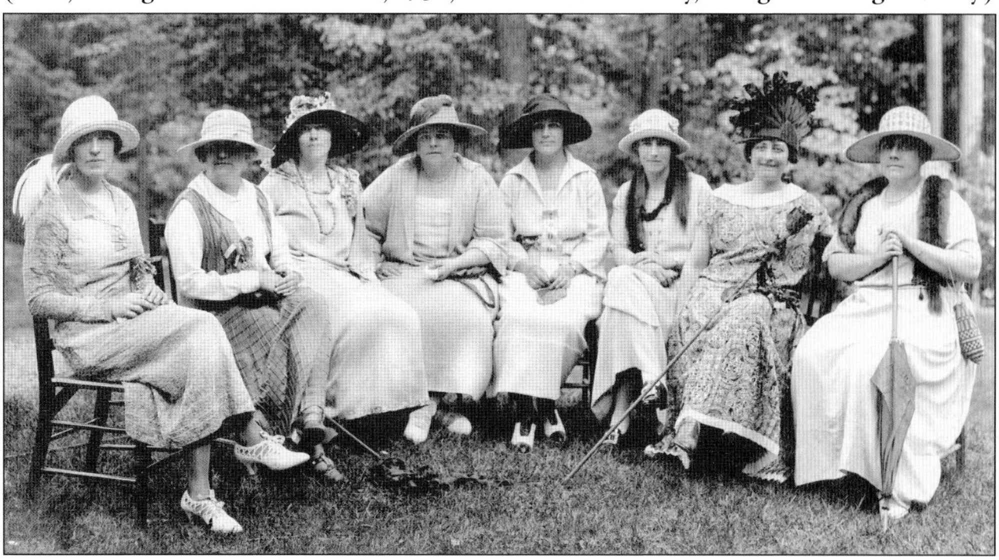

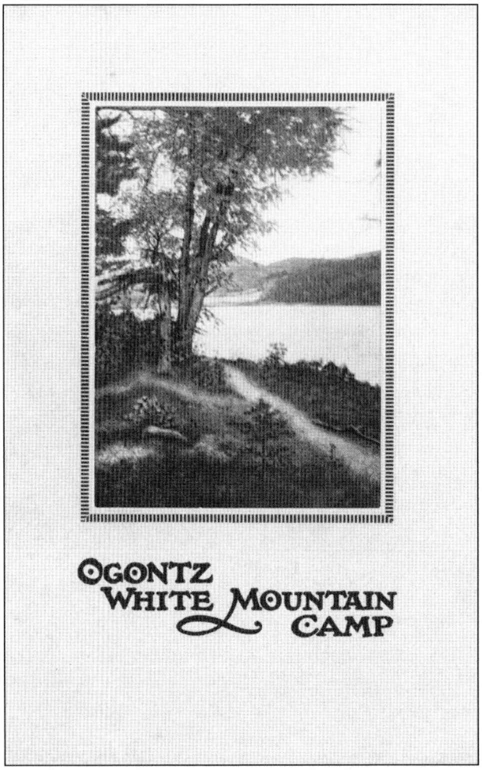

This is the cover of a brochure introducing the Ogontz White Mountain Camp, a summer project launched by Abby Sutherland in 1923 to complement and extend the experience of the Ogontz School. Located in Lisbon, New Hampshire, about 90 miles south of the Canadian border, the camp was 560 acres of prime White Mountains real estate surrounding a spring-fed lake. (The Ogontz School Archives, date unknown, Penn State University, Abington College Library.)

Ogontz White Mountain Camp is believed to be the brainchild of Sutherland's husband, William Furbey Brown, a rugged cowboy whom she met during a vacation in Colorado and married in 1917. His way of contributing to the ongoing physical and cultural well-being of "Abby's girls," the camp contained a golf course, tennis courts, archery and rifle ranges, horseback riding, and of course, the beautiful lake seen here. (The Ogontz School Archives, date unknown, Penn State University, Abington College Library.)

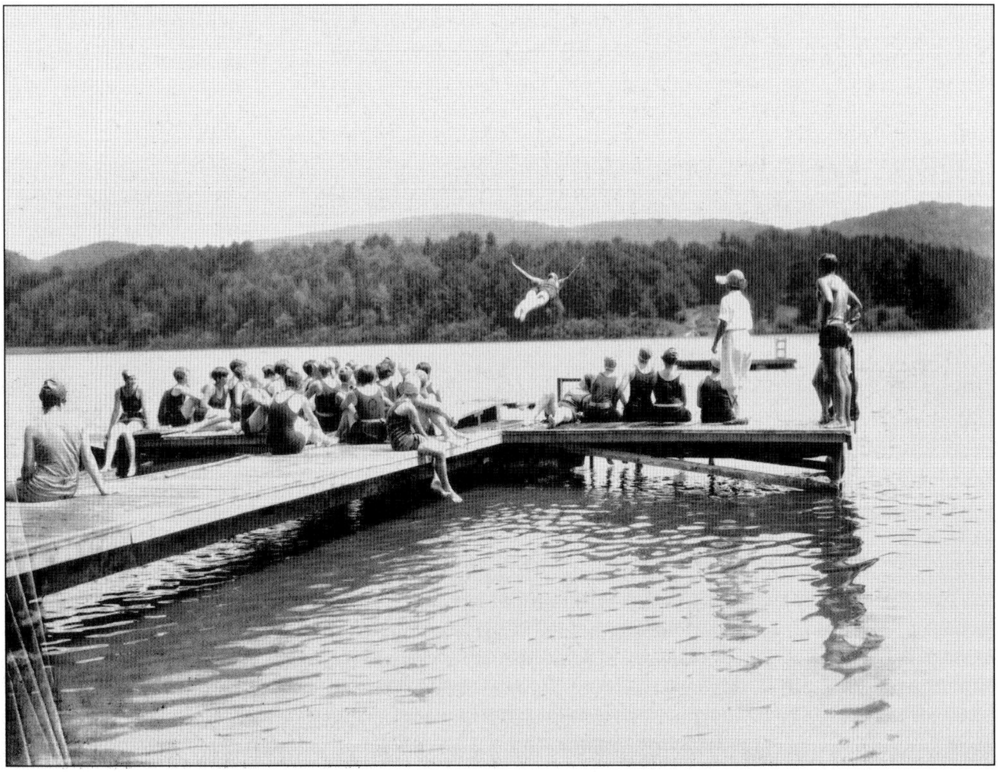

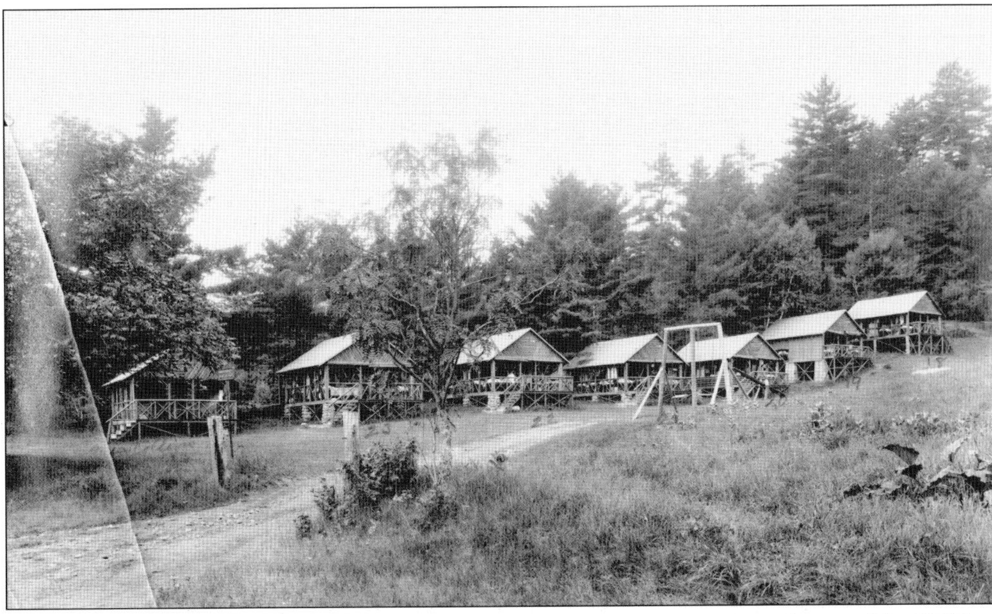

Here is a view of the original cabins at Ogontz White Mountain Camp, designed by William Furbey Brown, who, it is said, participated in the actual construction of the cabins. When Abby Sutherland died in 1961, the camp was passed on to her nephew, Donald, under whose cared it thrived into the 1960s. Under new management, it still functions as a camp today. (The Ogontz School Archives, date unknown, Penn State University, Abington College Library.)

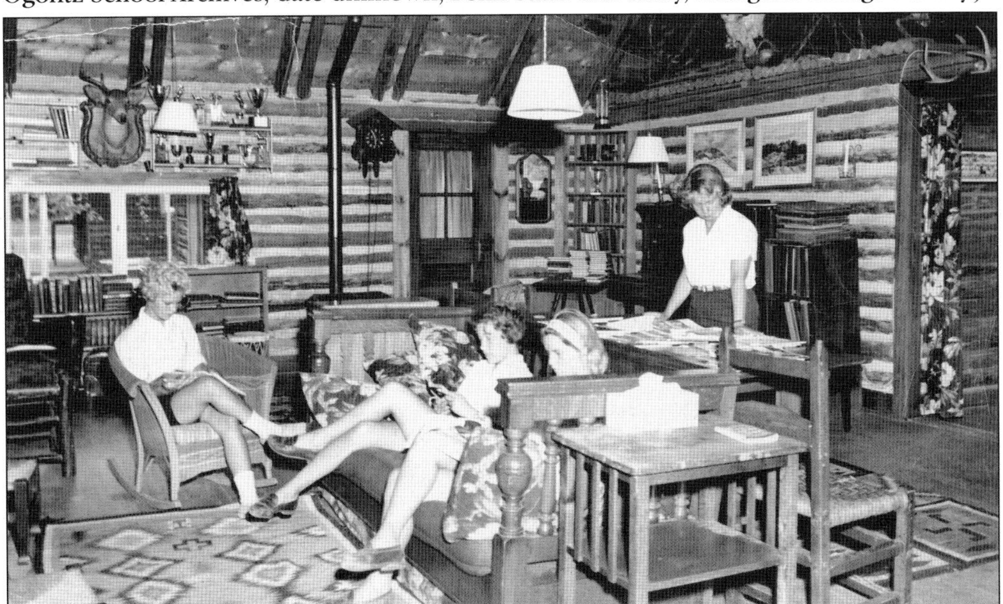

Ogontz White Mountain campers are seen relaxing inside one of their cabins. With Abby Sutherland at the helm, the camp provided for more than simply outdoors activities, although the familiar Ogontz military drill was part of camp routine. There were arts and crafts, theatrical productions, musical performances, storytelling, and poetry readings. Sutherland made tutoring available in practically any college subject. (The Ogontz School Archives, date unknown, Penn State University, Abington College Library.)

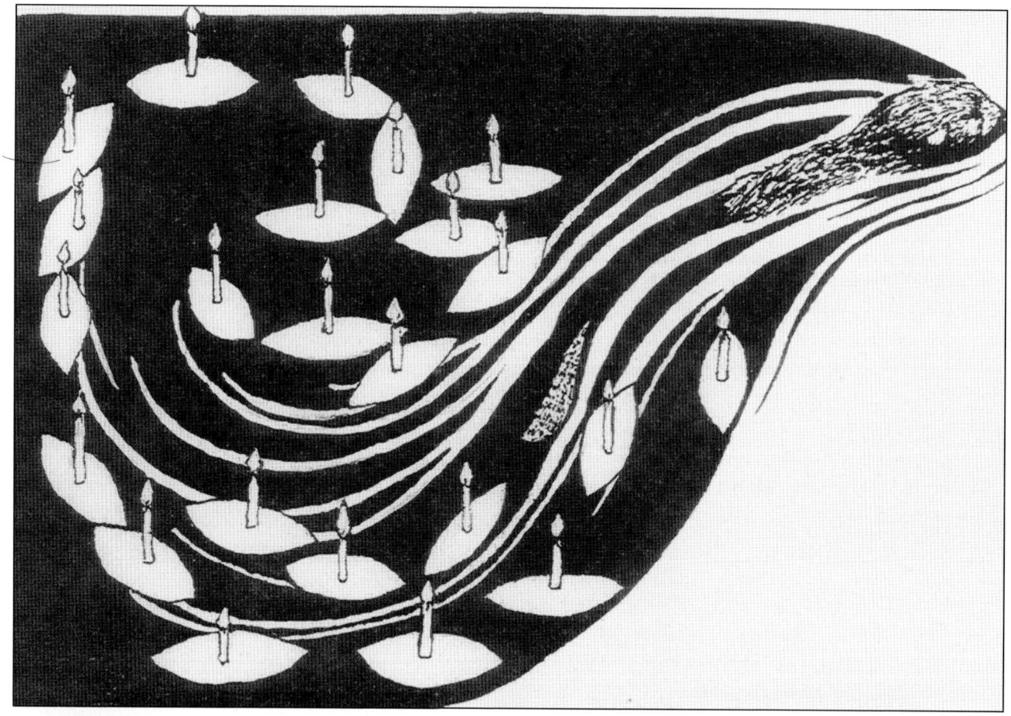

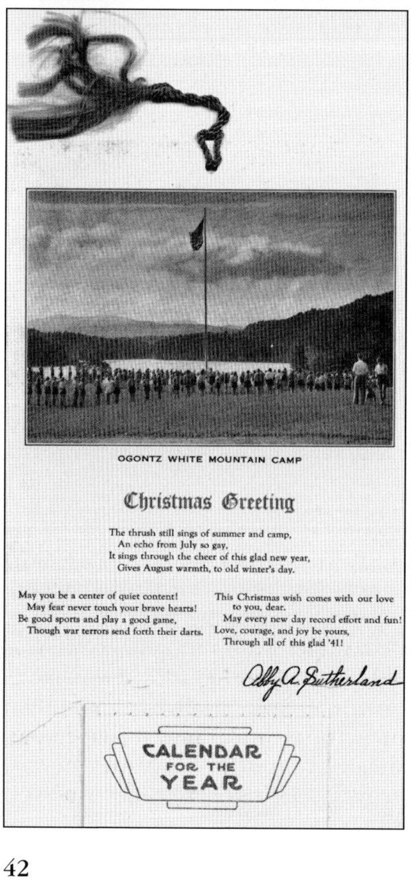

The Candlelight Ceremony concluded the final night of the camp season. Each camper would set a little candlelit wooden boat off into Ogontz Lake, using Abby Sutherland's words, "We are setting afloat on the lake three flame-winged wishes—one for our individual good, one for a near friend, one for the camp." This drawing by artist Rod Torbert is a fanciful expression of the ceremony, featuring candlelit boats set in motion by the unseen swing of a beaver's tail. Beavers are still known to frolic by the lake. At left is Abby Sutherland's Christmas greeting and calendar for 1941, depicting the saluting of the flag at Ogontz White Mountain Camp. (Above, the Ogontz School Archives, date unknown, Penn State University, Abington College Library; left, the Ogontz School Archives, 1941, Penn State University, Abington College Library.)

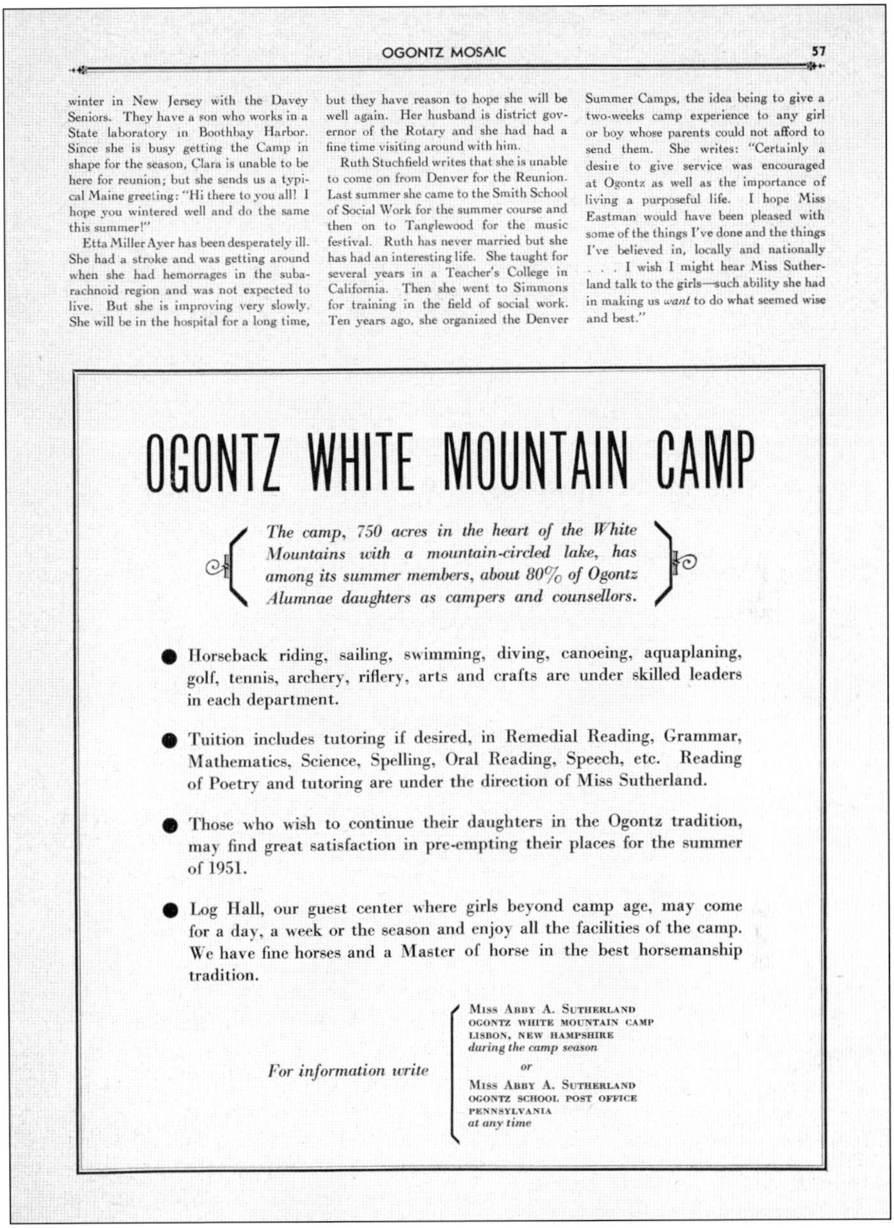

winter in New Jersey with the Davey Seniors. They have a son who works in a State laboratory in Boothbay Harbor. Since she is busy getting the Camp in shape for the season, Clara is unable to be here for reunion; but she sends us a typical Maine greeting: "Hi there to you all! I hope you wintered well and do the same this summer!"

Etta Miller Ayer has been desperately ill. She had a stroke and was getting around when she had hemorrages in the subarachnoid region and was not expected to live. But she is improving very slowly. She will be in the hospital for a long time, but they have reason to hope she will be well again. Her husband is district governor of the Rotary and she had had a fine time visiting around with him.

Ruth Stuchfield writes that she is unable to come on from Denver for the Reunion. Last summer she came to the Smith School of Social Work for the summer course and then on to Tanglewood for the music festival. Ruth has never married but she has had an interesting life. She taught for several years in a Teacher's College in California. Then she went to Simmons for training in the field of social work. Ten years ago, she organized the Denver Summer Camps, the idea being to give a two-weeks camp experience to any girl or boy whose parents could not afford to send them. She writes: "Certainly a desire to give service was encouraged at Ogontz as well as the importance of living a purposeful life. I hope Miss Eastman would have been pleased with some of the things I've done and the things I've believed in, locally and nationally . . . I wish I might hear Miss Sutherland talk to the girls—such ability she had in making us *want* to do what seemed wise and best."

For Ogontz girls and their friends who had been enjoying the Ogontz White Mountain Camp since its founding in 1923, this advertisement in the July 1950 issue of *Ogontz Mosaic* must have been quite a relief. Even though Abby Sutherland had decided to donate the Ogontz School to Penn State College (later Penn State University), effective after the end of the spring 1950 semester, Ogontz White Mountain Camp would continue. Even though no one was certain the camp would outlive the school, it actually did, thriving for decades in the hands of Abby Sutherland, then her nephew, Donald Sutherland, after she died in 1961, and then run by Ogontz graduates until the end of the 20th century. Today, under new management, the camp is occupied continually from Memorial Day through Labor Day by various musical and arts groups and hosts weddings and other special events. (The Ogontz School Archives, 1950, Penn State University, Abington College Library.)

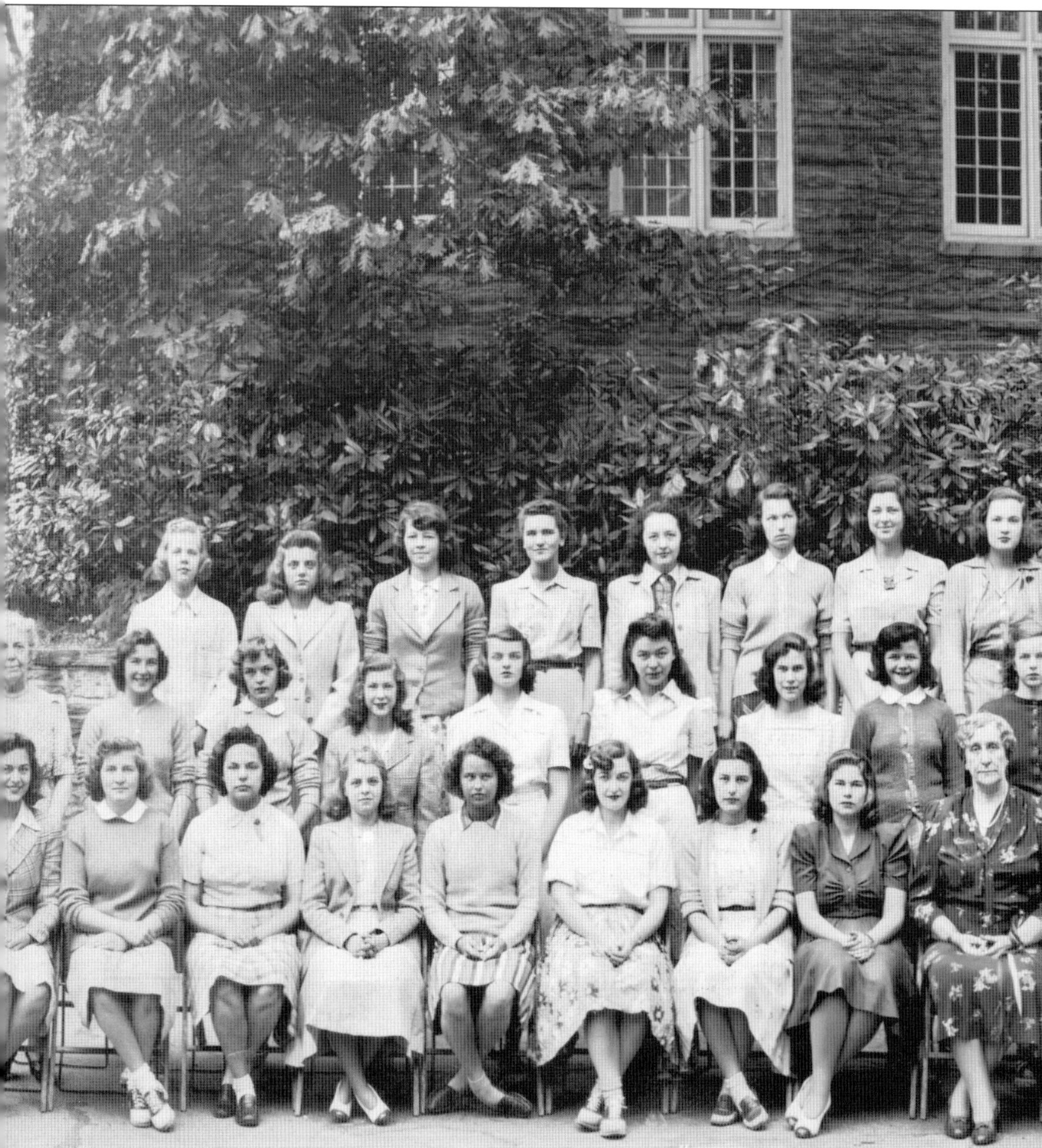

Against the backdrop of Sutherland Building, the Kin Club of 1941 gathers before its annual dinner. Founded in 1929 by Abby Sutherland at the suggestion of girls whose mothers had been students and devoted friends of their alma mater, the Kin Club met once a month to reminisce and confirm the traditions that made the school so dear to its graduates. The younger alumnae would enjoy searching for pictures of their mothers or grandmothers from

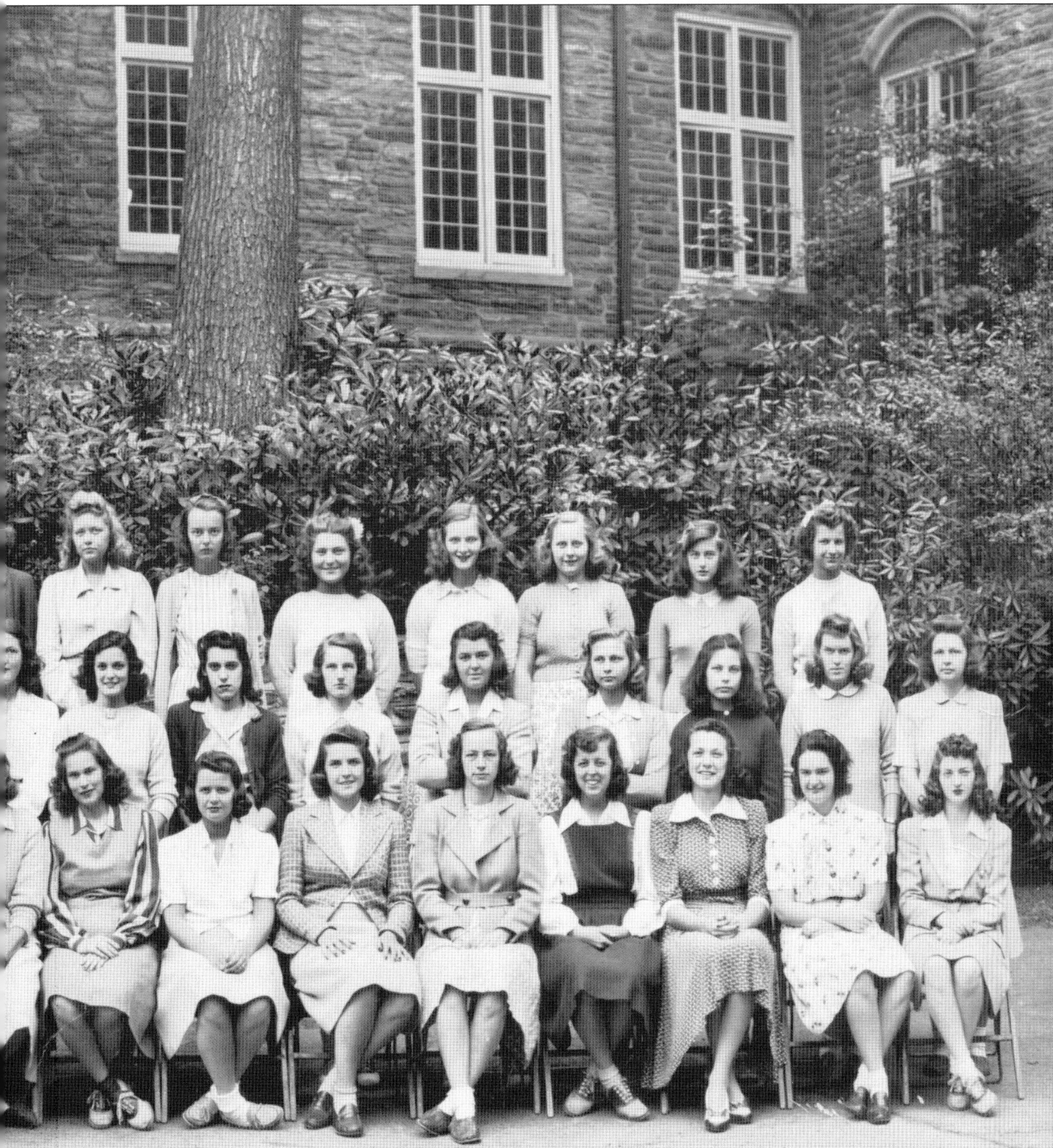

among the photographs of classes as far back as 1883 hanging on the walls of Sutherland. According to Dr. Laura Fattal, a former art history teacher at Penn State Ogontz, by the time the Ogontz School closed in 1950, approximately 55 percent of the student body had close relatives who had attended the school. (The Ogontz School Archives, 1941, Penn State University, Abington College Library.)

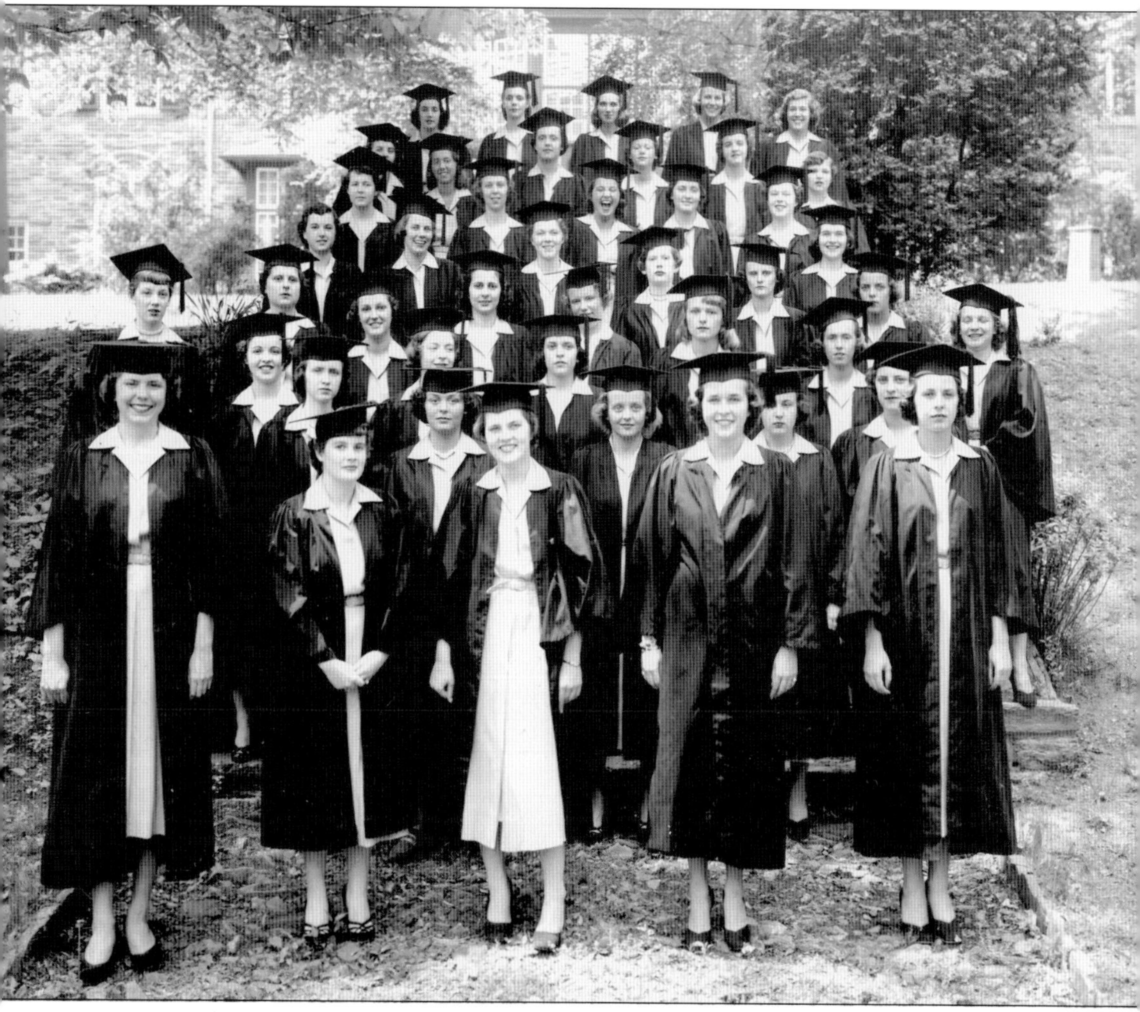

Here it is, the class of 1950, the final graduating class of the Ogontz School. The times had clearly changed. The kind of education these fine young ladies had been receiving for the past 100 years had come to an end. It was clear to Abby Sutherland, even in the early years of the 20th century, when she began introducing an academic track to the curriculum, that finishing schools would have a termination date. The education of the elite young ladies of Ogontz prepared them to become wives to ambassadors and to the cultural, political, and professional and business elite. Education was becoming more democratic, as the new Penn State Ogontz Center would soon show. (The Ogontz School Archives, 1950, Penn State University, Abington College Library.)

Three

Ogontz Evolves into Abington

Faculty, deans, and chancellors can be eloquent, incisive, and persuasive. But sometimes a student's simple insights are even more transcendent. How does one best explain the difference between the school's first century of education and the more than 65 years that followed?

On one hand were the privileged young ladies who fused their milieux and values with those of their inspiring principals at the Chestnut Street Female Seminary and the Ogontz School for Young Ladies. On the other is the new breed of students, who have infused Penn State Ogontz and Penn State Abington with a fresh new spirit.

Listen to the words of Matthew Guckin, a student who played basketball for Penn State Ogontz in the mid-1980s. A dropout after an unsuccessful freshman year, Guckin returned a year later after a life-changing stint of hard labor in the construction field and, inspired by teachers like Dr. Leonard Mustazza, applied himself both on and off the court. According to author Rachel Simon, Penn State Abington's former writer-in-residence in her lovely book *This Time This Place: Penn State at Abington 1950–2000*, Guckin described the "good, ordinary people" around him as "Not too sophisticated, or glamorous, or pretentious. They were no-nonsense, salt-of-the-earth, regular folk. That's the kind of student who goes to Penn State [Ogontz/Abington]."

Guckin's estimate does not denigrate the achievements of all who came before him, for they are considerable; it is merely a reflection of the changing face and soul of modern education—Penn State Ogontz/Abington style.

This chapter reflects on the gradual metamorphosis of Penn State Ogontz into the magnetic institution it is today. That evolution includes new spaces where students study and play as well as leaders in the faculty and administration who inspire them to become the best they can be.

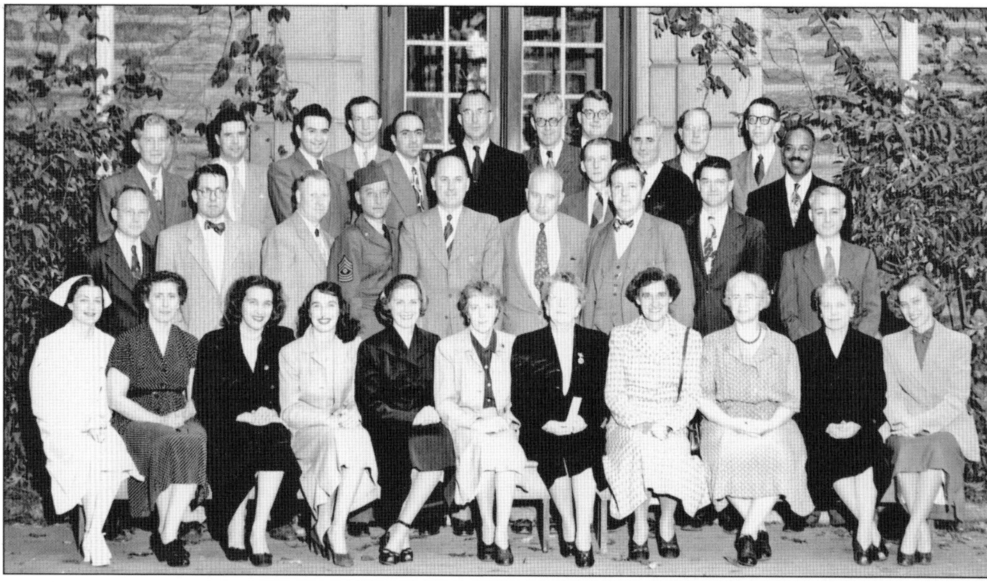

Oh, how the college has grown! Numbering less than three dozen when this photograph was taken, the faculty beginning the fall 1951 semester were fewer than the students enrolled in a typical class in psychology or mathematics today. In 1951, Penn State College (later University) merged its Ogontz and Swarthmore centers into the Penn State Ogontz Center, with 258 students enrolled predominantly in liberal arts. There was no tuition at the time, but students were charged $195 per semester in general fees. In the photograph below, Dinah Geiger (left), a beloved presence on campus for more than 40 years and assistant to the director of academic affairs Dr. John Pixton (right), is seen working with Pixton as E. Koenig looks on." (Above, the Ogontz School Archives, 1951, Penn State University, Abington College Library; below, the Ogontz School Archives, 1964, Penn State University, Abington College Library.)

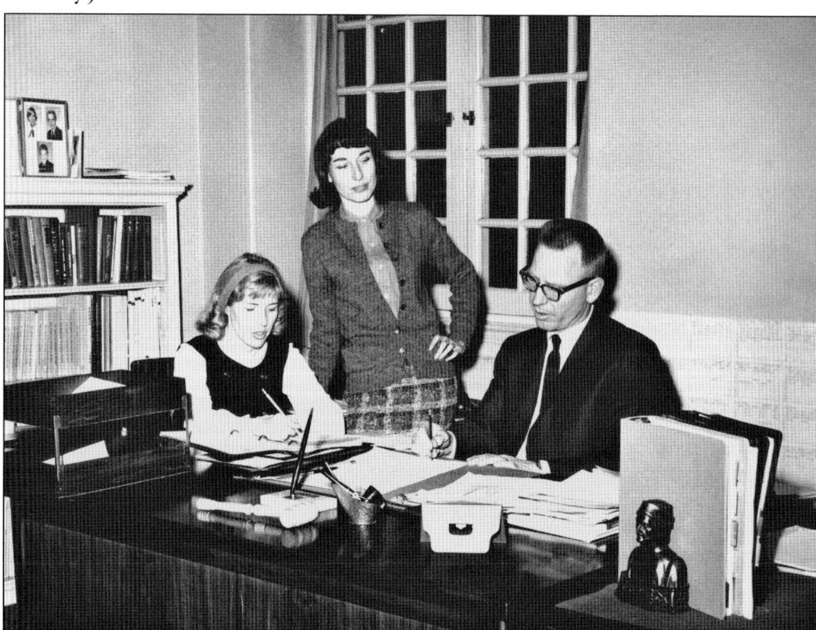

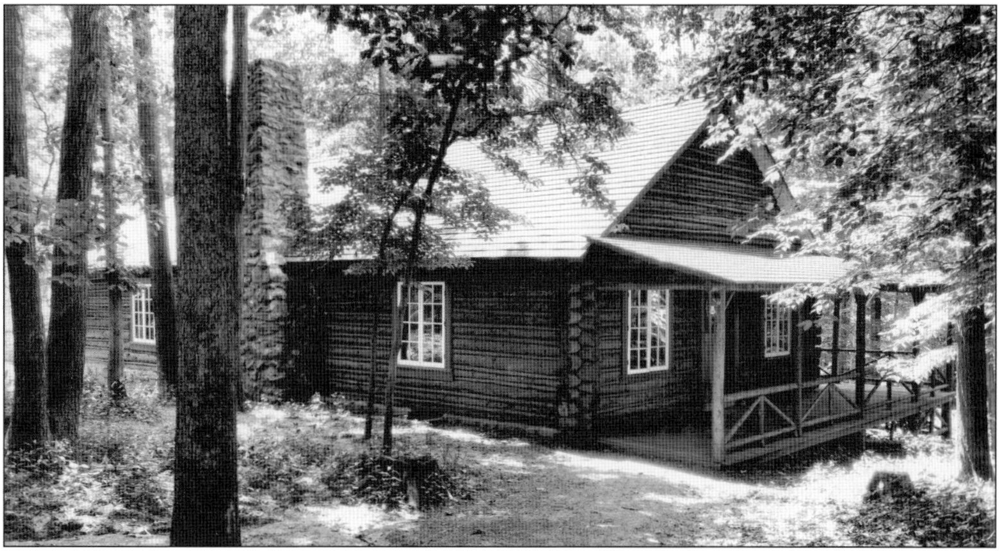

Demolished in the early 1960s, the rough-hewn log cabin built by Abby Sutherland's husband, William Furbey Brown, in the 1920s served as a student and faculty hangout during the first decade of the new school's life. It was there, just down the hill from the imposing shadow of the Sutherland Building, that students and teachers could grab a light snack between classes, chat informally, and get to know each other better. (The Ogontz School Archives, c. 1950s, Penn State University, Abington College Library.)

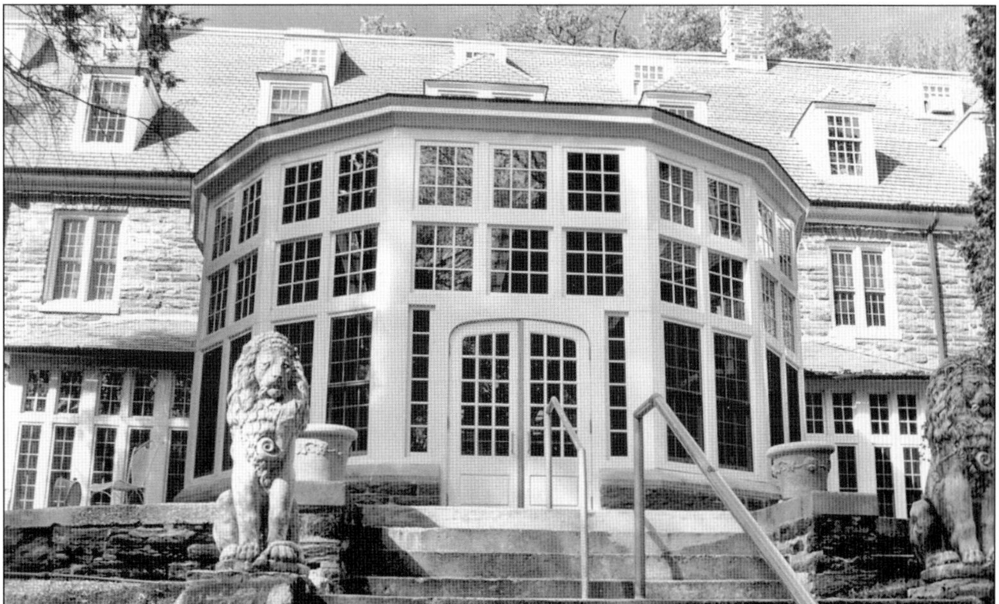

Area resident J. Liddon Pennock Jr. gave these stately lions to the college to stand as sentinels outside the entrance to the solarium in Sutherland. A landscape designer, floral artist, and cultural activist, he was renowned for his floral decorations at the Nixon White House as well as society weddings. The college still has a close relationship with nearby Meadowbrook Farm, the estate and gardens he cultivated in Abington Township. (The Ogontz School Archives, date unknown, Penn State University, Abington College Library.)

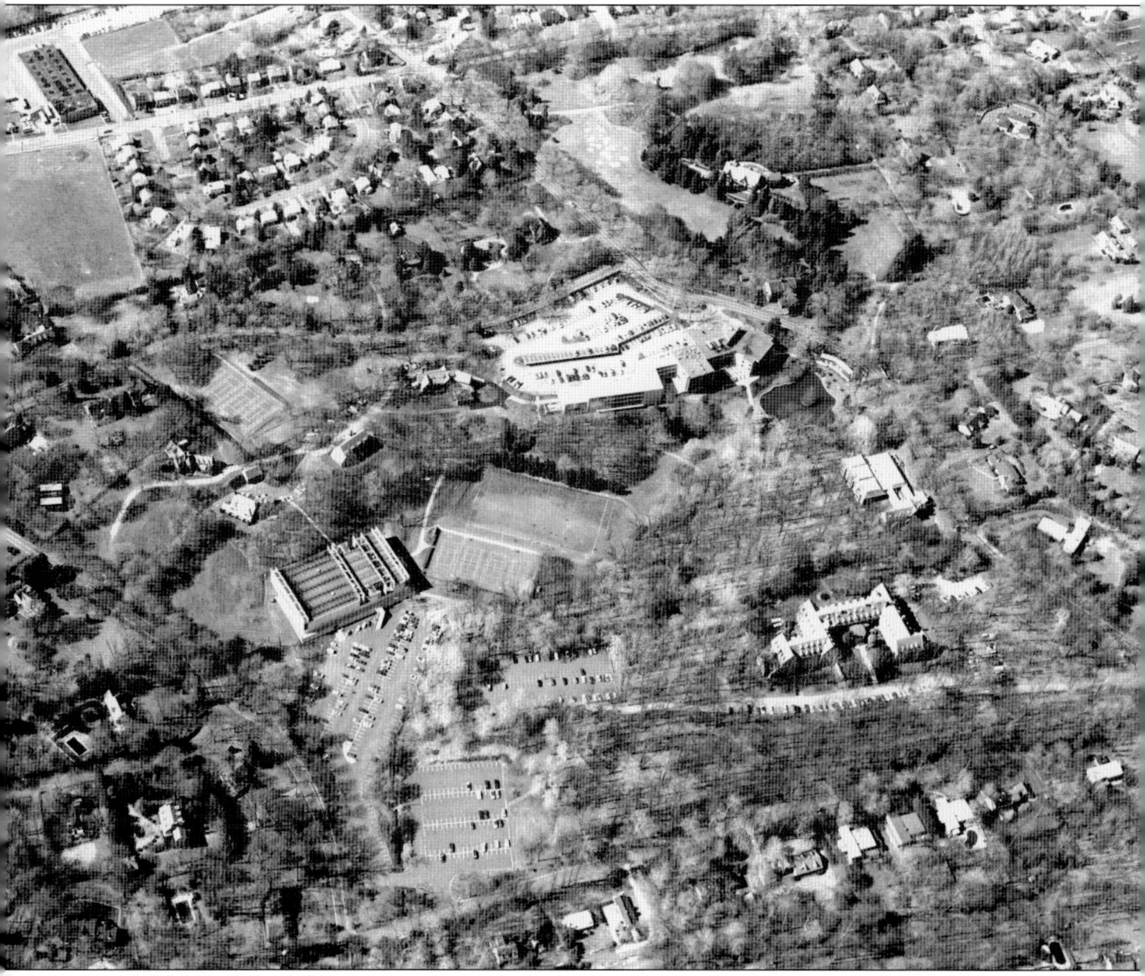

Just 11 years after its birth as Penn State Ogontz, it was clear that the former sedate Ogontz School for Young Ladies had grown into quite a different beast. That increasingly detectable roar that neighbors began to hear was the sound of automobile engines. It was not simply the result of higher enrollment. It was also that, in 1957, the dormitories on the second and third floors of Sutherland had to close to make way for new classrooms. The college had officially become a commuter campus. Thus began a challenge the well-heeled young ladies at the Ogontz School never had to face. The moaning and groaning about parking shortages and excessive parking fines began to fill the pages of the campus newspapers when the students themselves were not taking up placards and protesting to the administration for relief. (The Ogontz School Archives, 1961, Penn State University, Abington College Library.)

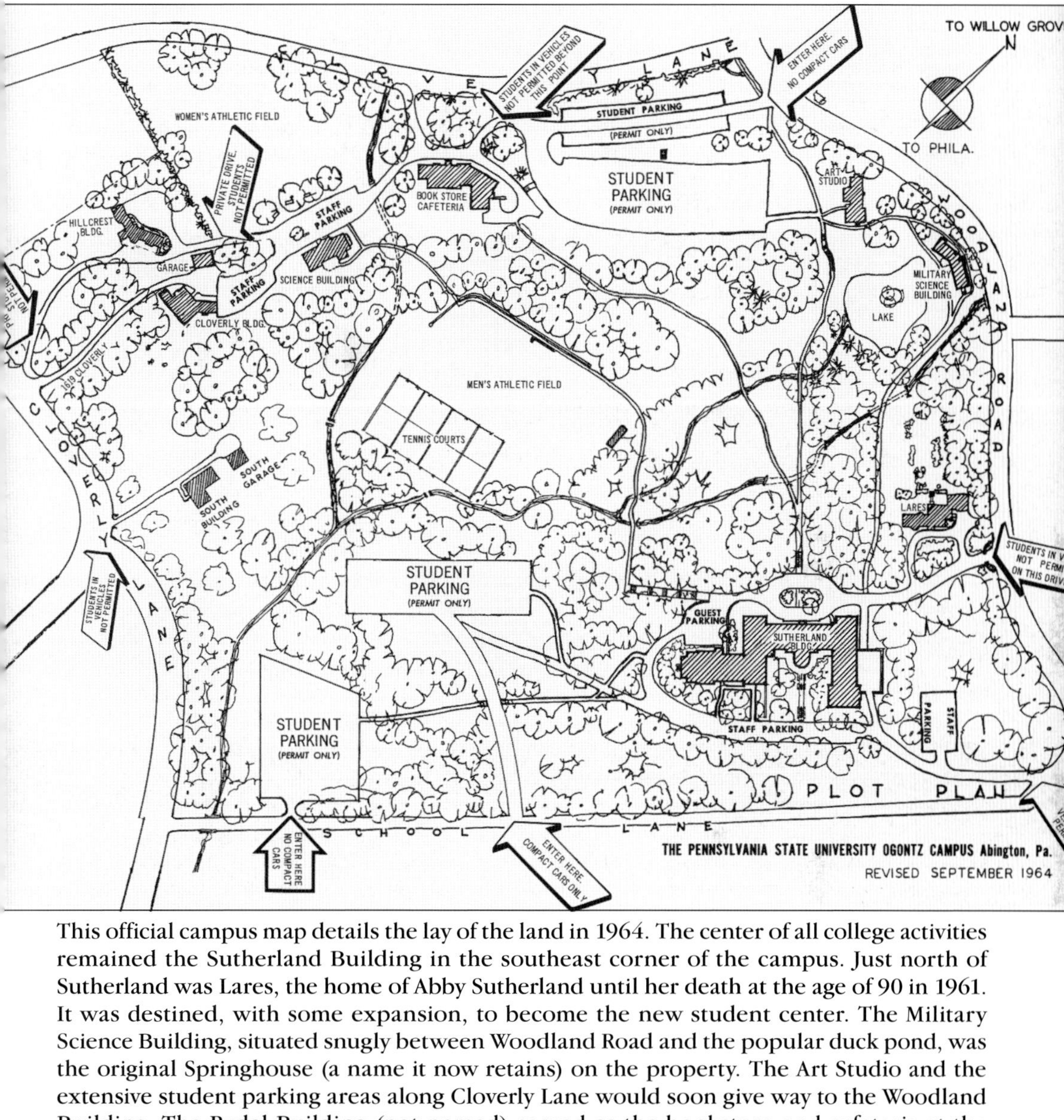

This official campus map details the lay of the land in 1964. The center of all college activities remained the Sutherland Building in the southeast corner of the campus. Just north of Sutherland was Lares, the home of Abby Sutherland until her death at the age of 90 in 1961. It was destined, with some expansion, to become the new student center. The Military Science Building, situated snugly between Woodland Road and the popular duck pond, was the original Springhouse (a name it now retains) on the property. The Art Studio and the extensive student parking areas along Cloverly Lane would soon give way to the Woodland Building. The Rydal Building (not named) served as the bookstore and cafeteria at the time. Down the path from Rydal were the science building (now the Conference Center) and Cloverly Building. Both were designed by Horace Trumbauer. Right up the hill is aptly named Hillcrest, a former private residence that later became the residence of the school's directors. After the college purchased more than two acres of land along Cloverly Lane, the tennis courts, men's athletic field, the South Building, parking areas, and garages would soon be reconfigured as the Physical Education Building. (The Ogontz School Archives, 1964, Penn State University, Abington College Library.)

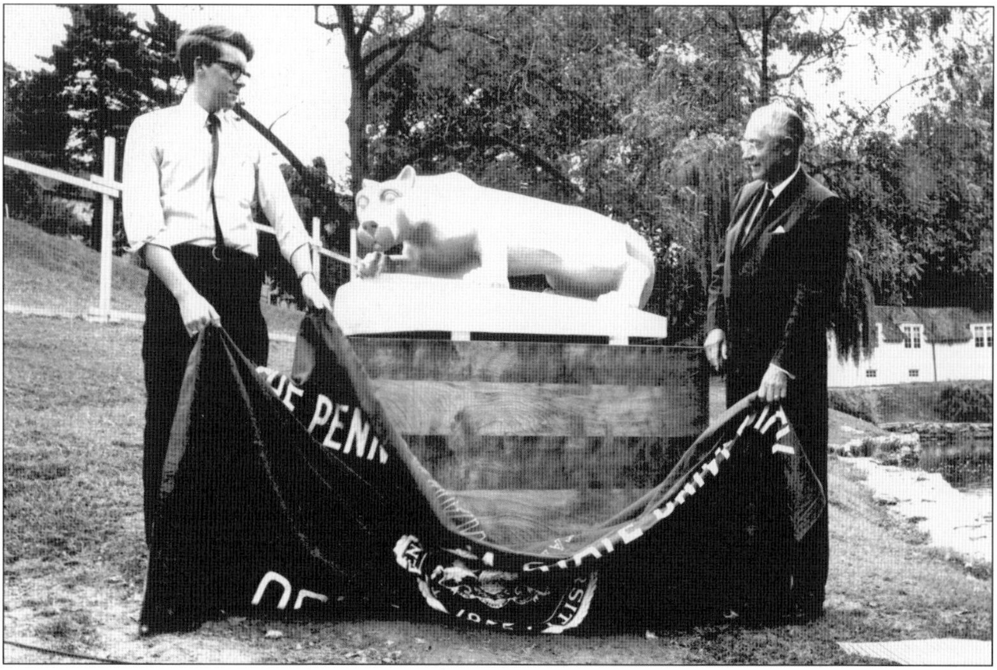

On September 25, 1969, during the ground breaking for the new Woodland Building, Penn State University president Eric A. Walker presents a replica of the iconic Nittany Lion at University Park to Sam Wood, president of the Student Government Association. Woodland would become the first new building constructed on campus since the Trumbauer buildings of the 1920s. (University Relations Department, Penn State Abington.)

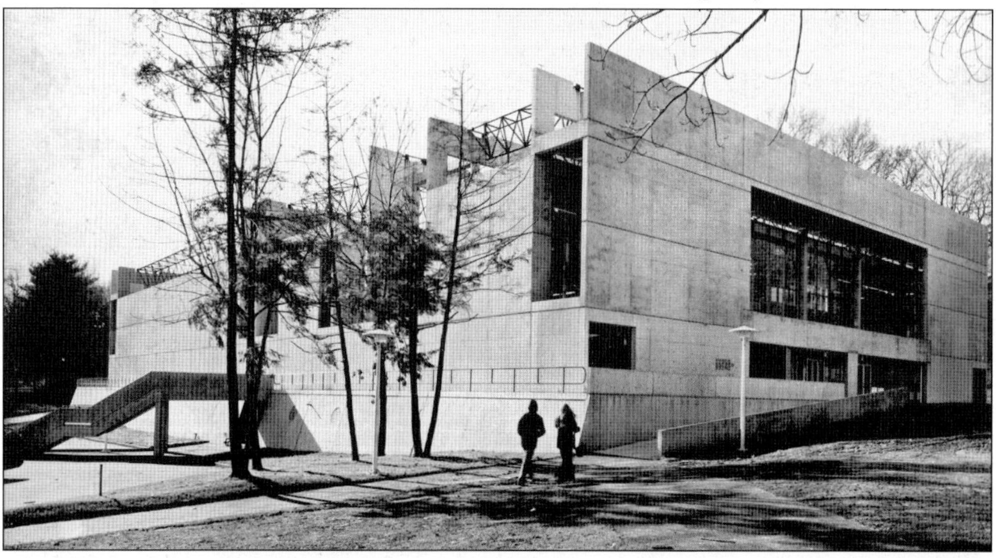

The massive scale of the boxlike Physical Education Building proved quite controversial when its design was presented in the early 1970s. Its huge, modernist footprint would clearly dominate the charming Trumbauer buildings dating to the first two decades of the century. But it was ultimately approved; it was completed in 1973, and it won a design award. It has served the college's physical education needs well ever since. (The Ogontz School Archives, c. 1973, Penn State University, Abington College Library.)

Wes Olsen, who arrived on campus in the 1970s, loved calisthenics far more than calculus. A member of the bowling team affectionately dubbed "The Misfits," Olsen graduated from Penn State but could not stay away from Ogontz for long. Not long after his return, he was managing the physical education department and coaching the golf team. After he died, a golf tournament was named in his honor. (University Relations Department, Penn State Abington.)

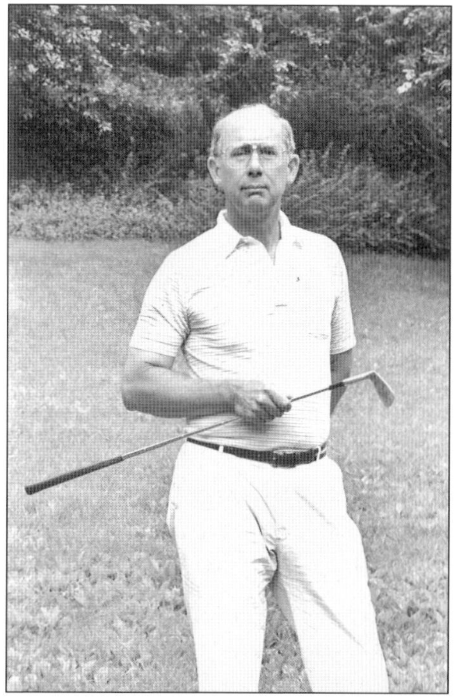

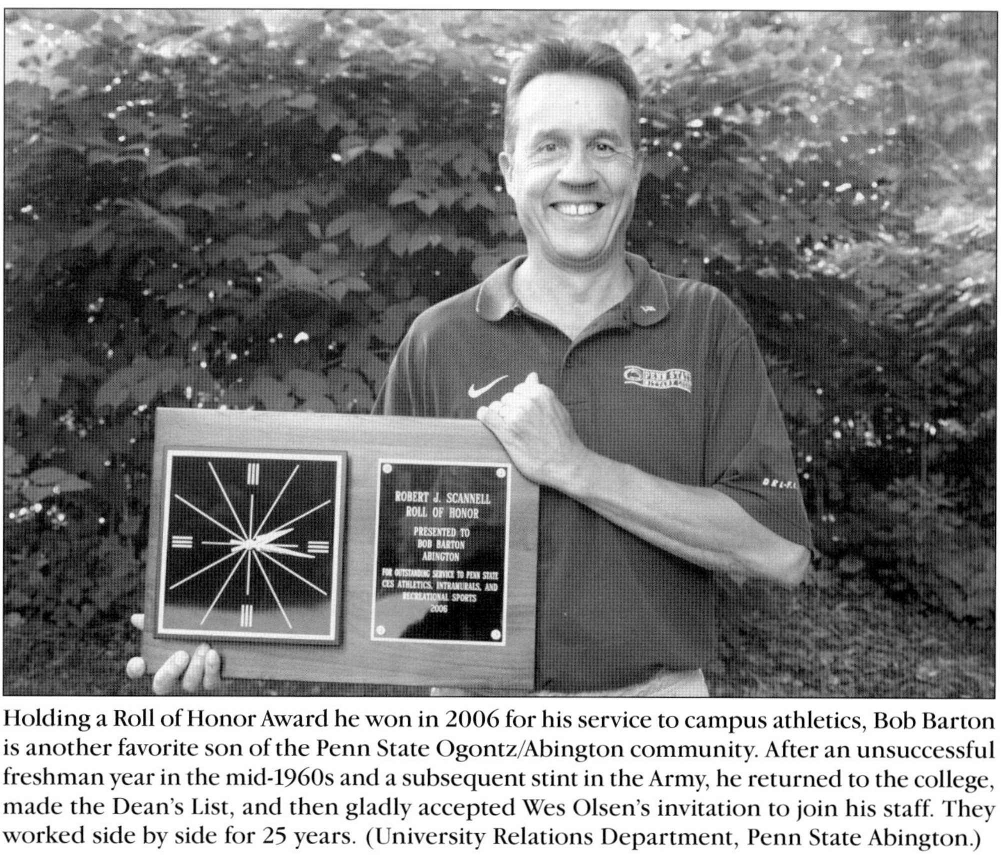

Holding a Roll of Honor Award he won in 2006 for his service to campus athletics, Bob Barton is another favorite son of the Penn State Ogontz/Abington community. After an unsuccessful freshman year in the mid-1960s and a subsequent stint in the Army, he returned to the college, made the Dean's List, and then gladly accepted Wes Olsen's invitation to join his staff. They worked side by side for 25 years. (University Relations Department, Penn State Abington.)

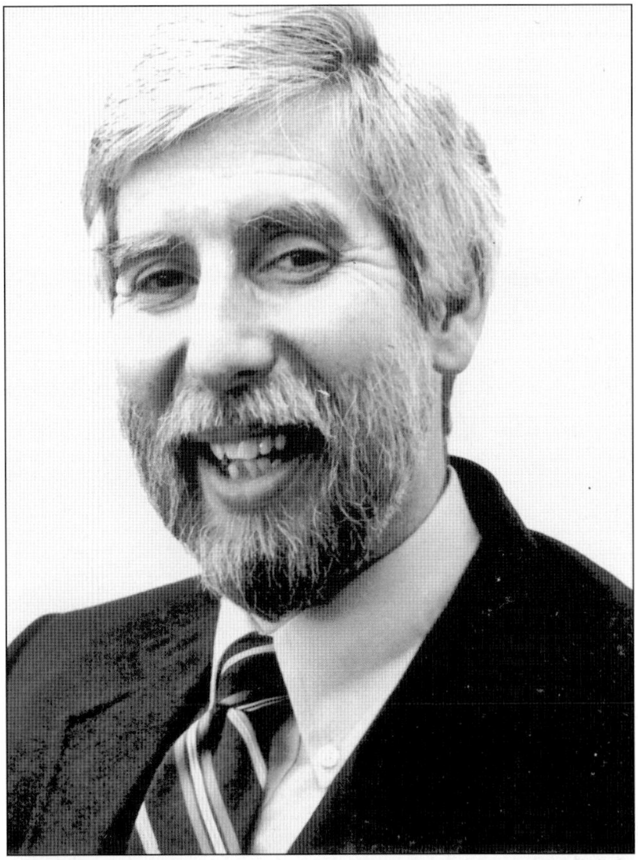

Dr. Robert Bernoff began his career at Penn State Ogontz as a highly regarded science teacher. His success in the classroom and educational vision led to his elevation to the position of dean and chief executive officer of the college. He retired with the distinguished rank of professor emeritus of science and general chemistry. He is seen below (far right) at the college's 1986 commencement with the commencement speaker, Pennsylvania state senator Hardy Williams, class of 1986 graduate Elizabeth Lundgren, and winner of the Outstanding Alumni Award Harry I. Levit, class of 1965. (Left, the Ogontz School Archives, date unknown, Penn State University, Abington College Library; below, the Ogontz School Archives, 1986, Penn State University, Abington College Library.)

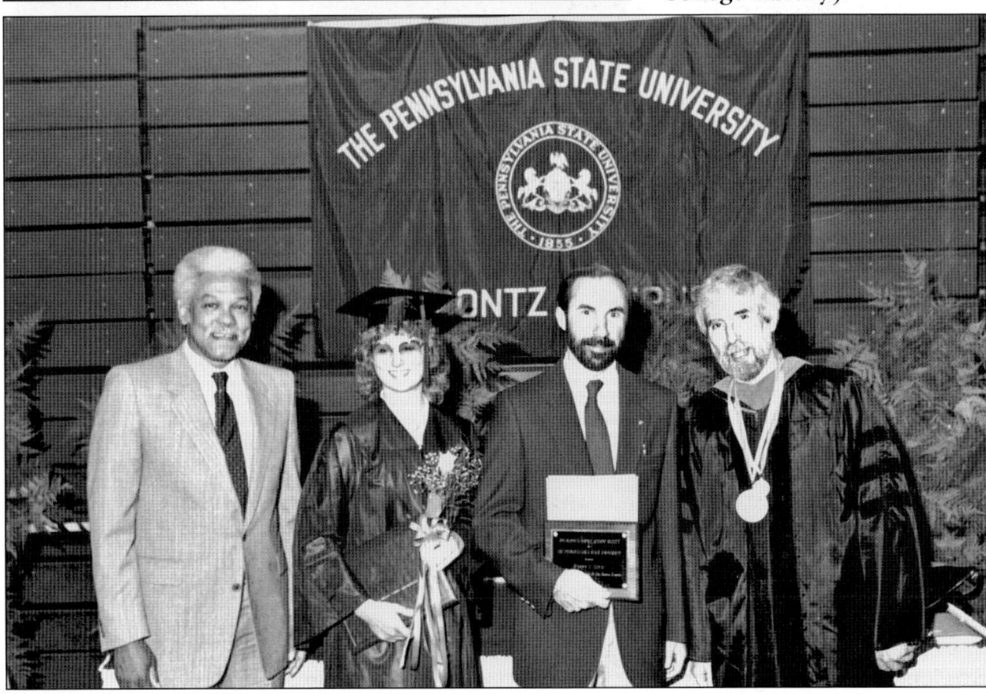

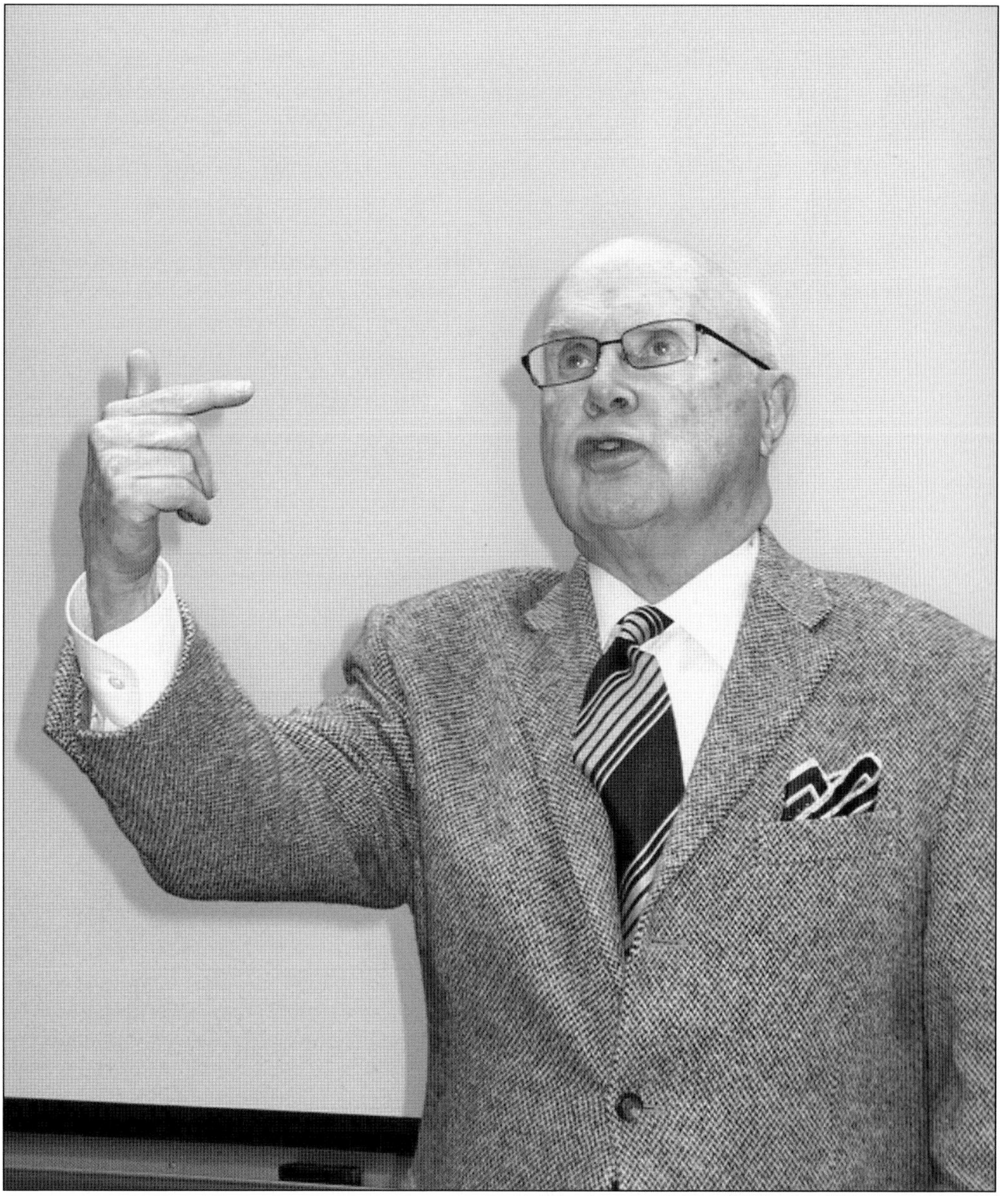

Dapper, dramatic, dedicated to finding creative ways to induce students to care about the performing arts, Dr. Moylan C. Mills, known to many as "Mike," broke onto the Penn State Ogontz scene in the mid-1960s. Dr. Mills is professor emeritus of integrative arts at the Pennsylvania State University, and he has taught film, theater, and popular culture courses at Penn State Abington. The founder and former head of the college's Department of Integrative Arts and former director of academic affairs and interim chief executive officer for Abington College, Dr. Mills has been a familiar figure on and off campus as a major contributor to the college's cultural arts program. He also writes extensively on film, literature, and theater, most recently on Irish films for the essay collection *Contemporary Irish Cinema* and on South American films and religious philosophy for *JAISA: The Journal of the Association for Interdisciplinary Studies in the Arts*. He has received the Lindback and Amoco awards for excellence in teaching. (University Relations Department, Penn State Abington.)

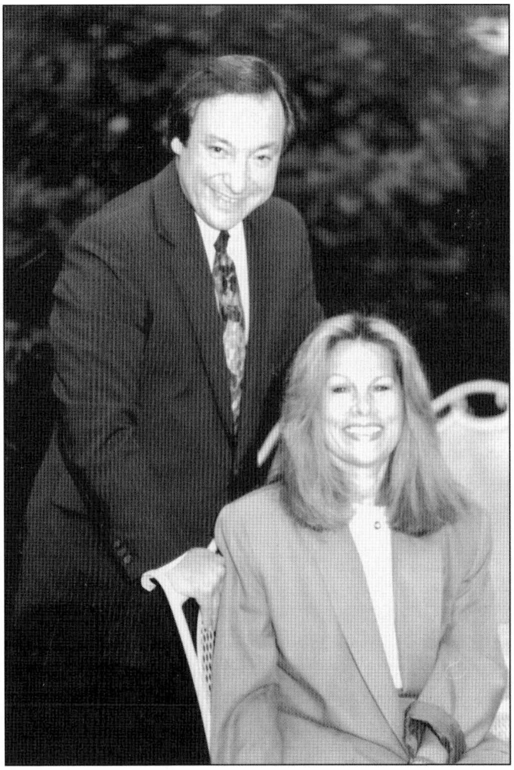

Penn State Abington faculty value the role of researcher as well as teacher. As such, Dr. Leonard Mustazza, distinguished professor of English and American Studies and former associate dean for academic affairs, has more than fulfilled his roles. He is seen left with campus colleague Dr. Vicki Abt, professor of sociology and American studies, after the 1997 publication of their book *Coming After Oprah: Cultural Fallout in the Age of the TV Talk Show*. Dr. Abt also appeared on Oprah Winfrey's talk show that year. Dr. Mustazza, who has written dozens of books, articles, and reviews, is renowned as one of the country's leading voices on Frank Sinatra. He is seen below with graduating senior Theresa Sheasley at the 1997 commencement after being presented with the college's first Lion Heart Award, honoring the graduating class's most inspiring faculty, administrative, or staff member. (Both, the Ogontz School Archives, 1997, Penn State University, Abington College Library.)

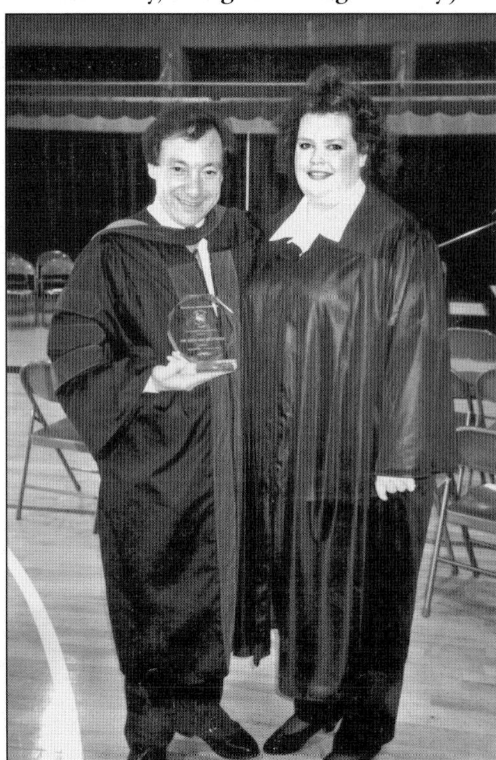

Assistant director of academic affairs when Penn State Abington became a four-year college in 1997 and its first Arts and Humanities Division head, Dr. Ellen Knodt helped steer the college forward. Her optimistic belief that within five years, half of the student body would be upper-level proved to be uncannily accurate. She is especially pleased at how well upper-level students have adapted to their roles as mentors and leaders to the underclassmen. (The Ogontz School Archives, 2000, Penn State University, Abington College Library.)

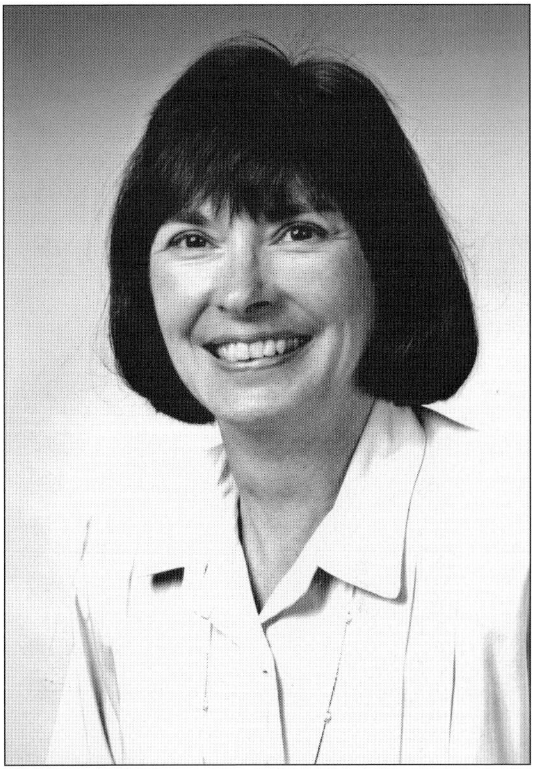

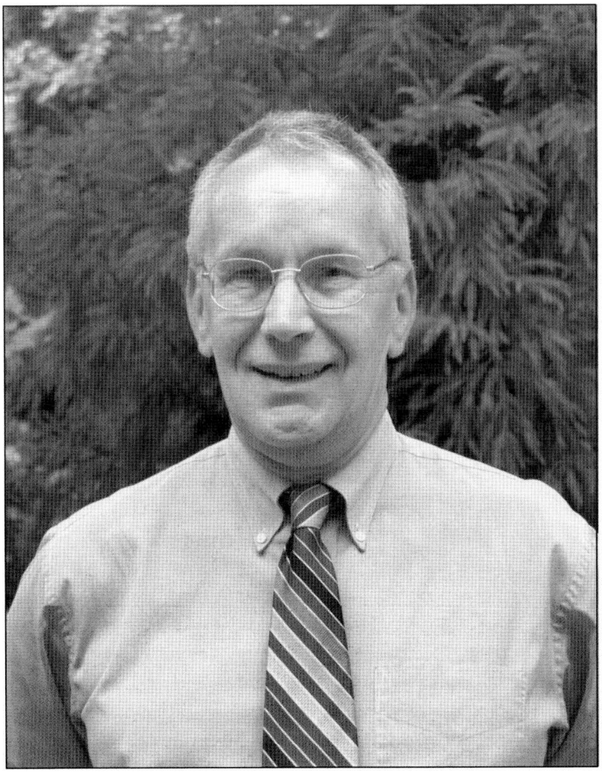

Aside from his role as a teacher of English, Dr. Thomas R. Smith, seen here in 2015, served the college twice as head of the Arts and Humanities Division, from July 2006 to December 2007 and from July 2012 to June 2015. In the intervening years, as interim director of the Advising Center, he also played a pivotal role in revamping the college's complex advising system and initiating what would develop into the New Student Orientation program. (University Relations Department, Penn State Abington.)

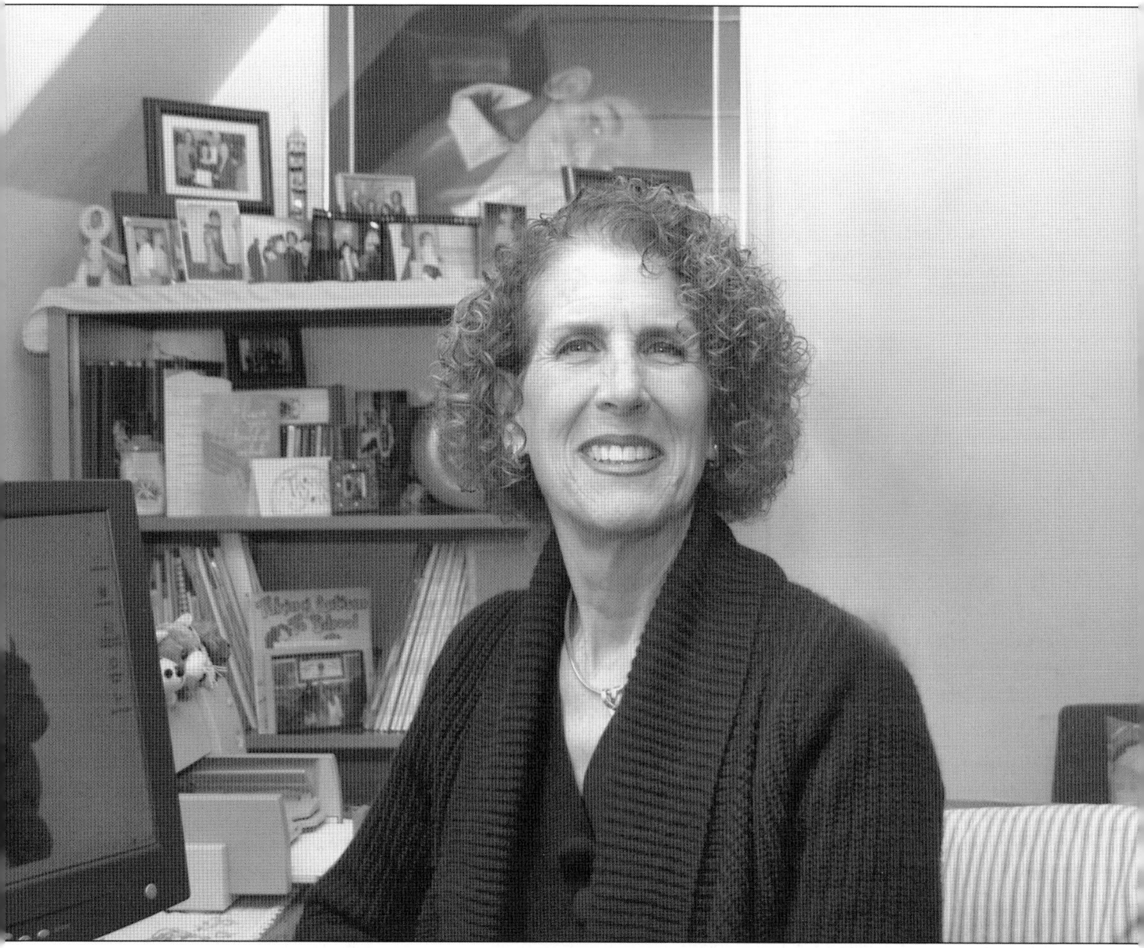

Known for her consistently high academic standards and her fierce ethical values, Dr. Judith Newman has been a mainstay on campus since she arrived at the college in 1967. An associate professor of human development and family studies, she has actively participated in the college's growth from a two-year college offering courses on a 10-week quarter system to a degree-granting four-year college. When she arrived, she observed that the student body was basically middle-class Caucasian, speaking one language. But today, she is gratified to see what she calls "a rainbow of skin tones" and a multiplicity of languages being spoken in the halls, as Penn State Abington has become one of the most diverse colleges in the commonwealth. The college also provides services for students with disabilities. Dr. Newman has also been the recipient of the college's Outstanding Teacher Award (2004 and 2012) and Outstanding Service Award (2015). (Dr. Judith Newman.)

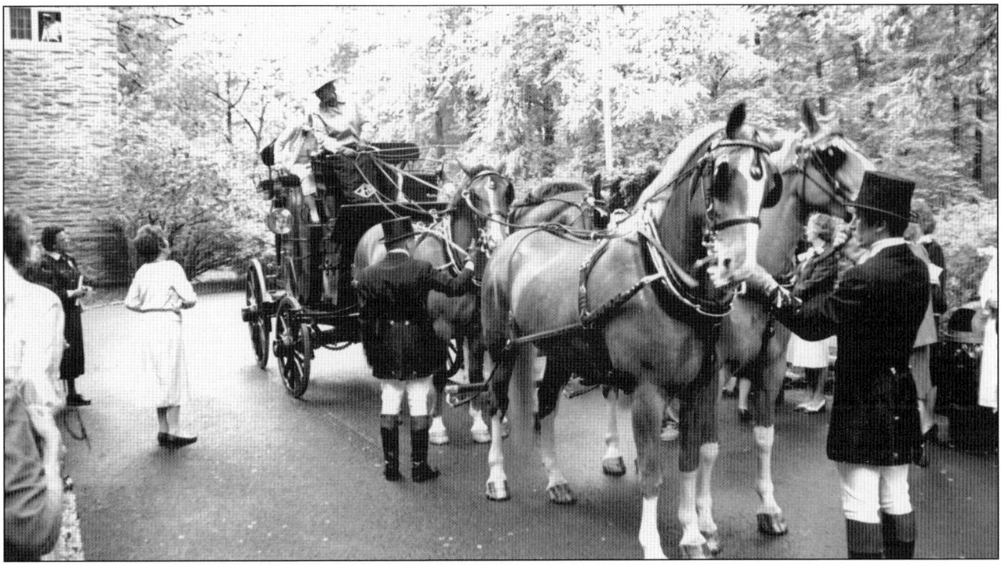

The Reunion of 1985 on the grounds of Penn State Ogontz was a really big deal. It celebrated 35 years of education at the site where Abby Sutherland once presided over a group of elite young ladies at the Ogontz School. The festivities during that first week of June 1985 included horse-and-buggy rides replicating the cultural trips Abby's girls would take to Philadelphia or trips to the Wissahickon for sleigh rides and nature walks. In a *Philadelphia Inquirer* article printed shortly after the reunion, Wyncote resident Elizabeth McFarland, class of 1940, recalled her days at the Ogontz School, where she received her education from grammar school through junior college. She said, "We walked down stairs with books on our head. We took tea properly. And we could go out and borrow a baby to learn how to care for it. It was primarily a finishing school that taught you social graces and prepared you for family responsibilities." (Both, the Ogontz School Archives, 1985, Penn State University, Abington College Library.)

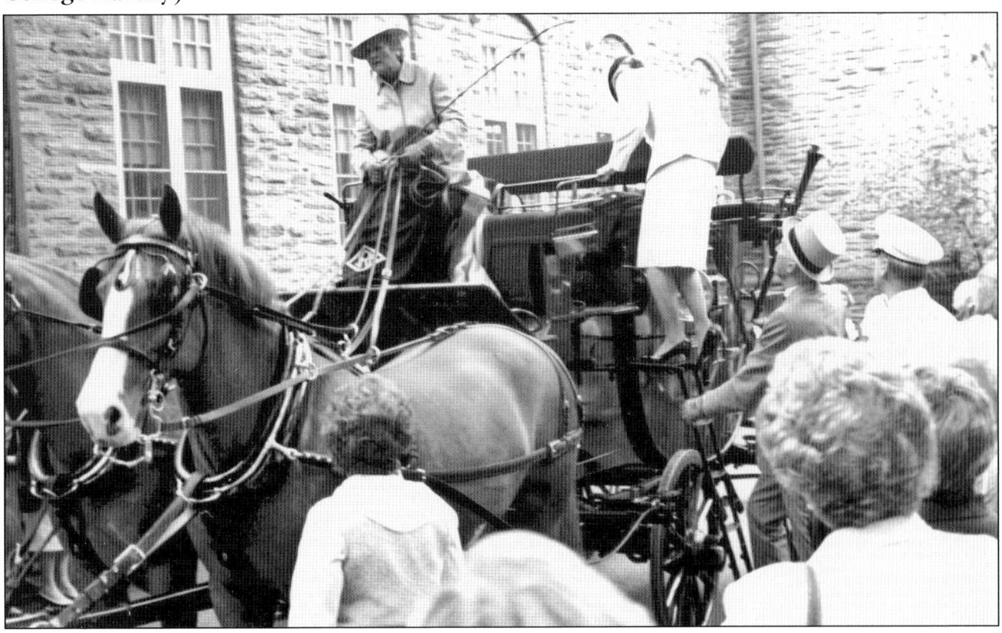

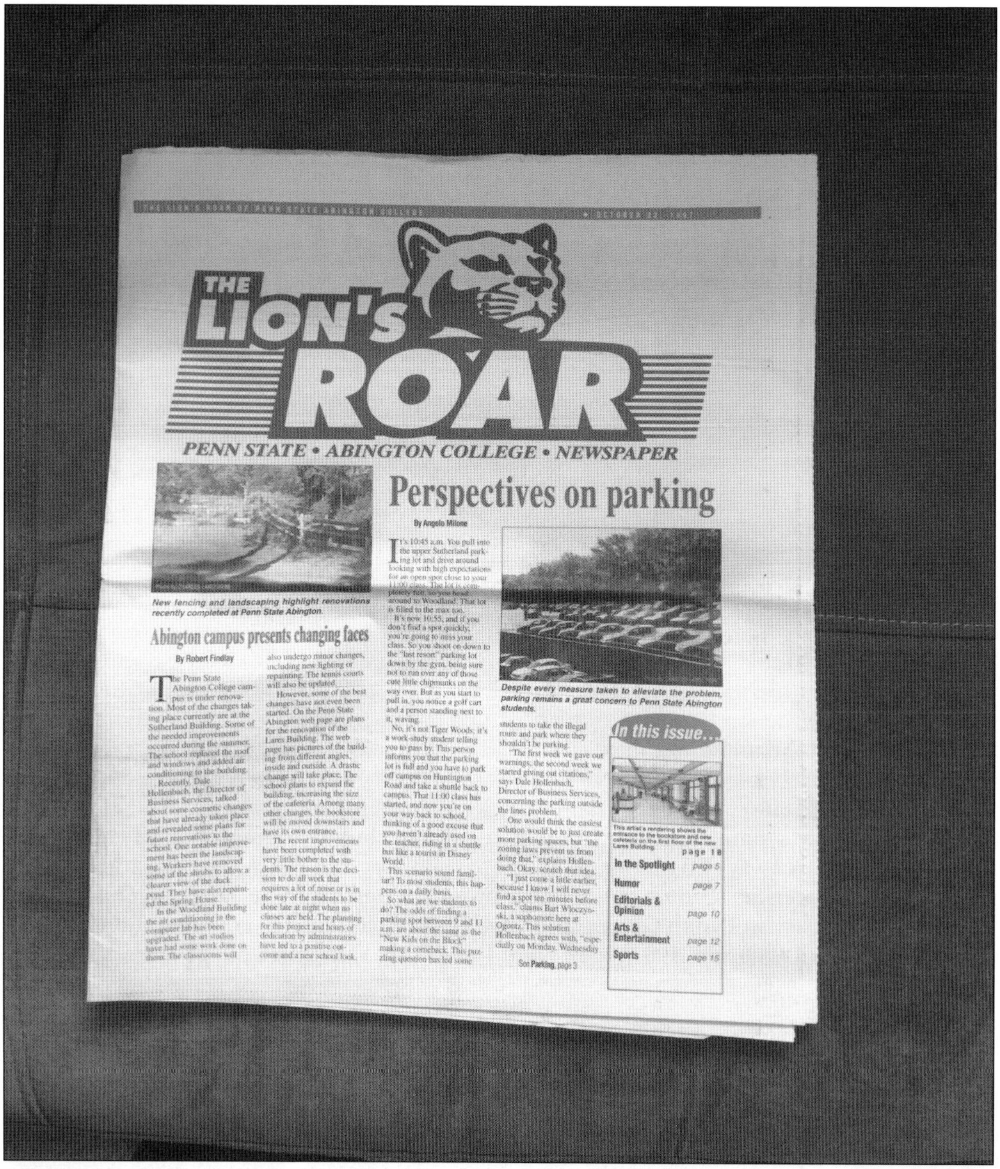

THE LION'S ROAR

PENN STATE • ABINGTON COLLEGE • NEWSPAPER

New fencing and landscaping highlight renovations recently completed at Penn State Abington.

Abington campus presents changing faces

By Robert Findlay

The Penn State Abington College campus is under renovation. Most of the changes taking place currently are at the Sutherland Building. Some of the needed improvements occurred during the summer. The school replaced the roof and windows and added air conditioning to the building.

Recently, Dale Hollenbach, the Director of Business Services, talked about some cosmetic changes that have already taken place and revealed some plans for future renovations to the school. One notable improvement has been the landscaping. Workers have removed some of the shrubs to allow a clearer view of the duck pond. They have also repainted the Spring House.

In the Woodland Building the air conditioning in the computer lab has been upgraded. The art studios have had some work done on them. The classrooms will also undergo minor changes, including new lighting or repainting. The tennis courts will also be updated.

However, some of the best changes have not even been started. On the Penn State Abington web page are plans for the renovation of the Lares Building. The web page has pictures of the building from different angles, inside and outside. A drastic change will take place. The school plans to expand the building, increasing the size of the cafeteria. Among many other changes, the bookstore will be moved downstairs and have its own entrance.

The recent improvements have been completed with very little bother to the students. The reason is the decision to do all work that requires a lot of noise or is in the way of the students to be done late at night when no classes are held. The planning for this project and hours of dedication by administrators have led to a positive outcome and a new school look.

Perspectives on parking

By Angelo Milone

It's 10:45 a.m. You pull into the upper Sutherland parking lot and drive around looking with high expectations for an open spot close to your 11:00 class. The lot is completely full, so you head around to Woodland. That lot is filled to the max too.

It's now 10:55, and if you don't find a spot quickly, you're going to miss your class. So you shoot on down to the "last resort" parking lot down by the gym, being sure not to run over any of those cute little chipmunks on the way over. But as you start to pull in, you notice a golf cart and a person standing next to it, waving.

No, it's not Tiger Woods; it's a work-study student telling you to pass by. This person informs you that the parking lot is full and you have to park off campus on Huntington Road and take a shuttle back to campus. That 11:00 class has started, and now you're on your way back to school, thinking of a good excuse that you haven't already used on the teacher, riding in a shuttle bus like a tourist in Disney World.

This scenario sound familiar? To most students, this happens on a daily basis.

So what are we students to do? The odds of finding a parking spot between 9 and 11 a.m. are about the same as the "New Kids on the Block" making a comeback. This puzzling question has led some students to take the illegal route and park where they shouldn't be parking.

"The first week we gave out warnings; the second week we started giving out citations," says Dale Hollenbach, Director of Business Services, concerning the parking outside the lines problem.

One would think the easiest solution would be to just create more parking spaces, but "the zoning laws prevent us from doing that," explains Hollenbach. Okay, scratch that idea.

"I just come a little earlier, because I know I will never find a spot ten minutes before class," claims Bart Wloczynski, a sophomore here at Ogontz. This solution Hollenbach agrees with, "especially on Monday, Wednesday

See **Parking**, page 3

Despite every measure taken to alleviate the problem, parking remains a great concern to Penn State Abington students.

In this issue...

This artist's rendering shows the entrance to the bookstore and new cafeteria on the first floor of the new Lares Building.
page 18

One more sign that the former two-year college had arrived as a four-year degree-granting institution was the appearance of the latest incarnation of the campus newspaper. After years of on-and-off success at getting the all-commuter student body to sustain its commitment to a campus newspaper, it finally happened. On October 27, 1997, the *Lion's Roar* burst upon the scene, reflecting on the old and the new. One of the articles on page one lamented the ongoing parking problems that had plagued the campus since the Sutherland dormitories closed in 1957, while the other featured renovations to the campus landscape and upgrades in various buildings. Under the astute leadership of associate dean for academic affairs Dr. Leonard Mustazza and Arts and Humanities Division head Dr. Ellen Knodt, the *Lion's Roar* would become the major project of a new course, ENGL 110 (Newspaper Practicum). The paper would be published twice each semester, and students could take the course up to three times to assure the paper's continuity. (The Ogontz School Archives, 1997, Penn State University, Abington College Library.)

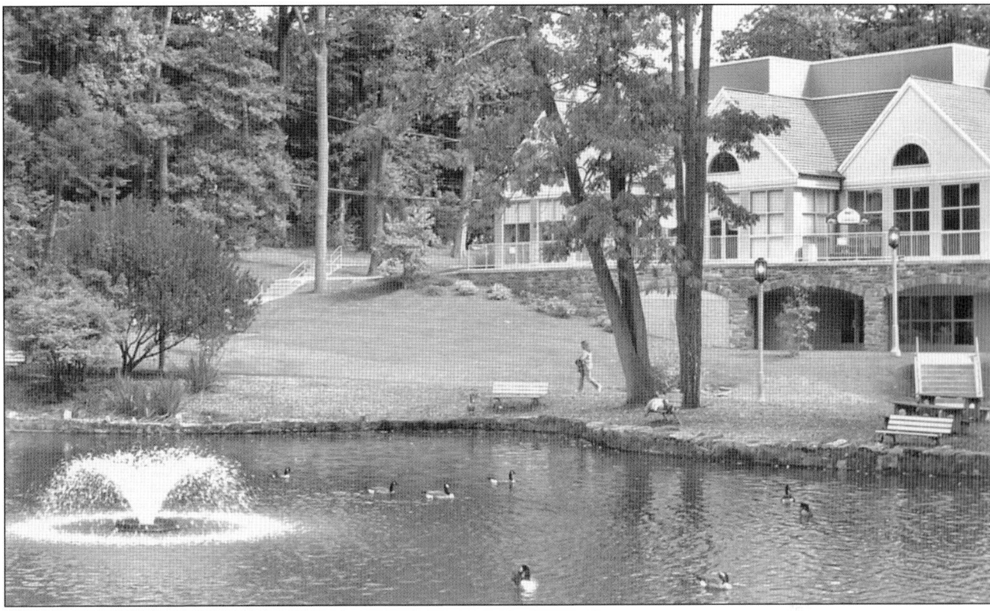

The years have been kind to Lares, one of the oldest buildings on campus. Designed in 1923 by Julian Abele, chief designer for the Horace Trumbauer firm, Lares was built from stone quarried on the property to be the home of Abby Sutherland, the principal and owner of the Ogontz School. Sutherland's actual residence looks essentially the same as it did in 1923, but the beginnings of the renovated building (above) can be seen at the far left. After Sutherland died in 1961, Lares began to house the dining hall and the bookstore and became the site of weekly Friday evening student concerts, soon replacing the log cabin as the chief hangout on campus. But after an ongoing facelift that began two years earlier, Lares had grown substantially by 1999, now featuring a brand-new cafeteria offering hot and cold foods, a state-of-the-art bookstore, faculty and dean's dining rooms, and areas where students could study and meet, all within view of the popular duck pond. (Both, University Relations Department, c. 2000s, Penn State Abington.)

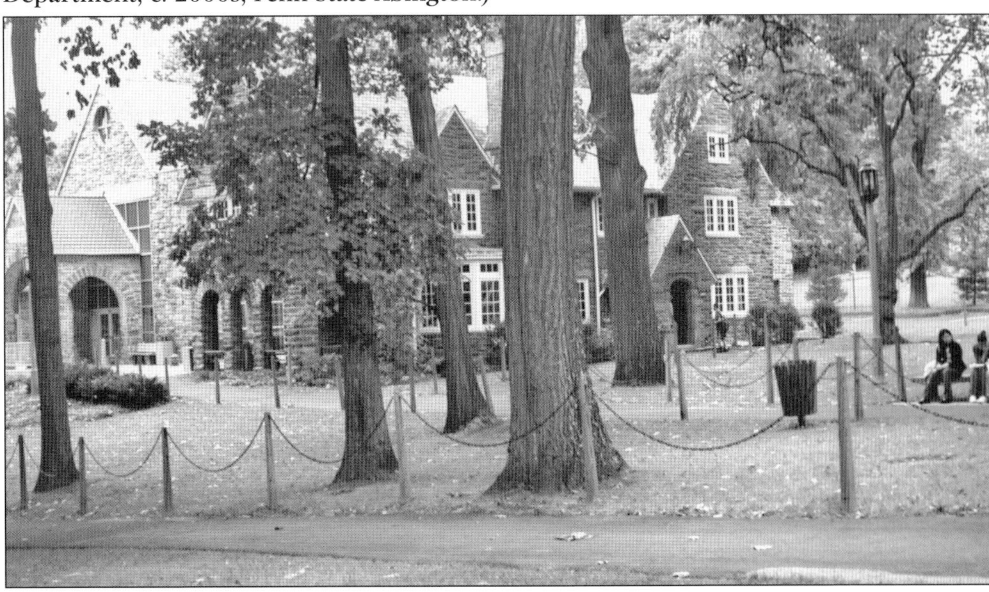

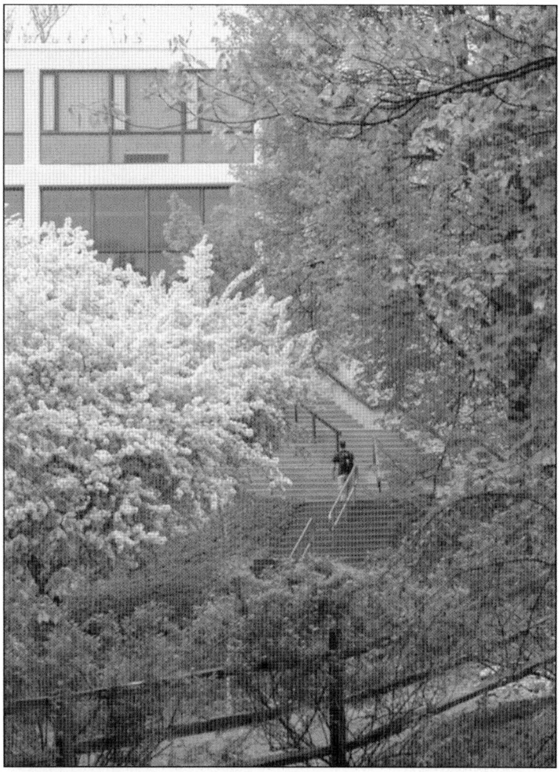

These steep stairs, no more daunting than the rugged hills that students traverse every day to reach classes spread out across the campus, lead up to Woodland, the modern building (completed in 1973) that houses the library, major science and computer labs, classrooms, an auditorium, art studios, and a new art gallery, as well as administrative offices, lounges, and a snack bar. (University Relations Department, c. 2000s, Penn State Abington.)

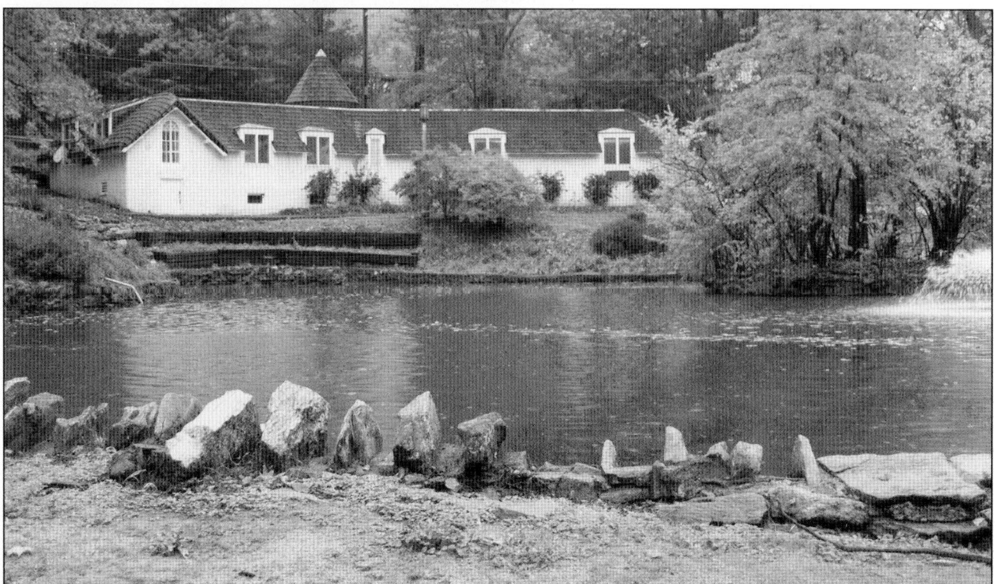

The charming Springhouse, the oldest structure on campus, dating back to 1901, is wedged between Woodland Road on the far side of the building and the duck pond. Over the years, it has served in many capacities, originally as a storage area for dairy products made on the Herring Estate, then as a laboratory and classroom building, including military science. Today, classes are again offered there. (University Relations Department, c. 2000s, Penn State Abington.)

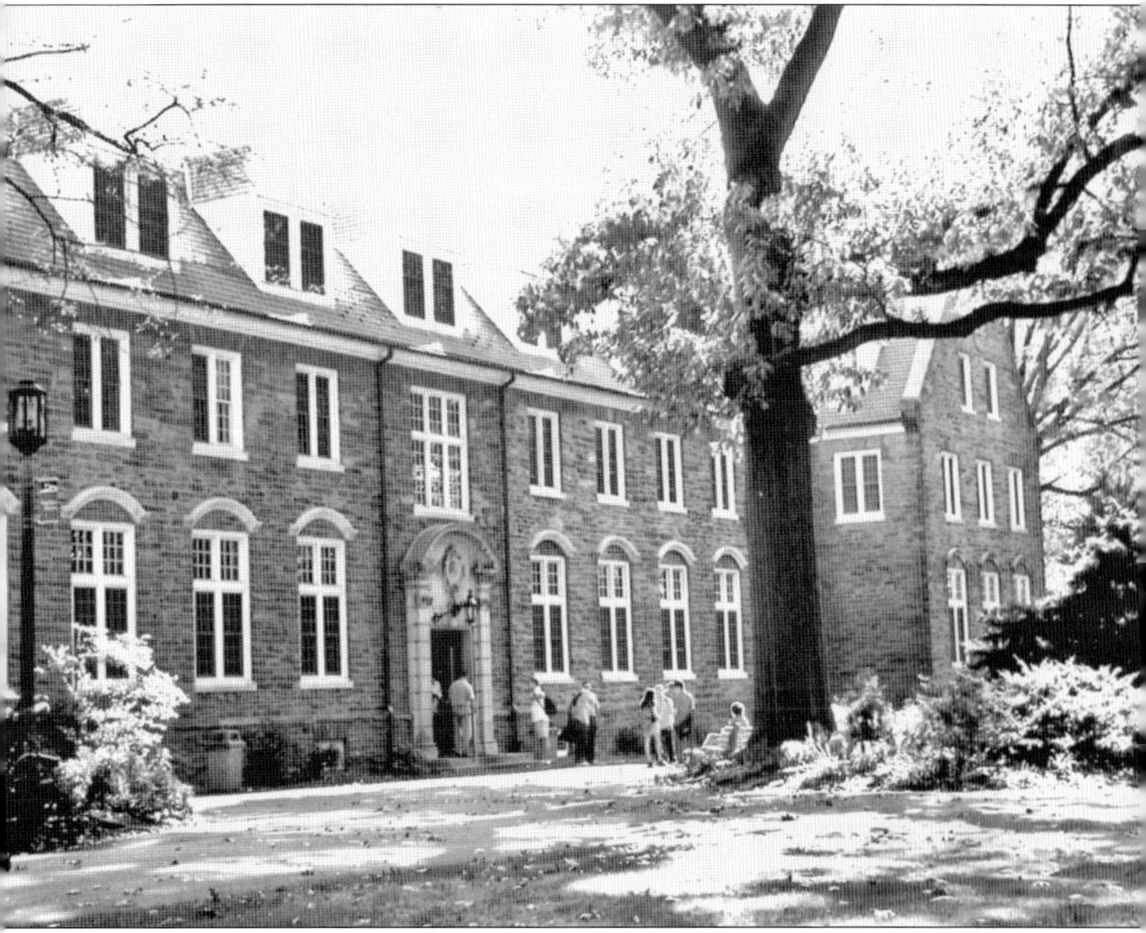

Oh, the history this building has seen! Like the campus itself, the Sutherland Building, constructed by Julian Abele for the Horace Trumbauer firm in 1916–1917, is now more than 100 years old. Pictured in 2008, it has held up well, serving as the new home for the Ogontz School until 1950, when Abby Sutherland turned it over to the Penn State College. It might be hard to believe that the cramped quarters of the stately old English manor house once easily housed dozens of fine young ladies in well-ordered dormitories, classrooms, and athletic facilities, including a swimming pool. Gradually, as the Ogontz campus grew, the dormitory rooms disappeared, as did the swimming pool. Now the building holds the main administrative offices, the solarium, cozy faculty and student lounges, a sizable auditorium, and on the fourth floor—where students in the 1950s often spotted former principal Abby Sutherland looking down upon them—faculty offices and a lactation station. (University Relations Department, Penn State Abington.)

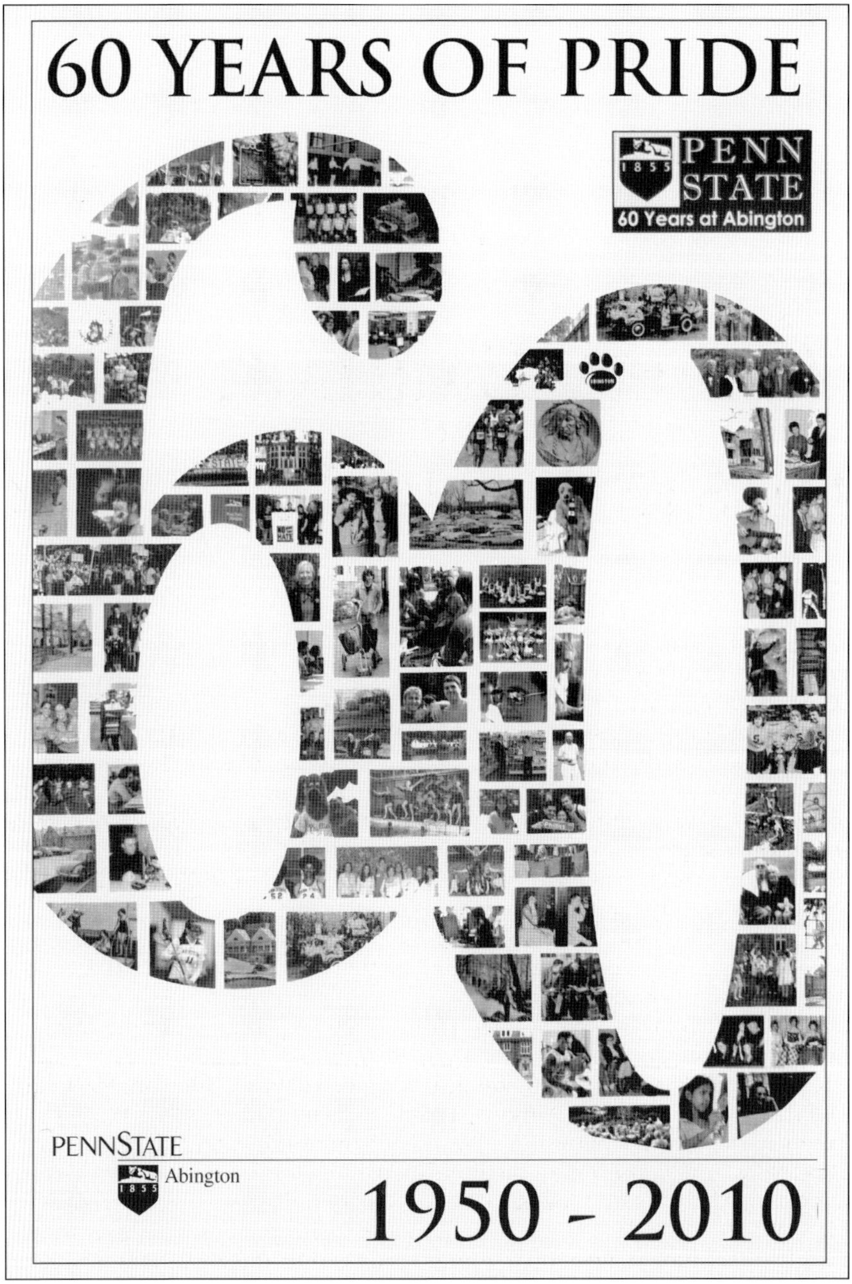

This is the official 2010 poster commemorating "60 Years of Pride," 60 years of education at Penn State Abington. Upon closer inspection, the viewer will see dozens of photographs recalling the long history of the college. There are photographs from the bobby-socks-and-poodle-skirted 1950s, the long-haired social revolutions of the 1960s and 1970s, and the more practical 1980s and 1990s, when the college—after years of being identified as Penn State Ogontz—finally officially became Penn State Abington in 1997. The images, culled from hundreds, show students, faculty, and administrators at work and at play over the course of 60 revolutionary and evolutionary years. (University Relations Department, Penn State Abington.)

Four

Amelia Earhart and Outstanding Students

Some of the most illustrious students who attended the Ogontz School, including many that accomplished truly great things, never even graduated. The surnames on the class lists—Cooke, Stetson, Curtis, DuPont, Gillette, Campbell, Corning, Sperry, Rothschild, and VanSciver, to name just a few—are a veritable who's who of the rich and famous.

Abby Sutherland proudly pointed out that 51 percent of her school's graduates went on to success in institutions of higher learning and then became leaders in various professions from medicine and law to publishing and aeronautics. Is there a more recognizable name among the former students than Amelia Earhart? Although she only attended the Ogontz School for three semesters, she inspired several other Ogontz girls to aeronautical careers, such as Betty Huyler, Winnabelle Coffee, and Cornelia Fort.

Dr. Jean Crump, a professor of pediatrics at the Women's Medical College; Dr. Belle Dixon Varker, whose practice aided needy children and mothers; and Dr. Marcia Patrick, who devoted herself to progressive improvement in hospital care, distinguished themselves in the field of medicine. Agnes Dodds became a noted attorney who represented women's civic groups. Wilma Sinclair became director of the bank of Steubenville, Ohio.

In the realm of music and the performing arts, Queena Mario Tillotson, Mary Curtis, and Evelyn Duerler made major contributions, as did Rose Tillotson (Queena Mario's sister) and Molly Costain in the world of publishing. Speaking of publishing, onetime Penn State Ogontz student Rod Nordland has become a distinguished Pulitzer Prize–winning journalist for the *New York Times*. Al Lord was a former chief executive officer of publicly traded, for-profit student lender Sallie Mae. Joel Myers, who gave weather reports on the Penn State Ogontz campus while still a student, went on to found AccuWeather, the world's leading commercial weather service.

Frances White Diehl, who attended the Ogontz School in 1910, was toastmistress for the school's final graduation ceremony and reunion in 1950. White Diehl later became a president of the National Council of Women, a key bridge between the women of America and the women in the rest of the world.

Readers will meet some of these good and great citizens over the course of this chapter.

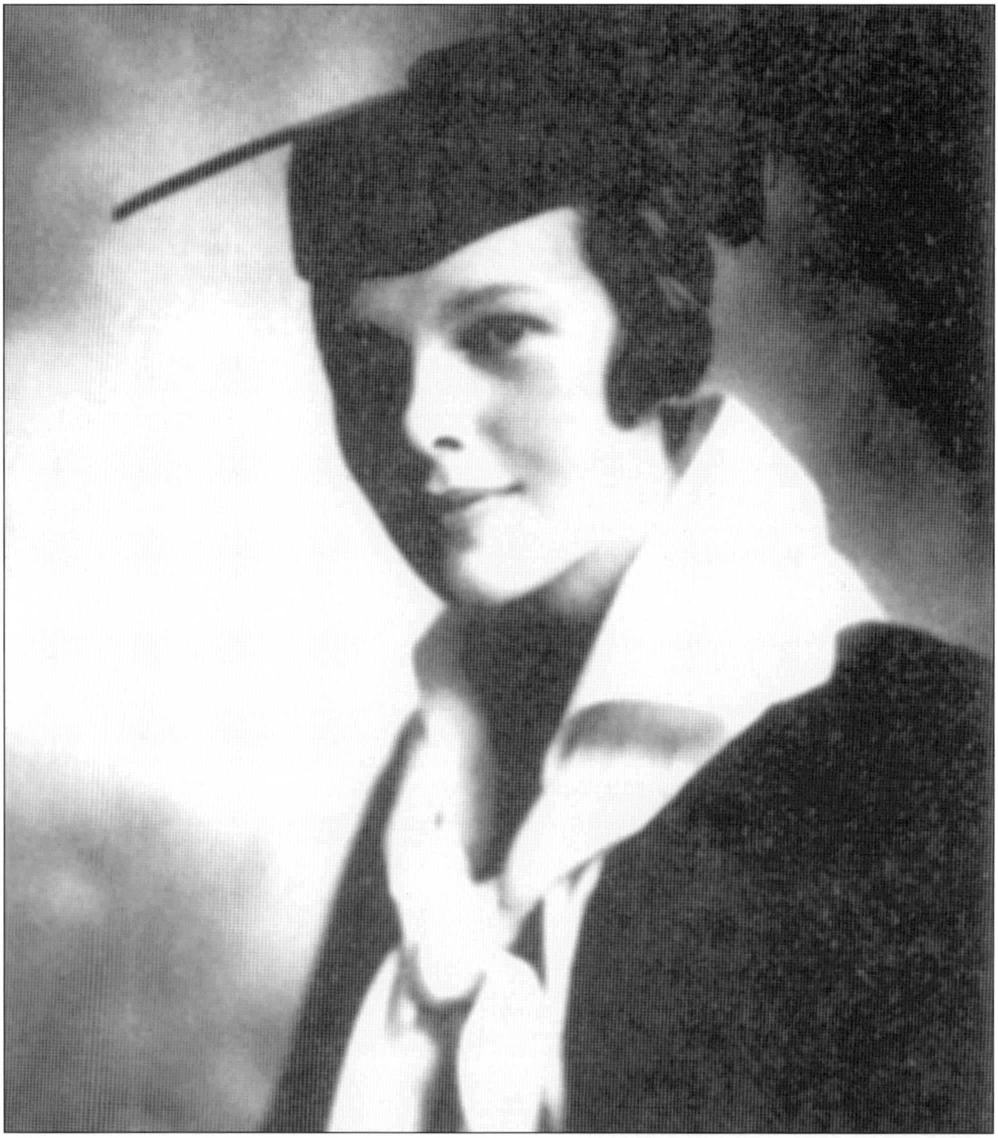

Although she appears in cap and gown in this 1917 photograph, Amelia Earhart never graduated from the Ogontz School. Traditionally, senior class members, like Earhart, donned their caps and gowns at Halloween each year, when the class leaders revealed their class motto, song, sponsor, and honorary members. Unlike most of her classmates, Earhart had not been brought up in luxury. Her father's failure in various ventures forced the family to move frequently, from her birthplace in Atchison, Kansas, to Chicago, where she graduated from Hyde Park High School, and ultimately to the Philadelphia area, where she hoped to attend Bryn Mawr College. The Ogontz School was a perfect step in that direction, and that was possible only because of a substantial inheritance her mother had received. At Ogontz, Earhart joined Alpha Phi but opposed what she found to be the sorority's elitism, as it excluded certain girls. When Alpha Phi rejected her proposal to extend admission to all students, she took her crusade to Abby Sutherland, whose solution was to disband all sororities. Principled and headstrong, Earhart already showed she was a natural leader. (The Ogontz School Archives, 1917, Penn State University, Abington College Library.)

Framed in Penn State Abington's archive room is Amelia Earhart's report card, which indicates that she was a fairly good student. She received "Excellent" grades in French II, German III, current events, art, and composition. Abby Sutherland praised Earhart's writing style and said that reading was an "adventure" for Earhart, who favored challenging authors such as George Bernard Shaw, Theodore Dreiser, Eugene O'Neill, and Fyodor Dostoyevsky. Earhart was less successful in Latin prose and chemistry lab, both of which she dropped, and in Bible, for which her final grade was "F" (or "Fair"). Ironically, Earhart had just been elected secretary and treasurer of the Christian Association. Before visiting her sister Muriel in Toronto during Christmas vacation in 1917, Earhart planned to return to Ogontz. She did for a few weeks in 1918 but decided to go back to Toronto to work with wartime amputees as a nurse's aide. (Both, the Ogontz School Archives, 1917, Penn State University, Abington College Library.)

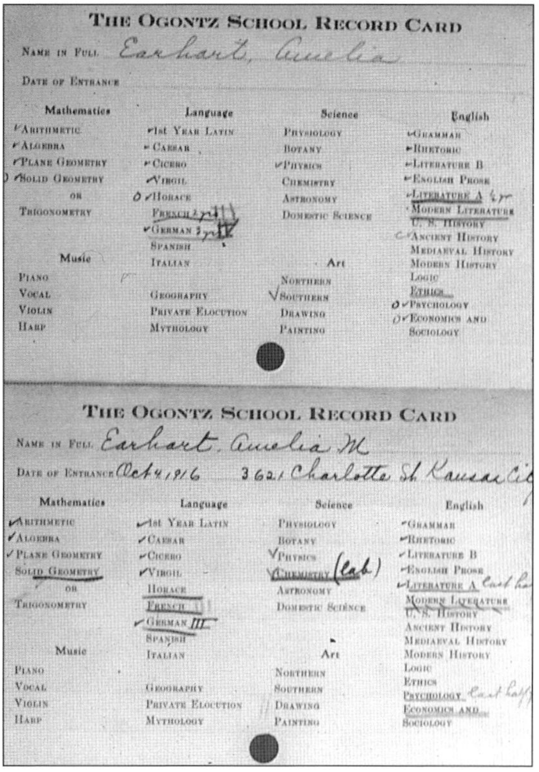

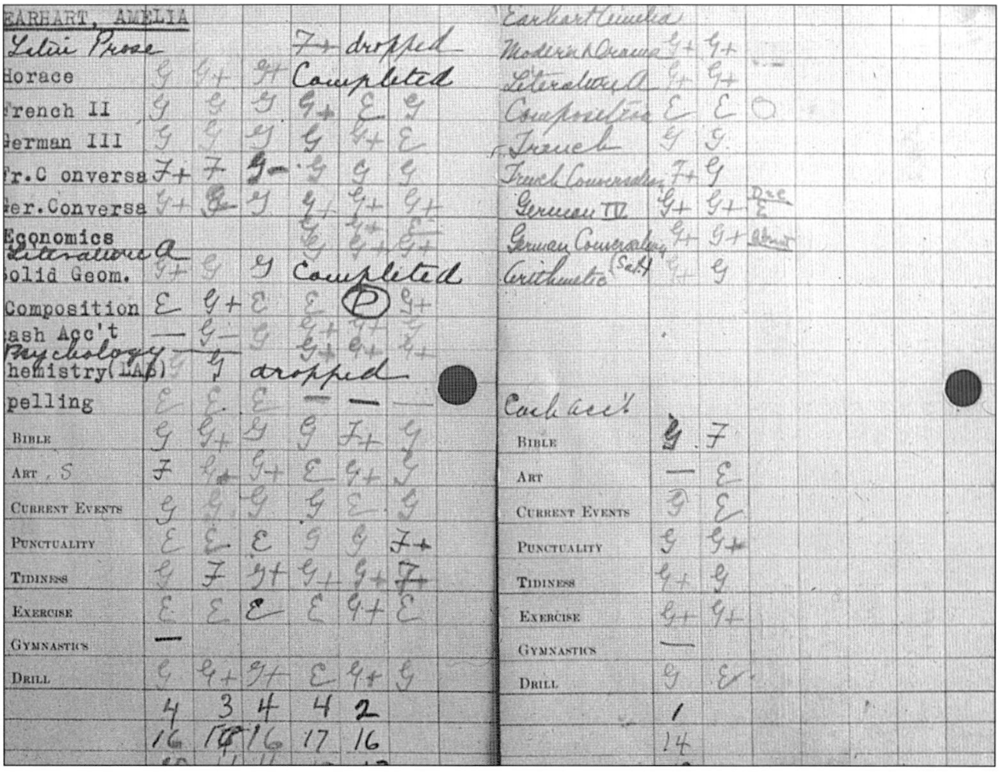

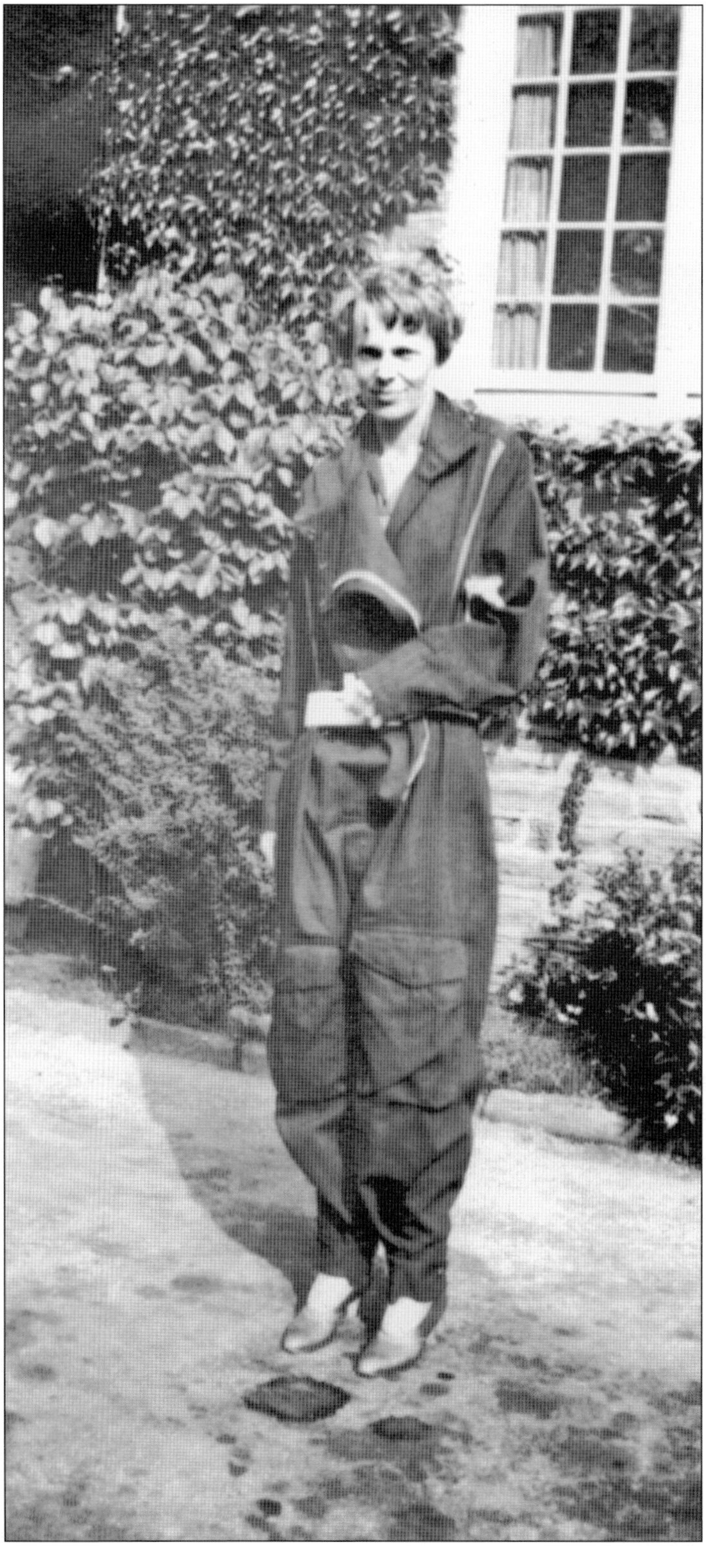

Earhart's ties to the school were strong. She returned several times, most notably on May 23, 1929, when this former corporal of the Ogontz Battalion was invited back for Battalion Day to help celebrate Col. Thomas D. Landon's 40th year as military director of the school. As a reviewing officer, Earhart was a major in the 381st Air Corps at the time. According to a report in the June 1929 *Ogontz Mosaic*, "She was charmingly modest as she took her reviews and the local friends' picture taking, and all the applause—and helped to pin the winning decorations on the girls in a way that won all hearts." In *Letters from Amelia: An Intimate Portrait of Amelia Earhart*, published in 1982, author Jean L. Backus describes Amelia Earhart's distinctive willowy appearance. She wrote, "The leggy strength of her slim body, the direct glance from her clear blue eyes, as full of wonder as a child's, the cropped hair, the cheerful grin, the breezy manner . . . were widely imitated by girls and women who adopted the 'Amelia Look.'" (The Ogontz School Archives, 1929, Penn State University, Abington College Library.)

Two years after becoming the first woman to cross the Atlantic in an airplane, Earhart was named an honorary member of the Ogontz School's class of 1930. In the class book, Abby Sutherland wrote, "Our ocean-daring Amelia, with the courage of a Viking and the gentleness of a true girl, challenges our admiration and that of the world." In 1937, Earhart and navigator Fred Noonan disappeared in her Lockheed Electra near Howland Island in the South Pacific. (The Ogontz School Archives, 1930, Penn State University, Abington College Library.)

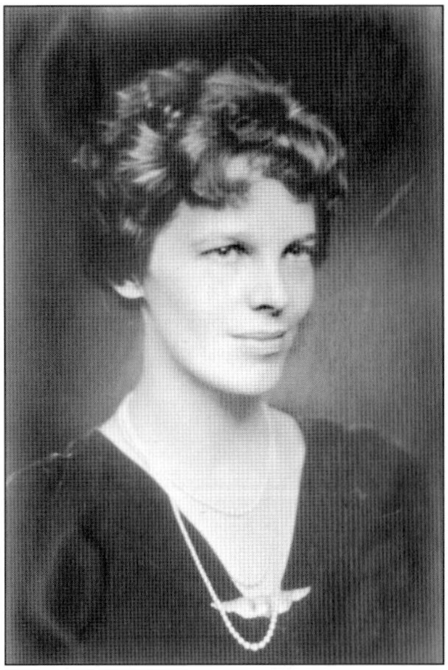

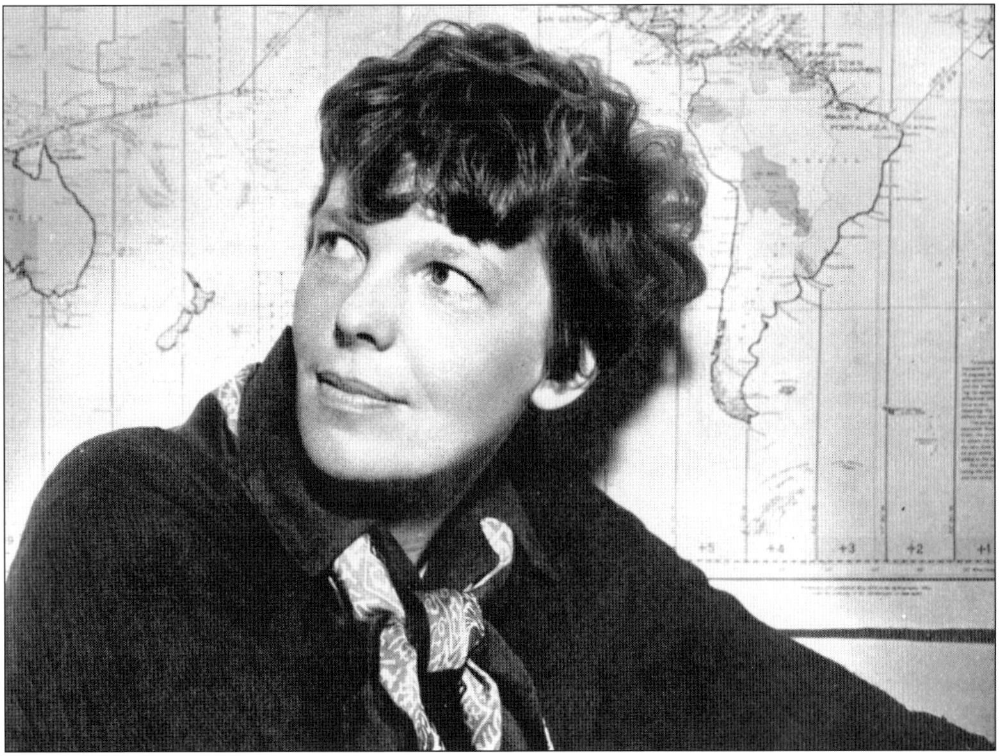

Beneath this photograph in the December 1937 *Ogontz Mosaic*, Abby Sutherland wrote, "Once on the drill field when she was a judge of Ogontz drill, a beautiful airplane flew over the field and just for that moment Amelia was not with us on the ground. She was in the air with the birdman who was flying over. Then I realized what air-mindedness meant and I knew she was a child of that new generation to whom the uncharted heavens were open and whose course might vie with eagles in their flight." (The Ogontz School Archives, 1937, Penn State University, Abington College Library.)

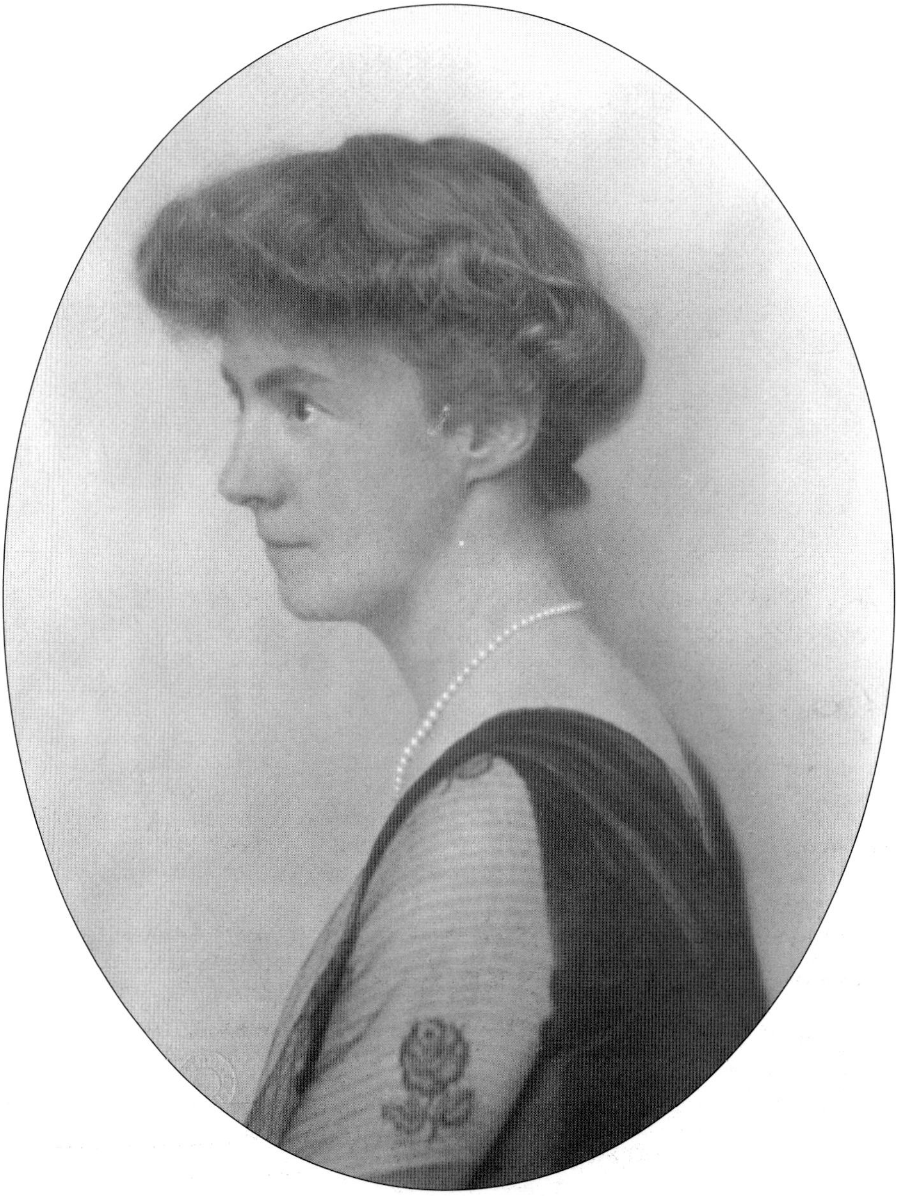

Mary Louise Curtis (1876–1970), the only daughter of Philadelphia publishing magnate Cyrus H.K. Curtis, attended the Ogontz School in the early 1890s. While still a teenager, under her mother's maiden name, Mary L. Knapp, she was writing for the *Ladies' Home Journal*, the publication her parents founded in 1883. She married the journal's longtime editor, Edward K. Bok, in 1896. Like many of her classmates at the Ogontz School, Curtis committed herself to civic and beautification programs and shared with her father a passion for nature and music. She played piano and organ and became involved with the Settlement School of Music. She served as the school's president in 1914 and in 1917 donated $150,000 to build the Settlement Music House. Seniors at the Ogontz School made Curtis an honorary member of the class of 1922. When her father died in 1933, she became the largest shareholder, director, and a vice president of Curtis Publishing. (Photograph by Mathilde Weil, 1898–1900, Photograph Collection, Curtis Institute of Music Archives.)

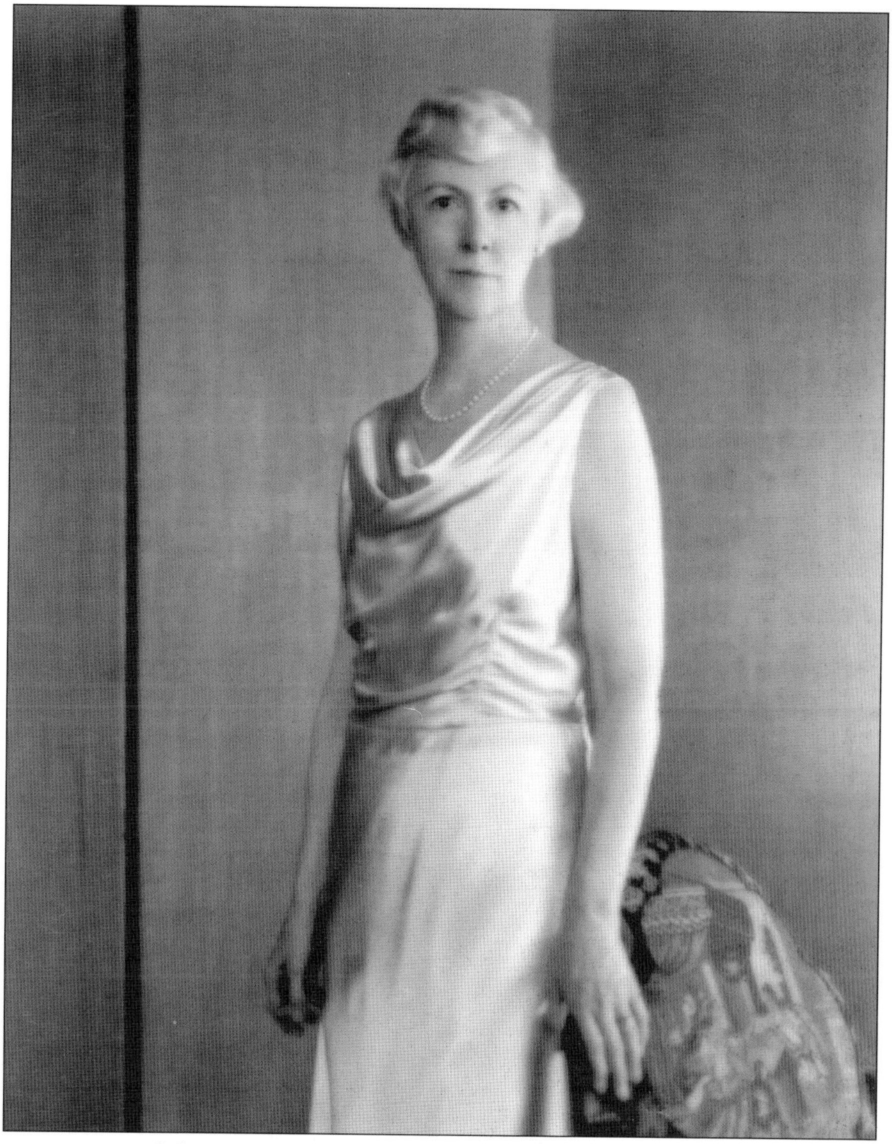

Major supporters of the arts, Edward K. and Mary Curtis Bok founded the Curtis Institute of Music at Eighteenth and Locust Streets in Philadelphia in 1924. With the assistance of their good friends Polish piano virtuoso Josef Hofmann and conductor of the Philadelphia Orchestra Leopold Stokowski, they attracted eminent music faculty and some of the finest music students in the world to the school. Stokowski also became director of the Curtis orchestra. In 1943, thirteen years after Edward died (1930), Mary married Efrem Zimbalist, the esteemed violinist and head of the Curtis Violin Department, which he directed until his death in 1968. She served the institute in various capacities until she died. Students, faculty, and staff, with whom she was very friendly, recall her arriving at work each day in a maroon car driven by a chauffeur in a matching uniform. The institute continues to prepare extraordinary young musicians for performing careers at the highest professional level. She also founded historic Curtis Hall Arboretum, whose landscaping was designed by Frederick Law Olmsted (the designer of New York's Central Park), in Wyncote. (Photograph by Albert Petersen, 1936, Photograph Collection, Curtis Institute of Music Archives.)

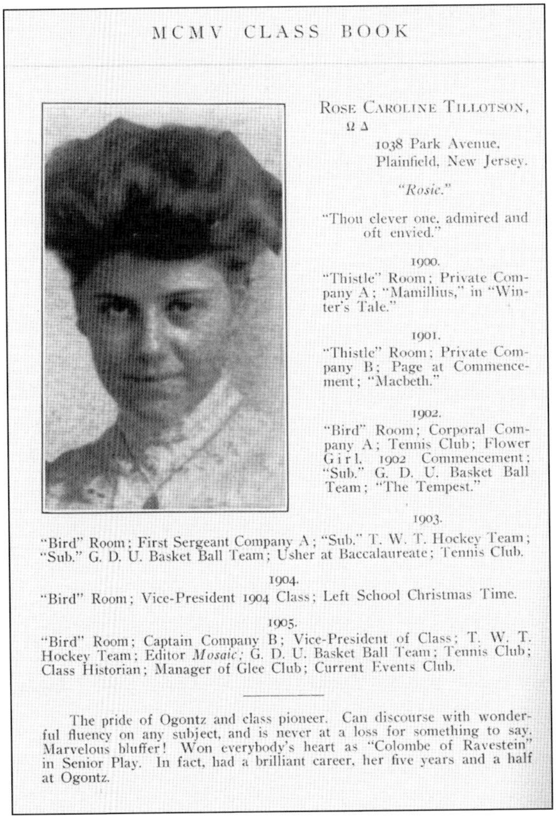

MCMV CLASS BOOK

Rose Caroline Tillotson, Ω Δ
1038 Park Avenue,
Plainfield, New Jersey.

"Rosie."

"Thou clever one, admired and oft envied."

1900.
"Thistle" Room; Private Company A; "Mamillius," in "Winter's Tale."

1901.
"Thistle" Room; Private Company B; Page at Commencement; "Macbeth."

1902.
"Bird" Room; Corporal Company A; Tennis Club; Flower Girl, 1902 Commencement; "Sub." G. D. U. Basket Ball Team; "The Tempest."

1903.
"Bird" Room; First Sergeant Company A; "Sub." T. W. T. Hockey Team; "Sub." G. D. U. Basket Ball Team; Usher at Baccalaureate; Tennis Club.

1904.
"Bird" Room; Vice-President 1904 Class; Left School Christmas Time.

1905.
"Bird" Room; Captain Company B; Vice-President of Class; T. W. T. Hockey Team; Editor *Mosaic;* G. D. U. Basket Ball Team; Tennis Club; Class Historian; Manager of Glee Club; Current Events Club.

The pride of Ogontz and class pioneer. Can discourse with wonderful fluency on any subject, and is never at a loss for something to say. Marvelous bluffer! Won everybody's heart as "Colombe of Ravestein" in Senior Play. In fact, had a brilliant career, her five years and a half at Ogontz.

On Rose Tillotson's page in the 1905 Class Book, her fellow graduates said that she "can discourse with fluency on any subject, and is never at a loss for something to say." So it is not surprising that Tillotson became a senior editor at *McClure's*, the famous muckraking magazine founded in 1893 to expose corruption in business and government. (The Ogontz School Archives, 1905, Penn State University, Abington College Library.)

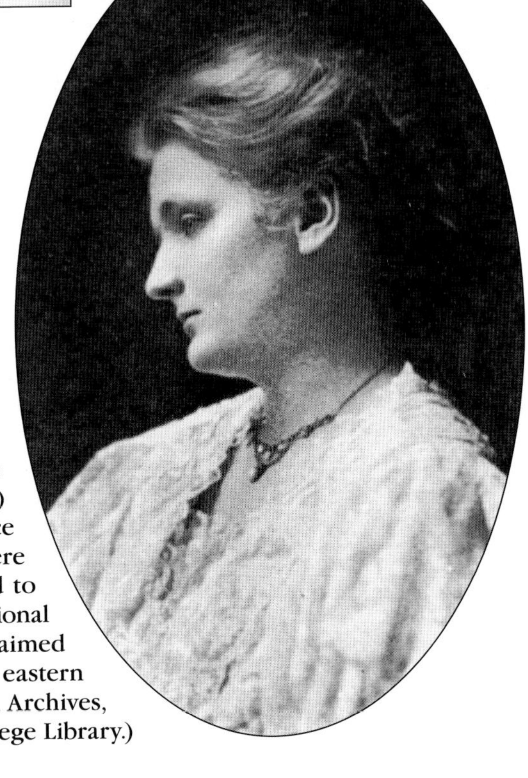

An editor of *Ogontz Mosaic* and class historian, Ada Stetson Peirce (class of 1906) was able to sate her passion for social justice and human rights in Tucson, Arizona, where she founded *Letter*, a quarterly dedicated to promoting dialogue on national and international problems, in the 1940s. She also gave acclaimed lectures on marriage and homemaking at eastern colleges in the 1920s. (The Ogontz School Archives, 1906, Penn State University, Abington College Library.)

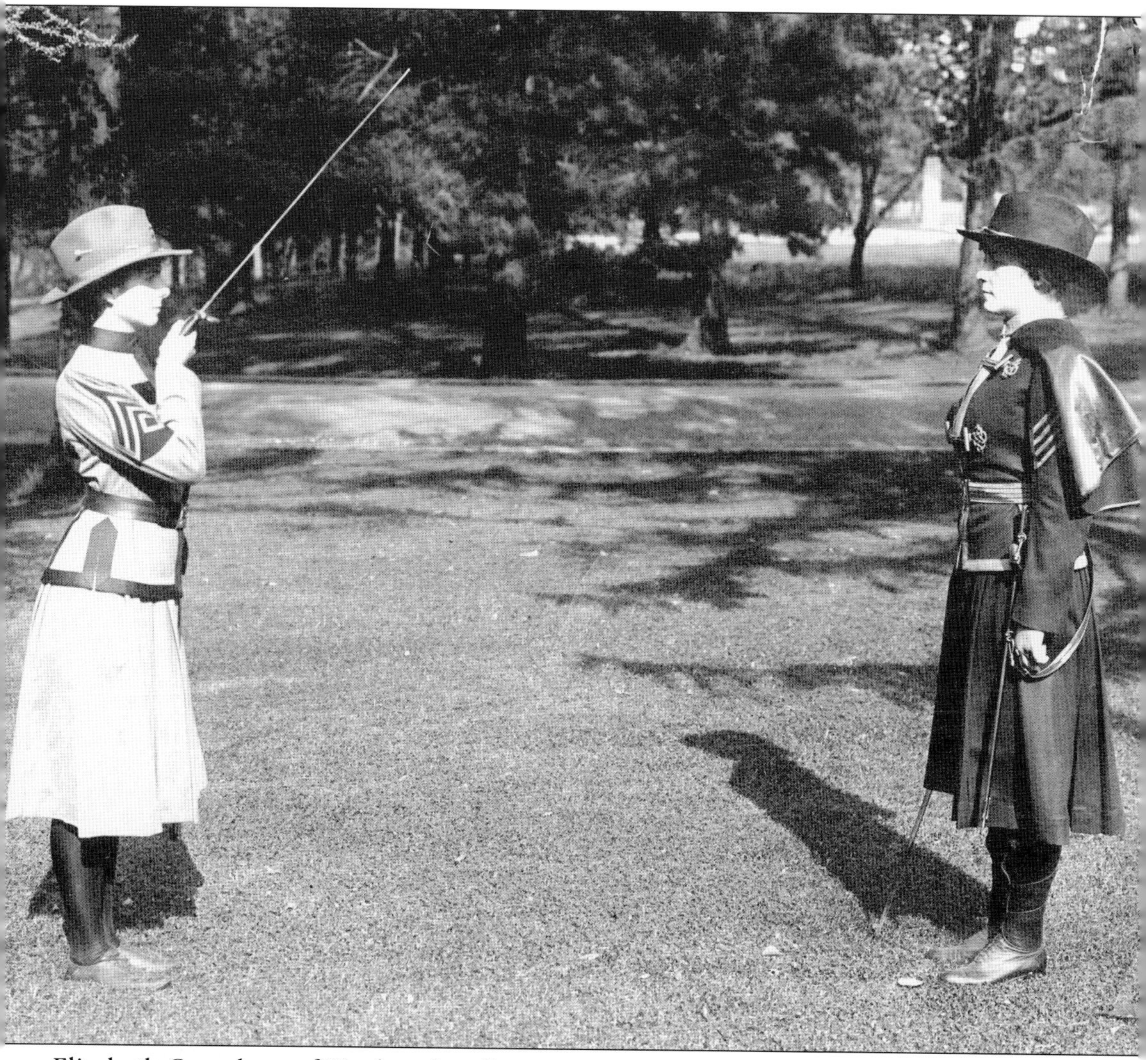

Elizabeth Carnahan, of Pittsburgh, a lieutenant, is saluting her superior officer, Hazel Hopkins, of Brooklyn, during military maneuvers on campus in 1916. Two of the most popular members of the class of 1916, they both appeared in the school's minstrel show in 1915 and were senior class officers in 1916, with Carnahan serving as secretary and Hopkins as vice president. Carnahan was business manager of the *Ogontz Mosaic* that year, secretary and treasurer of the Christian Association, and voted the most sincere member of her class. Hopkins was also May Queen during her senior year, played on the hockey and basketball teams, and was a member of the musical and dramatic clubs. Her classmates voted her best dancer and best looking member of her graduating class. (The Ogontz School Archives, 1916, Penn State University, Abington College Library.)

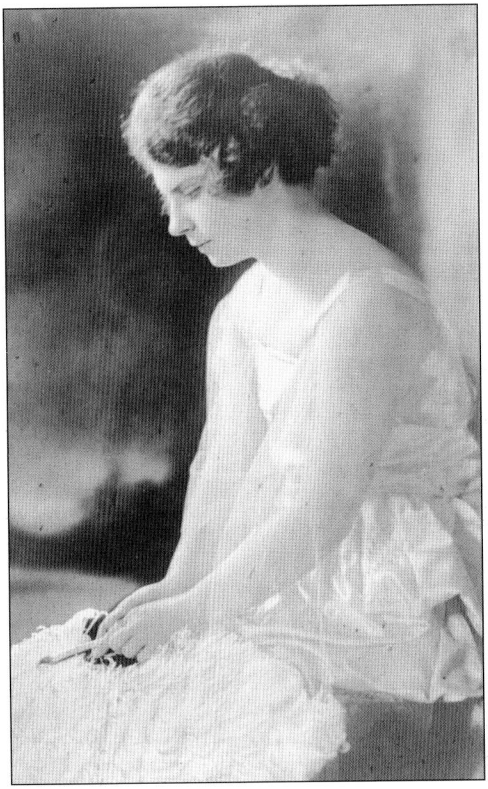

Seniors of the class of 1919 voted Mary Eleanor (Massey) Bridges the best informed and best conversationalist of their class, and teachers considered her an excellent artist. After graduating from the Ogontz School, she became known for her human and canine portraits and was a respected teacher, civic activist, and feminist. (The Ogontz School Archives, 1919, Penn State University, Abington College Library.)

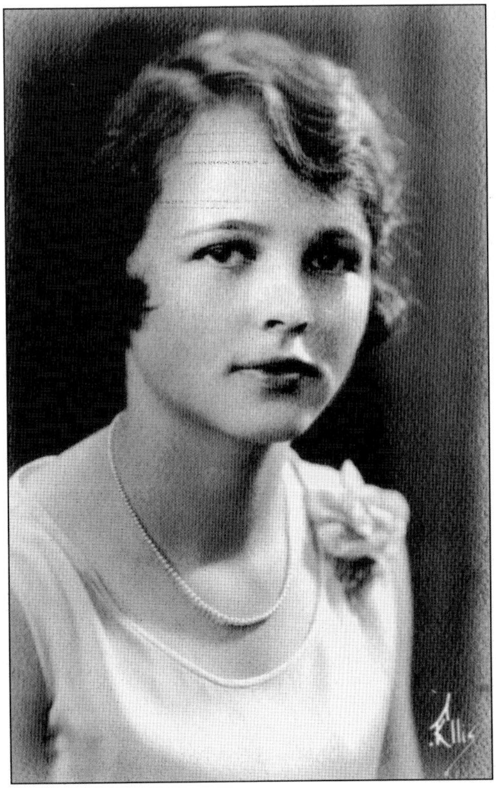

Elizabeth "Betty" (Huyler) Gillies, class of 1926, was one of several Ogontz School graduates to be inspired by Amelia Earhart. She became an aeronautics instructor and Women's Air Force Service Pilots squadron commander just before World War II and during the war ferried supplies and equipment by air. She also participated in the Annual All-Woman Transcontinental Air Race, terminating at the North Philadelphia Airport in 1957. (The Ogontz School Archives, 1926, Penn State University, Abington College Library.)

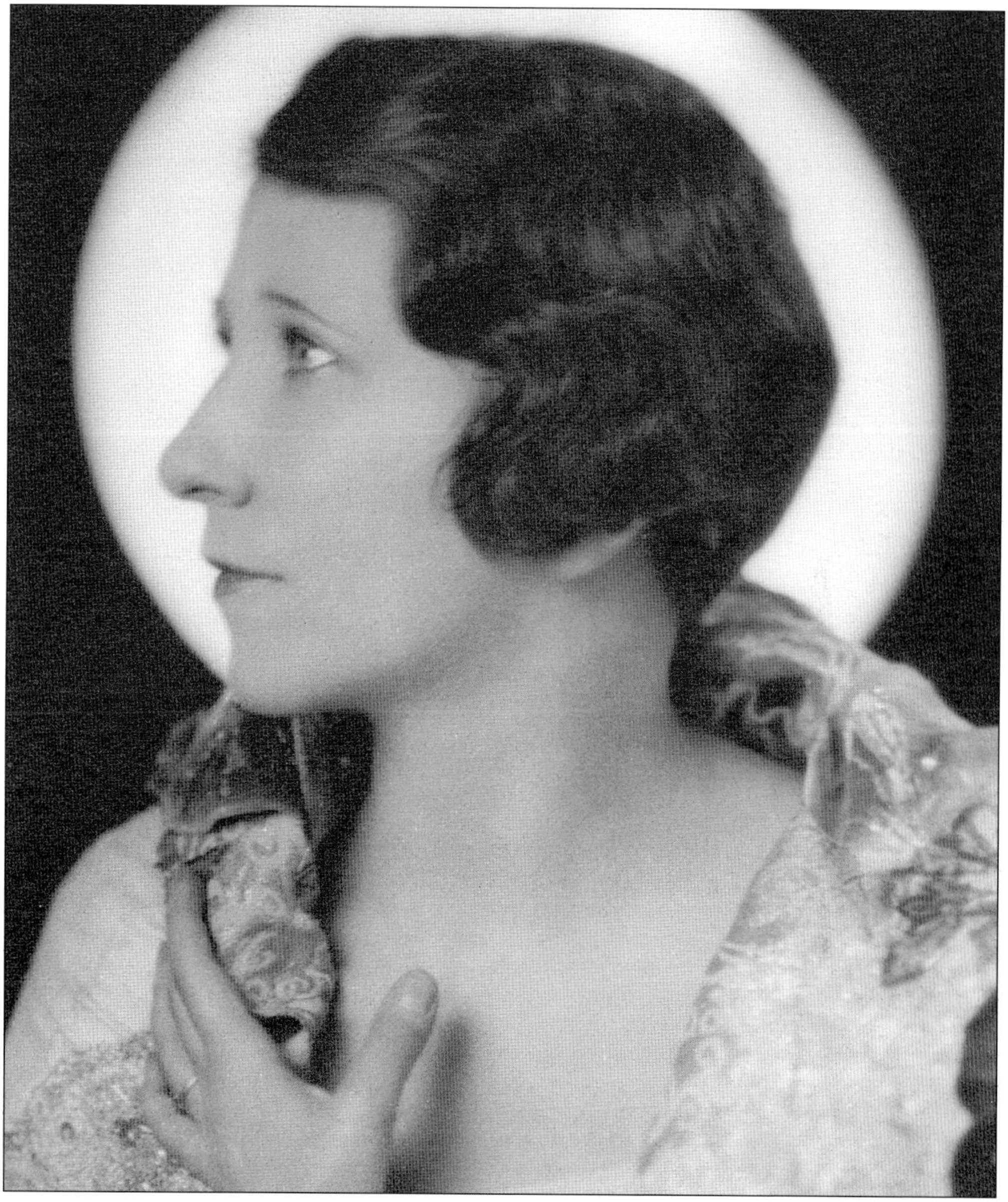

Born Queena Marian Tillotson, the Ogontz student who called herself Queena Mario throughout her career, became a noted soprano in the 1920s and 1930s. The younger sister of the Ogontz School's Rose Tillotson, Queena Mario attended the school in 1907 and 1908. Her studies with famed Polish soprano Marcella Sembrich paid off, as Queena Mario made her debut with the Metropolitan Opera on November 30, 1922. During her career, she gave 345 performances at that venerable venue. But until her death in 1951, she always found time to return to the Ogontz School to sing in recitals. After her final performance at the Met in 1938, she became a professor of voice training at New York's Juilliard School and then at Philadelphia's Curtis Institute, founded by fellow Ogontz student Mary Curtis. She ended her career as a writer of opera-themed murder mysteries under her given name and a newspaper columnist under the pen name of Florence Bryant. (Photograph by Albert Petersen, early 1920s, Photograph Collection, Curtis Institute of Music Archives.)

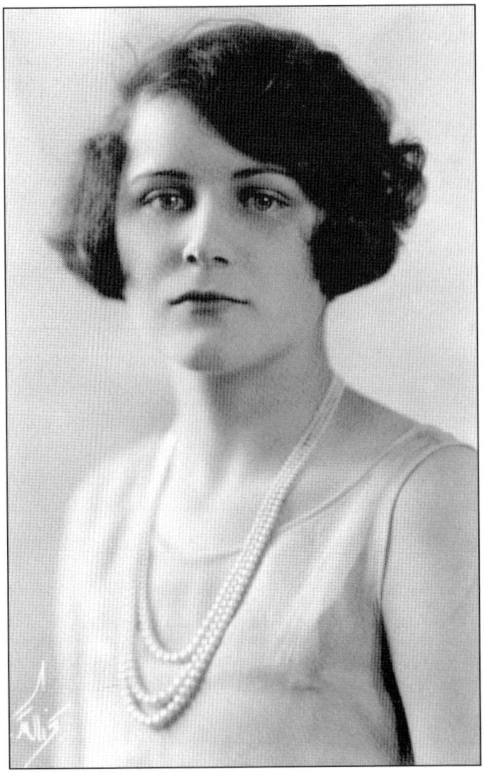

At Ogontz, Evelyn "Eve" Duerler was a member of the Glee Club and appeared in virtually every play and minstrel show the school presented during her years as a student. Voted the prettiest by the seniors of the class of 1925, Duerler became a well-known popular singer in light operas and on the big screen, using the stage name Evelyn Case. (The Ogontz School Archives, 1925, Penn State University, Abington College Library.)

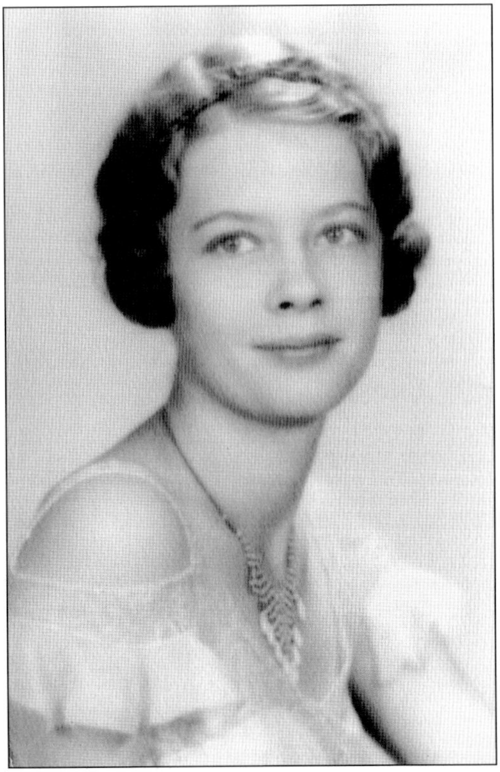

The daughter of best-selling novelist Thomas B. Costain, Molly Costain (class of 1932) became a novelist in her own right. She wrote *Queen Victoria*, one in a series of books for children, and for adults, *The Reluctant Queen*, *My Lord Brother the Lion Heart*, and other novels on the English monarchy. (The Ogontz School Archives, 1932, Penn State University, Abington College Library.)

Fred Rogers was surely thinking about his own dear mother, Nancy McFeely, when he wrote, "Parents are like the shuttles on a loom. They join the threads of the past with the threads of the future and leave their own bright patterns as they go." As successful as McFeely might have been as a student at the Ogontz School (she graduated in 1923), she is no doubt remembered best for bringing Fred Rogers into the world. The beloved host of *Mister Rogers' Neighborhood*, the longest running show in PBS history (1962 to 2001), Rogers can be seen holding his younger sister Nancy in the photograph below, which appeared in the December 1940 issue of *Ogontz Mosaic*. His father, James Hillis Rogers, was a prominent industrialist in Latrobe, Pennsylvania, and his mother was a dedicated community volunteer. The family was known as close-knit, loving, and philanthropic. (Right, the Ogontz School Archives, 1923, Penn State University, Abington College Library; below, the Ogontz School Archives, 1930, Penn State University, Abington College Library.)

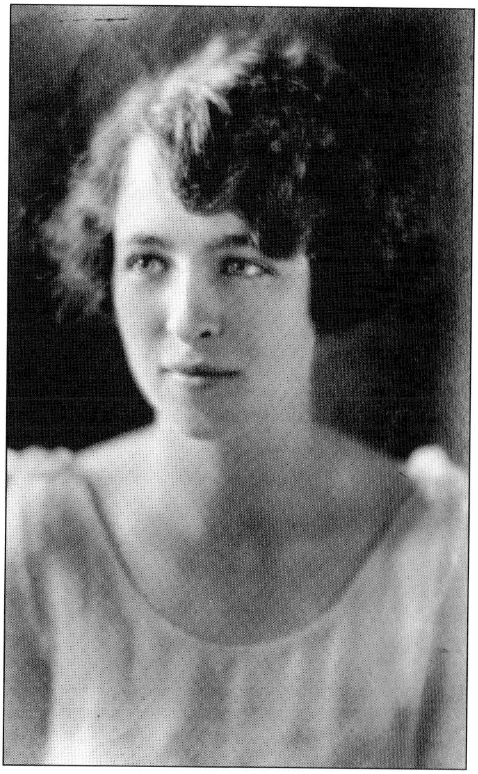

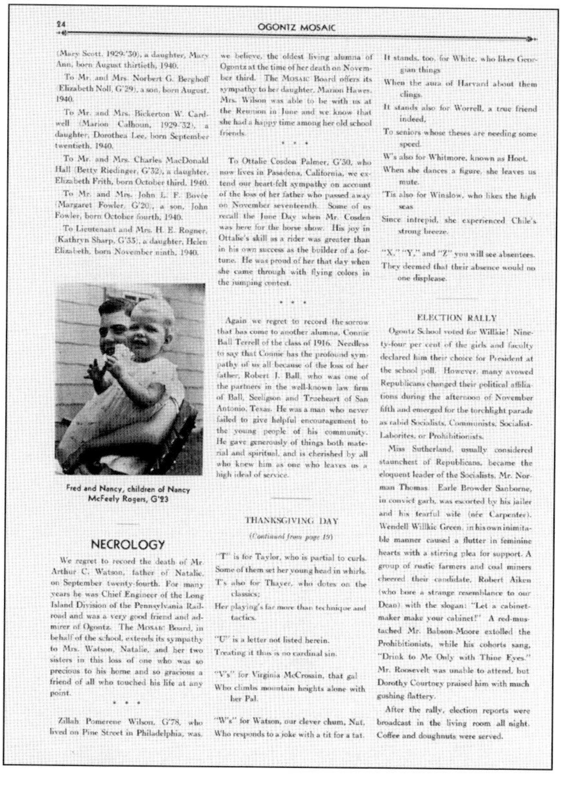

24 OGONTZ MOSAIC

(Mary Scott, 1929-'30), a daughter, Mary Ann, born August thirtieth, 1940.

To Mr. and Mrs. Norbert G. Berghoff (Elizabeth Noll, G'29), a son, born August, 1940.

To Mr. and Mrs. Bickerton W. Cardwell (Marion Calhoun, 1929-'32), a daughter, Dorothea Lee, born September twentieth, 1940.

To Mr. and Mrs. Charles MacDonald Hall (Betty Riedinger, G'32), a daughter, Elizabeth Frith, born October third, 1940.

To Mr. and Mrs. John L. F. Bovée (Margaret Fowler, G'20), a son, John Fowler, born October fourth, 1940.

To Lieutenant and Mrs. H. E. Rogner, (Kathryn Sharp, G'33), a daughter, Helen Elizabeth, born November ninth, 1940.

Fred and Nancy, children of Nancy McFeely Rogers, G'23

NECROLOGY

We regret to record the death of Mr. Arthur C. Watson, father of Natalie, on September twenty-fourth. For many years he was Chief Engineer of the Long Island Division of the Pennsylvania Railroad and was a very good friend and admirer of Ogontz. The Mosaic Board, in behalf of the school, extends its sympathy to Mrs. Watson, Natalie, and her two sisters in this loss of one who was so precious to his home and so gracious a friend of all who touched his life at any point.

* * *

Zillah Pomerene Wilson, G'78, who lived on Pine Street in Philadelphia, was, we believe, the oldest living alumna of Ogontz at the time of her death on November third. The Mosaic Board offers its sympathy to her daughter, Marion Hawes. Mrs. Wilson was able to be with us at the Reunion in June and we know that she had a happy time among her old school friends.

* * *

To Ottalie Cosdon Palmer, G'30, who now lives in Pasadena, California, we extend our heart-felt sympathy on account of the loss of her father who passed away on November seventeenth. Some of us recall the June Day when Mr. Cosden was here for the horse show. His joy in Ottalie's skill as a rider was greater than in his own success as the builder of a fortune. He was proud of her that day when she came through with flying colors in the jumping contest.

* * *

Again we regret to record the sorrow that has come to another alumna, Connie Ball Terrell of the class of 1916. Needless to say that Connie has the profound sympathy of us all because of the loss of her father, Robert J. Ball, who was one of the partners in the well-known law firm of Ball, Seeligson and Trueheart of San Antonio, Texas. He was a man who never failed to give helpful encouragement to the young people of his community. He gave generously of things both material and spiritual, and is cherished by all who knew him as one who leaves us a high ideal of service.

THANKSGIVING DAY

(*Continued from page 19*)

"T" is for Taylor, who is partial to curls.
Some of them set her young head in whirls.
T's also for Thayer, who dotes on the classics;
Her playing's far more than technique and tactics.

"U" is a letter not listed herein.
Treating it thus is no cardinal sin.

"V's" for Virginia McCrossin, that gal
Who climbs mountain heights alone with her Pal.

"W's" for Watson, our clever chum, Nat,
Who responds to a joke with a tit for a tat.
It stands, too, for White, who likes Georgian things
When the aura of Harvard about them clings.
It stands also for Worrell, a true friend indeed,
To seniors whose theses are needing some speed.
W's also for Whitmore, known as Hoot,
When she dances a figure, she leaves us mute.
'Tis also for Winslow, who likes the high seas
Since intrepid, she experienced Chile's strong breeze.

"X," "Y," and "Z" you will see absentees.
They deemed that their absence would no one displease.

ELECTION RALLY

Ogontz School voted for Willkie! Ninety-four per cent of the girls and faculty declared him their choice for President at the school poll. However, many avowed Republicans changed their political affiliations during the afternoon of November fifth and emerged for the torchlight parade as rabid Socialists, Communists, Socialist-Laborites, or Prohibitionists.

Miss Sutherland, usually considered staunchest of Republicans, became the eloquent leader of the Socialists, Mr. Norman Thomas. Earle Browder Sanborne, in convict garb, was escorted by his jailer and his tearful wife (née Carpenter). Wendell Willkie Green, in his own inimitable manner caused a flutter in feminine hearts with a stirring plea for support. A group of rustic farmers and coal miners cheered their candidate, Robert Aiken (who bore a strange resemblance to our Dean) with the slogan: "Let a cabinet-maker make your cabinet!" A red-mustached Mr. Babson-Moore extolled the Prohibitionists, while his cohorts sang, "Drink to Me Only with Thine Eyes." Mr. Roosevelt was unable to attend, but Dorothy Courtney praised him with much gushing flattery.

After the rally, election reports were broadcast in the living room all night. Coffee and doughnuts were served.

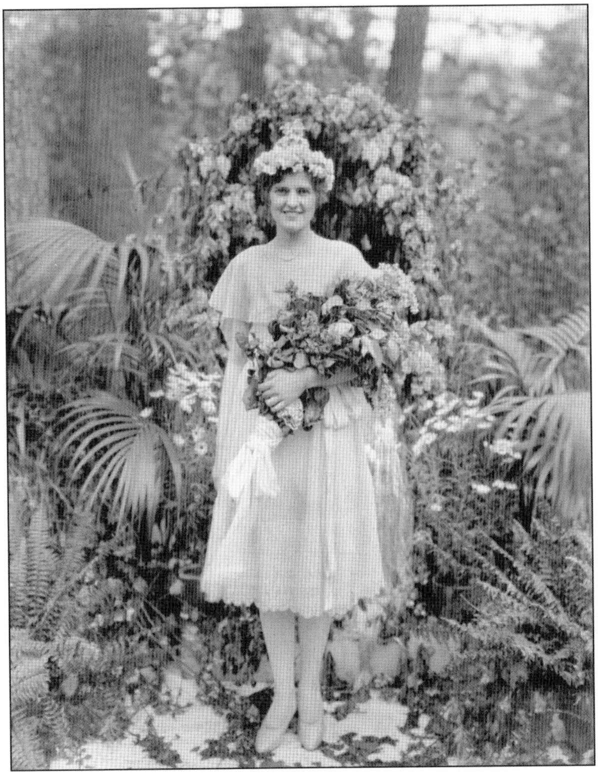

After weeks of discussion, as was the rule, the seniors of the class of 1926 chose Lovelady Hamilton—yes, that is her real name—as their May Queen. Spoken of with great affection by her classmates, Hamilton is seen here on the Ogontz School grounds during the celebration, holding the traditional bouquet of roses. (The Ogontz School Archives, 1926, Penn State University, Abington College Library.)

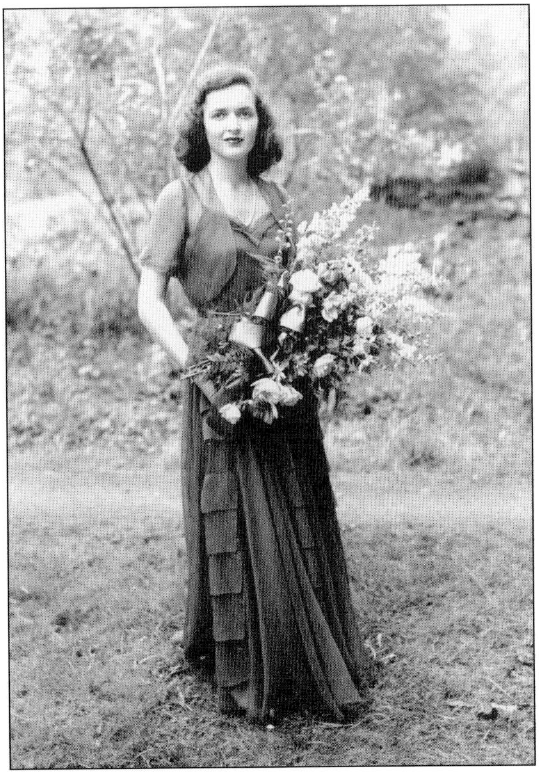

The popular Millicent Katherine Fritsch, who participated extensively in theatricals at the Ogontz School, graduated in 1946. Her classmates wrote about her in the 1946 Class Book: "With soulful eyes like liquid flame, / Sweet Millicent of voice divine, / Meets all our needs of *eye* and *ear*; / We're honored to be friend of thine." (The Ogontz School Archives, 1946, Penn State University, Abington College Library.)

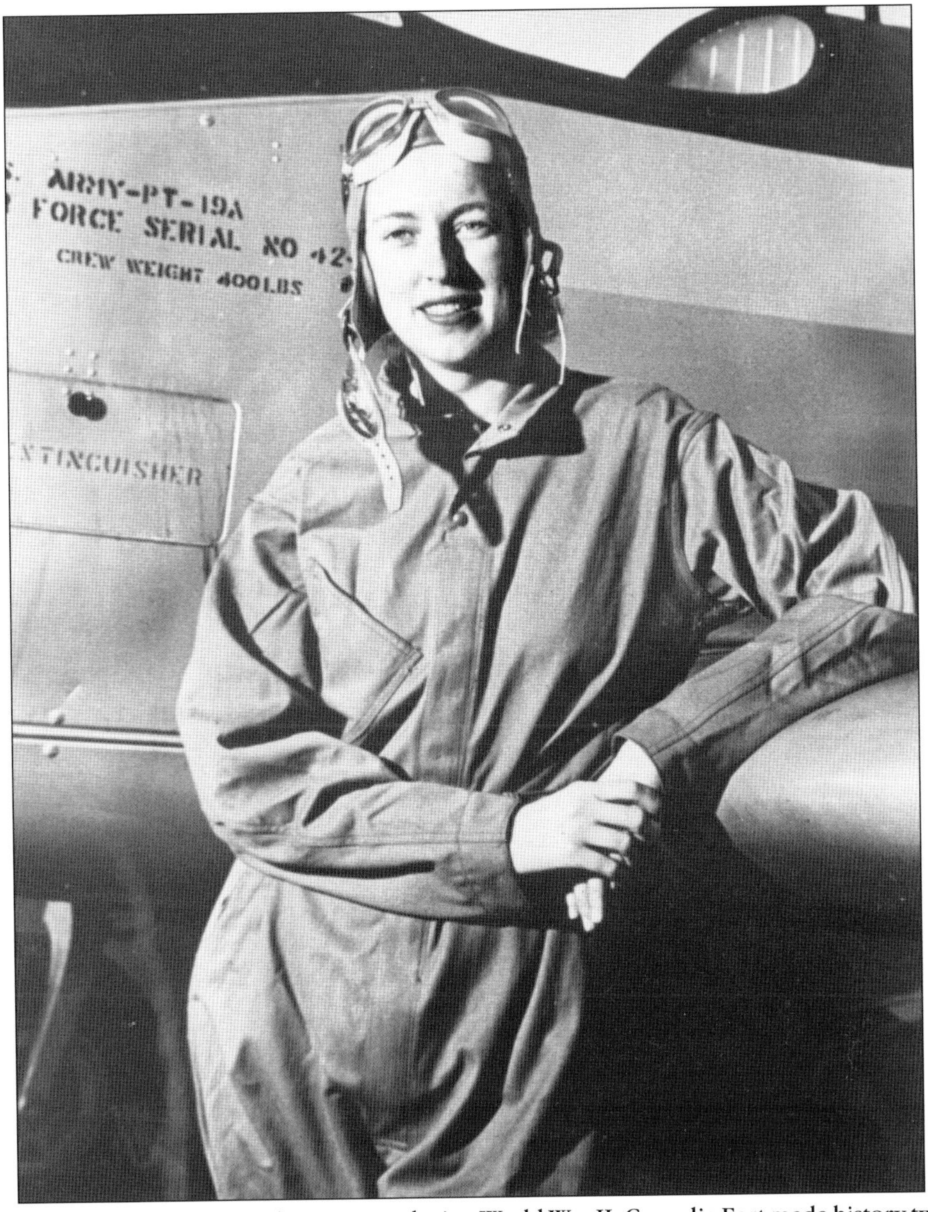

Renowned for her service to her country during World War II, Cornelia Fort made history twice during the turbulent war years. Most dramatically, she was aloft with a student pilot in Honolulu on December 7, 1941, when she spied a suspicious looking military aircraft approaching rapidly behind them. When she jerked the controls upward to avoid a midair collision, she saw the distinctive red sun of the Imperial Japanese Navy. Fort alerted headquarters immediately. The invasion of Pearl Harbor had begun. Seen here leaning against a PT-19A aircraft, Cornelia Fort was another Ogontz School "flygirl" inspired by the exploits of Amelia Earhart. The first female flight instructor in her hometown of Nashville, Tennessee, Fort was invited to join the newly formed Women's Auxiliary Ferrying Service, which freed male pilots for wartime duty. Ironically, during a routine ferrying mission in Texas on March 21, 1943, she was killed in a midair collision, becoming the first American woman to die on active military duty. (Nashville Public Library, Special Collections.)

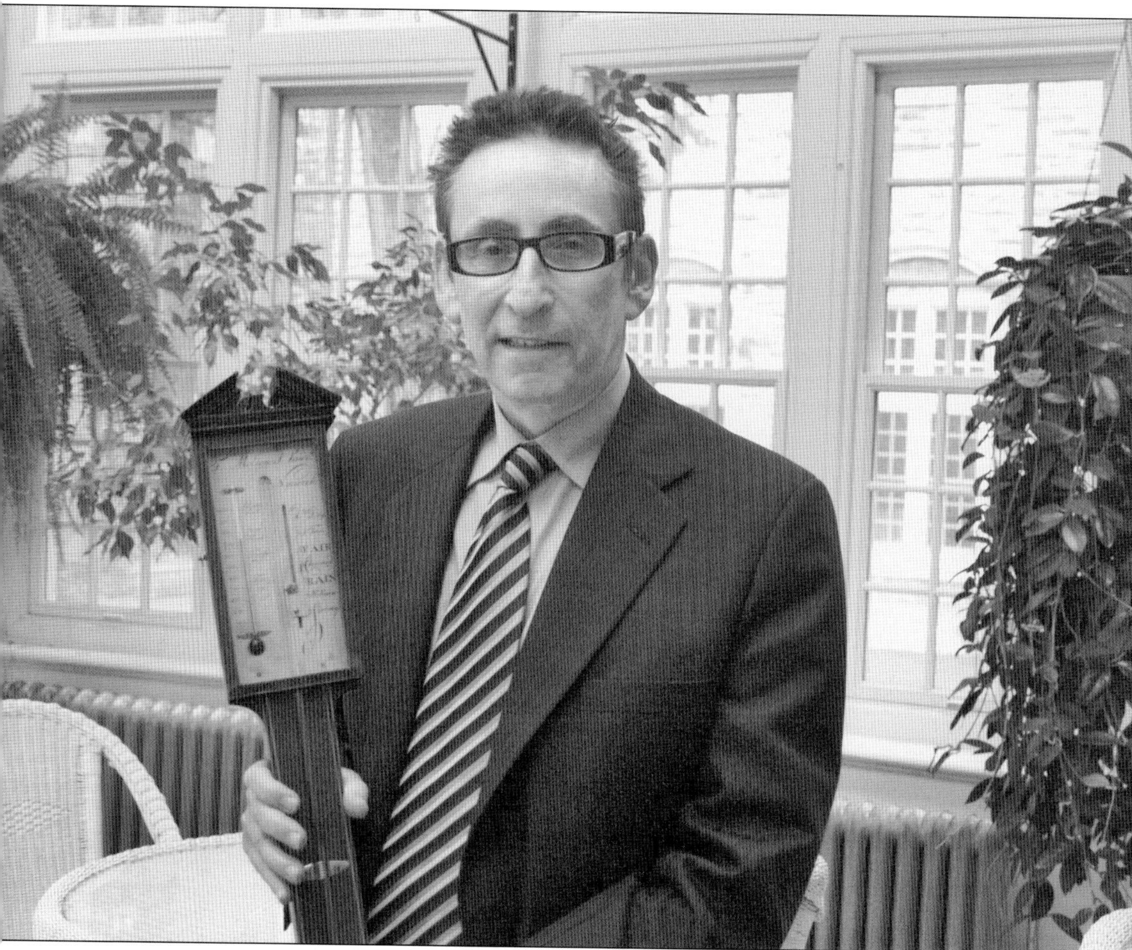

On a return visit to Penn State Abington on June 4, 2007, Dr. Joel Myers donated this mahogany stick barometer, created in 1820 by noted barometer maker Francis Molton of Norwich, England. That it came from his private collection of antique barometers is a measure of his fondness for the college. It might have been surprising to freshmen attending Penn State Ogontz in 1957 to hear Myers issuing weather forecasts from campus, but it was his boyhood dream to create a business based on predicting the weather. While he was a graduate student studying meteorology at Penn State University, he did just that, founding AccuWeather, the leading commercial weather service in the world. Its headquarters are at State College, where Myers has received three degrees in meteorology. The chairman and president of AccuWeather, Myers was a longtime trustee of the university, where he also served on the faculty for several years. *Entrepreneur* magazine recognized Myers as one of the 520 greatest entrepreneurs in American history, along with Steve Jobs, Bill Gates, and Thomas Edison. (University Relations Department, Penn State Abington.)

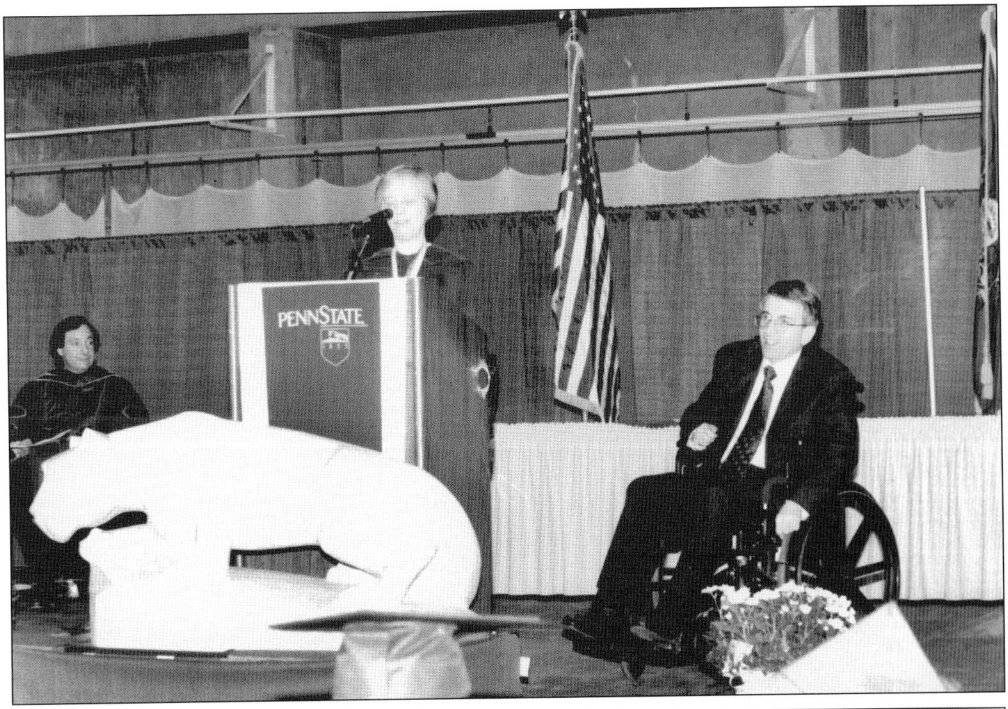

At the 1998 commencement, chancellor emerita Dr. Karen Wiley Sandler is announcing that Nicholas Maiale (right) was named Outstanding Alumnus. Former associate dean for academic affairs Dr. Leonard Mustazza is on the left. Maiale, an attorney who served the 183rd District as a Democratic member of the Pennsylvania House of Representatives from 1980 to 1992, got his first taste of politics at Penn State Ogontz. Former Penn State Abington writer in residence Rachel Simon writes that Maiale, a conservative from South Philadelphia, was upset that the college seemed to invite only antiwar speakers to campus in the late 1960s. So he wrote a letter to the *Philadelphia Inquirer* to criticize the school, whereupon Dean Robert Clappier invited Maiale to run for student government. Running for president on a platform of "community and togetherness," he won the 1970 election. He is seen at right with Chancellor Sandler after winning the Alumni Fellow Award, the most prestigious award given by the Penn State Alumni Association. (Above, University Relations Department, 1998, Penn State Abington; right, University Relations Department, 2001, Penn State Abington.)

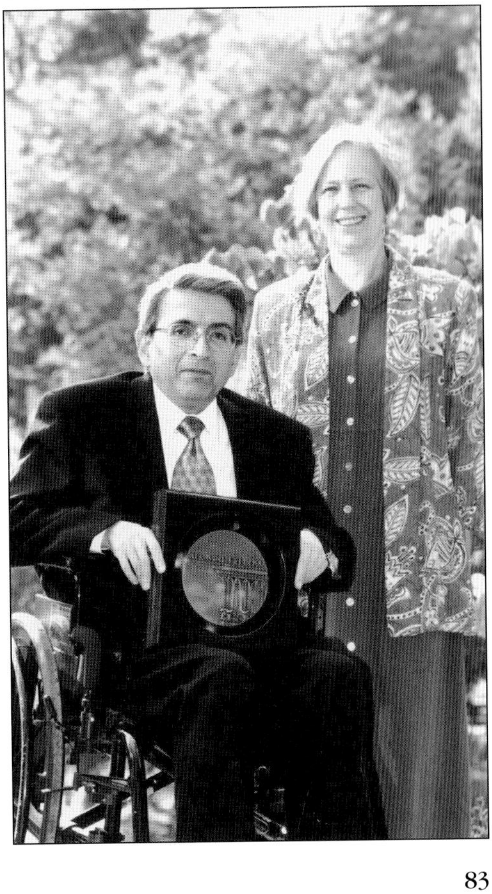

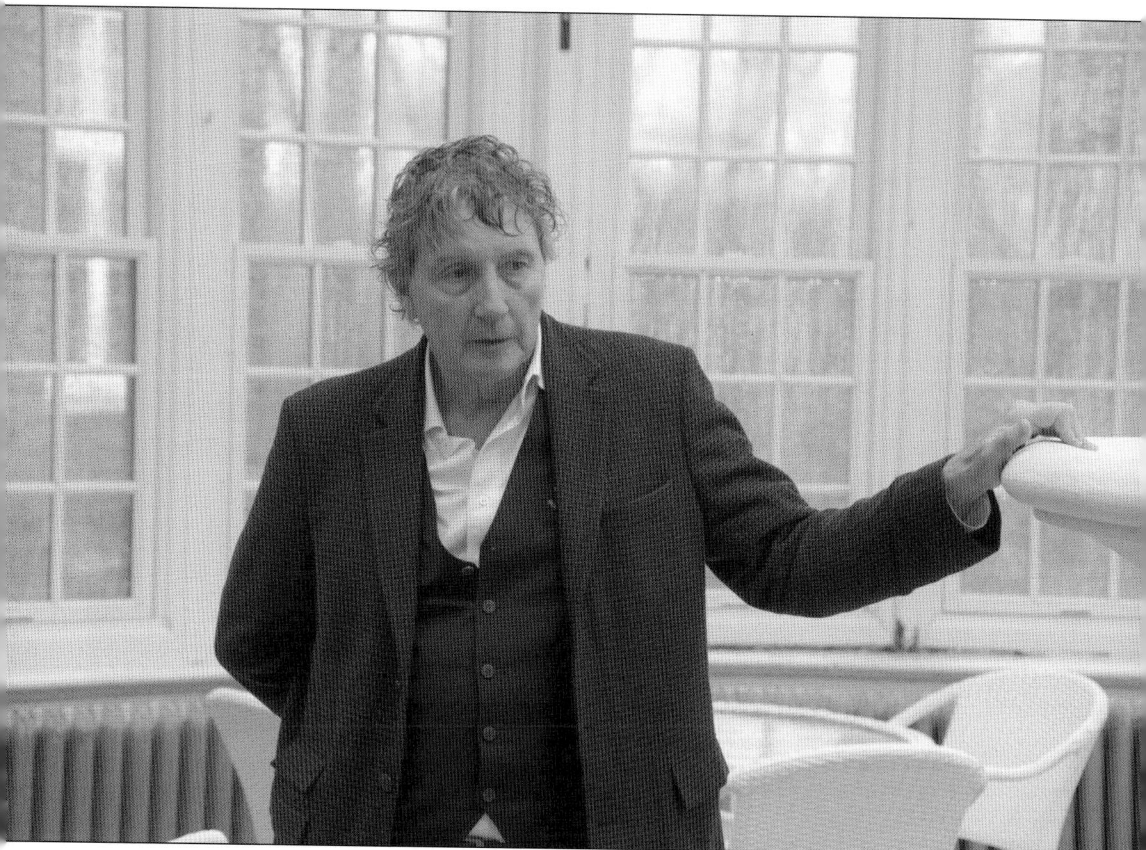

Rod Nordland, named editor of the *Ogontz Campus News* in 1969, has reached the pinnacle of success in his chosen field. A correspondent-at-large for the *New York Times* and the paper's Kabul bureau chief since 2013, Nordland has shared a Pulitzer Prize for reporting in the United States and was a Pulitzer finalist for international reporting. Visiting Penn State Abington on February 16, 2016, Nordland spoke of his extensive work as a foreign correspondent, starting with his hometown newspaper, the *Philadelphia Inquirer*, in the 1980s, then with *Newsweek*, where he was the magazine's chief foreign correspondent, and finally, with the *Times*, for which he has covered the Middle East and South Asia. His latest book, *The Lovers: Romeo and Juliet in Afghanistan*, is a personal reflection on tribal jealousies, religious customs, and honor killings in that war-torn land. (Photograph by Maria Narodetsky, University Relations Department, 2016, Penn State Abington.)

Five

Learning and Training

At the Chestnut Street Female Seminary and the Ogontz School, the faculty was chosen with great care. The salaries were far above average for the time. The living conditions, including accommodations, food, and service, were homey and inviting. And the dedication of the principals and key administrators was such that few of them married or raised families of their own. Their attention to the students and educational mission was clearly focused.

The teachers were all experts in their fields. The French teachers had either lived or studied in France, and the teachers of German had lived or studied in Germany. Music teachers could be members of the Philadelphia Orchestra. Art teachers might also be on the faculty of the Pennsylvania Academy of the Fine Arts. They traveled extensively and encouraged their students to follow in their footsteps.

Abby Sutherland was especially impressed by French teacher Mlle. Bôegli, at Ogontz from 1898 to 1901: "Her classroom work and table conversation were both thrilling and inspiring to students who admired her adventurous spirit. She started from Switzerland, where she was living, to the coast of Italy, then southeast, stopping at Australia, meeting wherever she went strange customs and interesting people. She gave lectures of her trip with interesting stereopticon views collected with care from Australia, the Pacific Islands, Japan and Asia."

The same kind of care has been taken with faculty selection since Penn State Ogontz came into being in 1950. Adhering to the rigorous standards of Penn State University, long known as one of the most significant research institutions in the country, the faculty are expected to be experts in their respective fields who also produce meaningful work—books, articles, symposia, inventions, artworks, and the like. But because the class size at Penn State Abington is much smaller than classes at University Park, Penn State Abington faculty can interact more effectively with their students.

This chapter also highlights the Ogontz School's famous military drills, ROTC activity, and more.

Former associate dean for academic affairs and teacher of English and American studies Dr. Leonard Mustazza said that he is most proud that, even though Penn State Abington has evolved into a formidable research institution, "We have never lost our love of teaching, and our students have responded brilliantly."

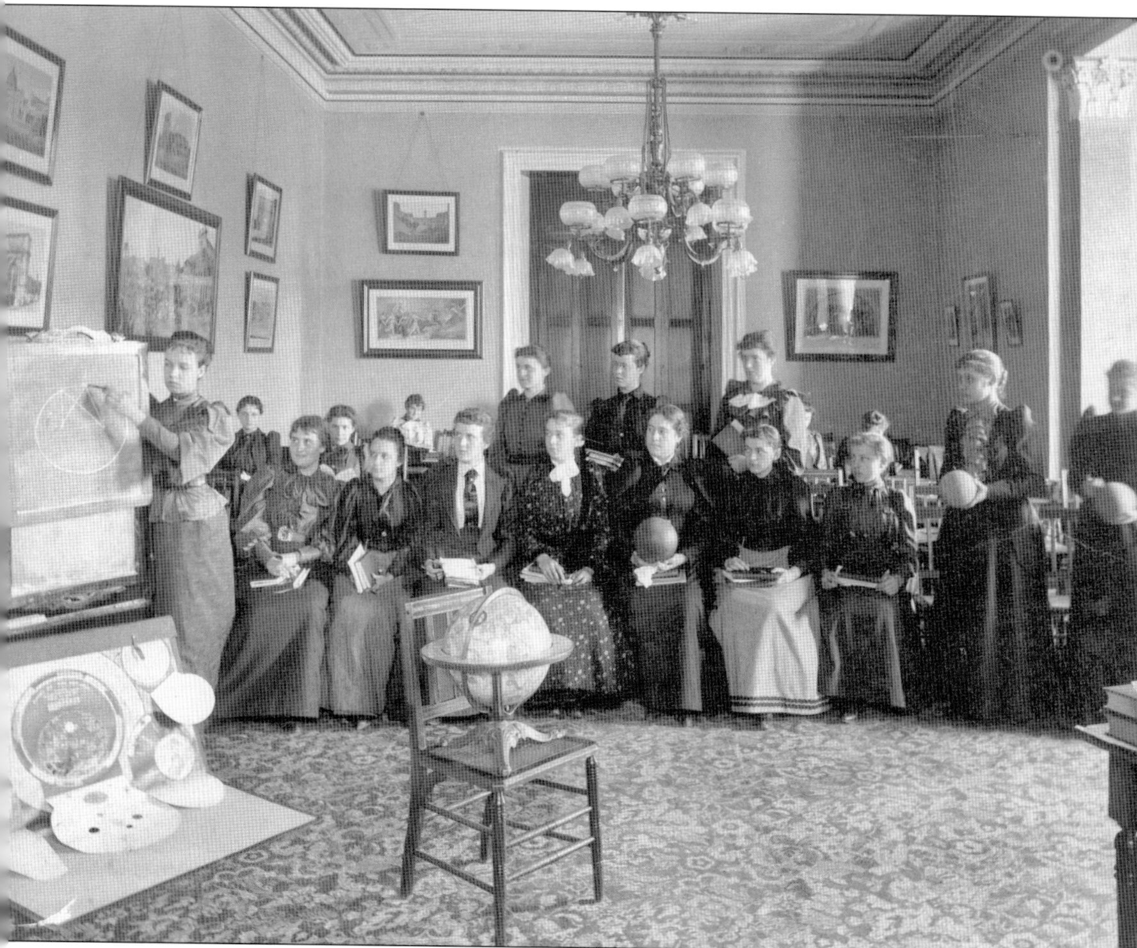

Astronomy class, which took place in the lower study parlor at the converted Jay Cooke mansion, was typical of the classroom ambience at the Ogontz School for Young Ladies. The building was furnished in ornate Victorian style; velvet carpets softened all the floors and stairs. There were high ceilings, artwork, and elegant furnishings in every room. In her history of the school, *100 Years of Ogontz*, Abby Sutherland wrote that this setting was "impressive even to girls from homes of affluence." Note how attentive the students are, holding their textbooks and/or gloves in their hands or laps as their teacher explains the boundaries of the physical universe. (The Ogontz School Archives, date unknown, Penn State University, Abington College Library.)

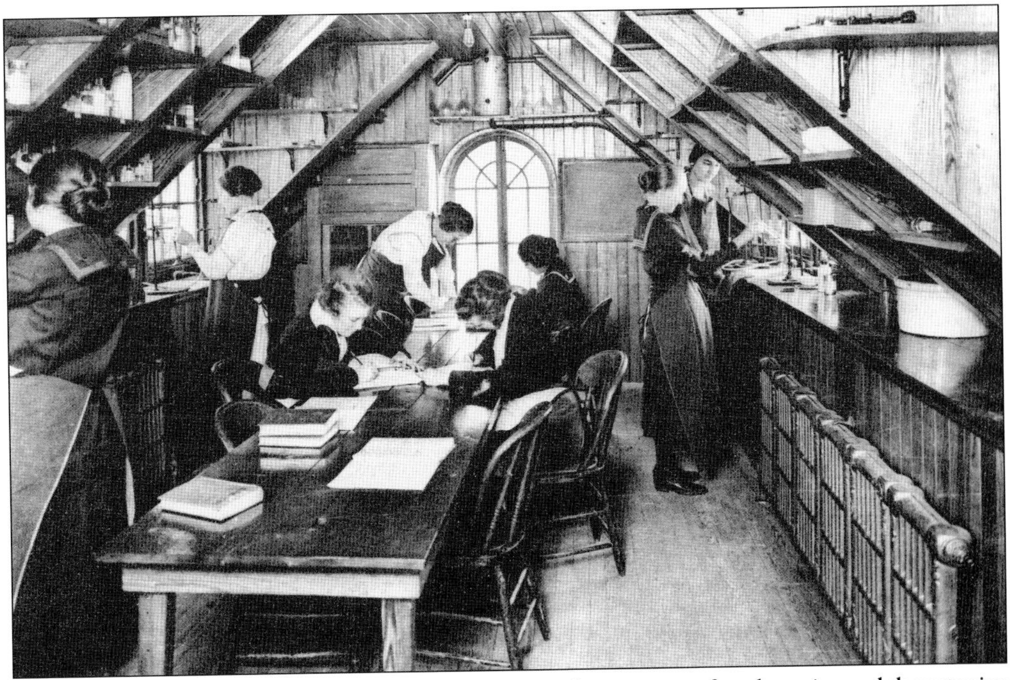

Far from the elegance of the Jay Cooke mansion, the quarters for the science laboratories at the new campus in Rydal must have come as a shock to the young girls of Ogontz. The photograph above shows students working on science projects either at long wooden tables with sturdy wooden chairs or doing measurements at counters beneath the curving wood shingle roof. According to Frederick Platt in his article "Horace Trumbauer in Rydal and Meadowbrook" in the *Old York Road Historical Society Bulletin* (Volume XLI, 1984), the setting in the photograph below might have been the Springhouse, converted from a summer house on the original Herring property into chemistry laboratories in 1932. Even the modernized chemistry laboratory pictured below seemed cramped for roughly a dozen students. (Both, the Ogontz School Archives, date unknown, Penn State University, Abington College Library.)

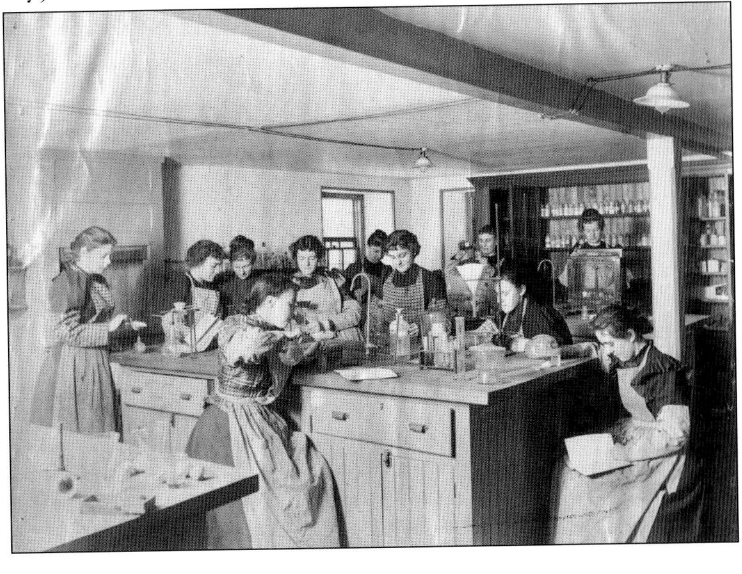

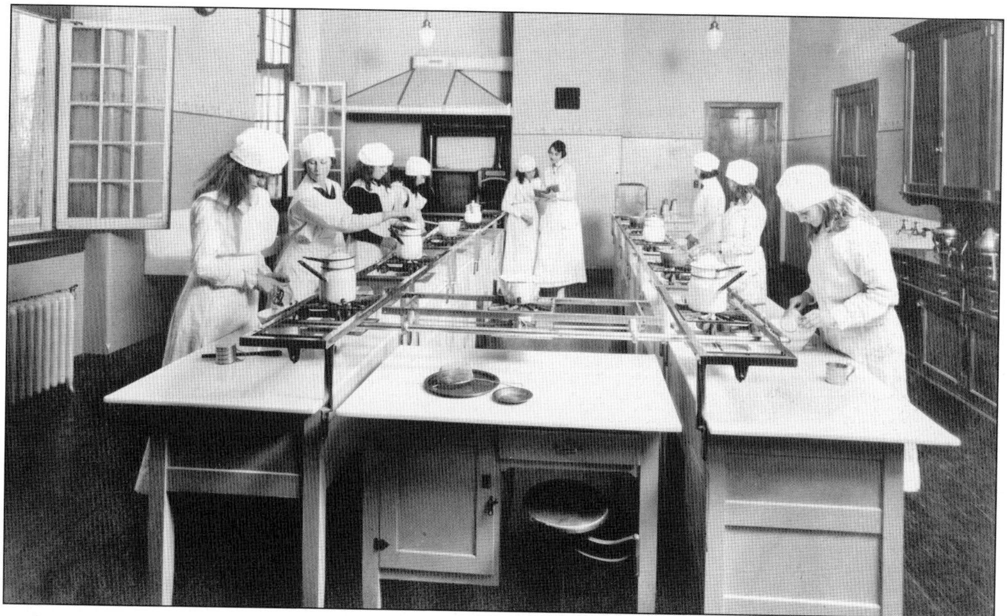

Judging from the first catalog of the Chestnut Street Female Seminary in 1850, the curriculum at the elite girls' school was as rigorous as those of the best college preparatory schools in the country. Mary Bonney and Harriet Dillaye planned a regular schedule of classes in basic subjects such as mathematics, history, and science. Abby Sutherland described the curriculum, paralleling that of Vassar College, as being "carried according to the college standard manner with searching tests and examinations." But it was still a finishing school, so classes like home economics were also part of the plan. Above, students are learning the fine arts of the kitchen. Below, students are studying and chatting in the comfortable library in the Sutherland Building. (Above, the Ogontz School Archives, date unknown, Penn State University, Abington College Library; below, the Ogontz School Archives, c. 1940s, Penn State University, Abington College Library.)

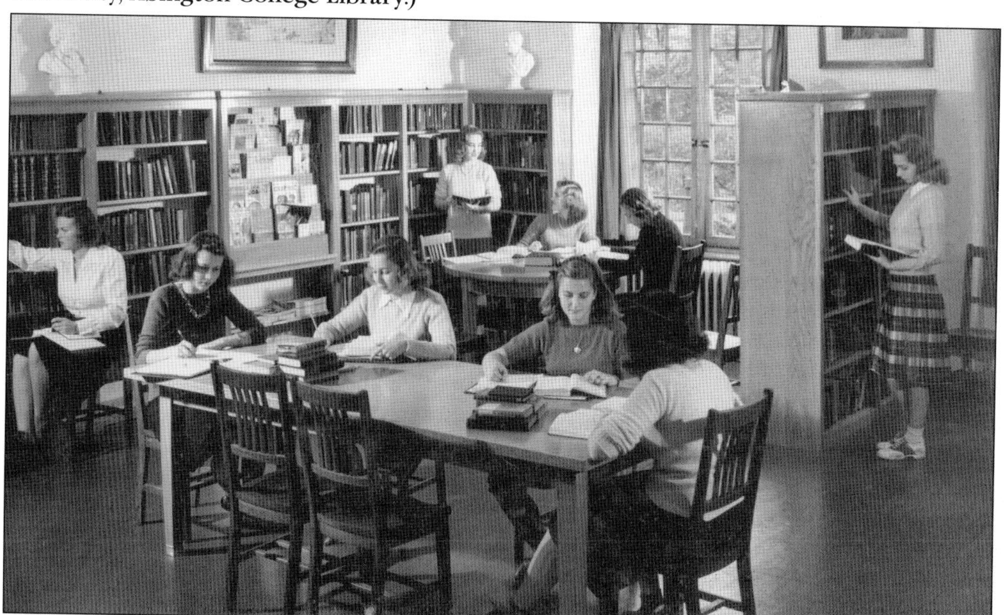

Although the technology might not be as sophisticated as the devices students take for granted today, the students in these photographs show what education at the Ogontz School in the 1940s looked like. The girl seen at right is working on an architectural rendering at her desk using an old-fashioned drawing compass. Below, the girl standing on the wooden platform, with help from a classmate, is doing an air gun painting on an oversized canvas. The process might be messy, but the results can be spectacular. (Both, the Ogontz School Archives, 1940s, Penn State University, Abington College Library.)

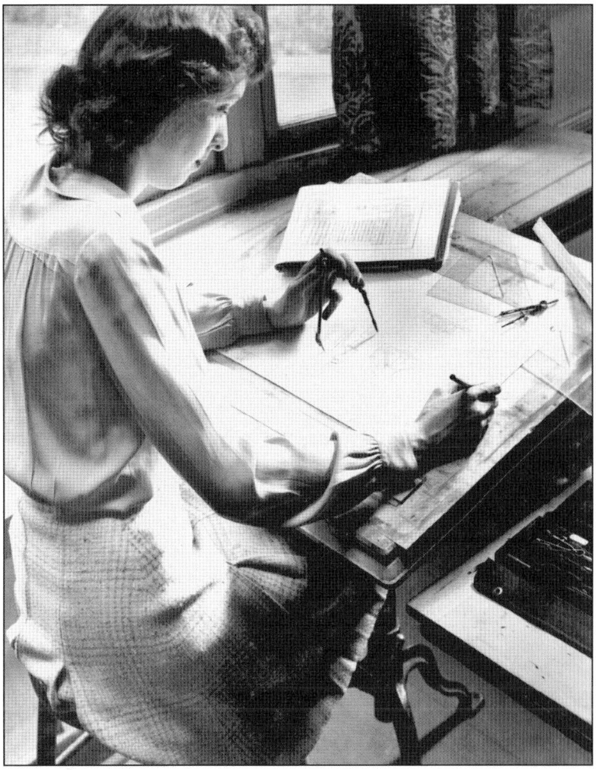

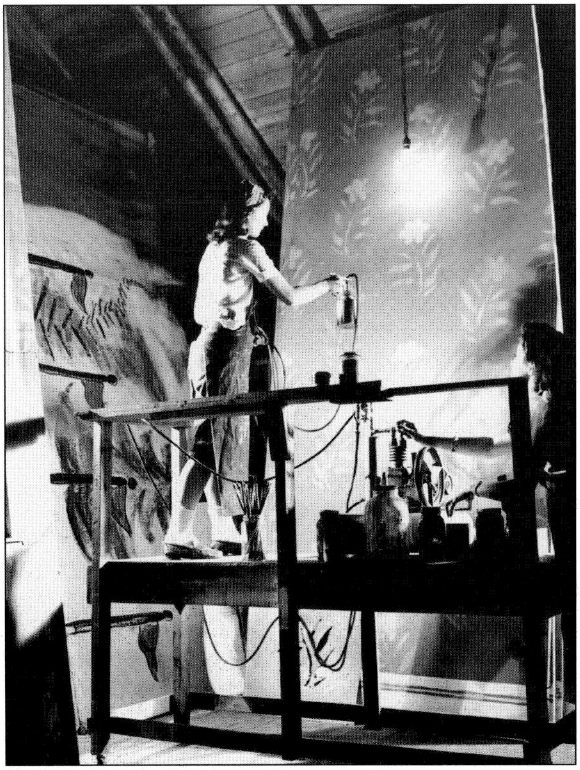

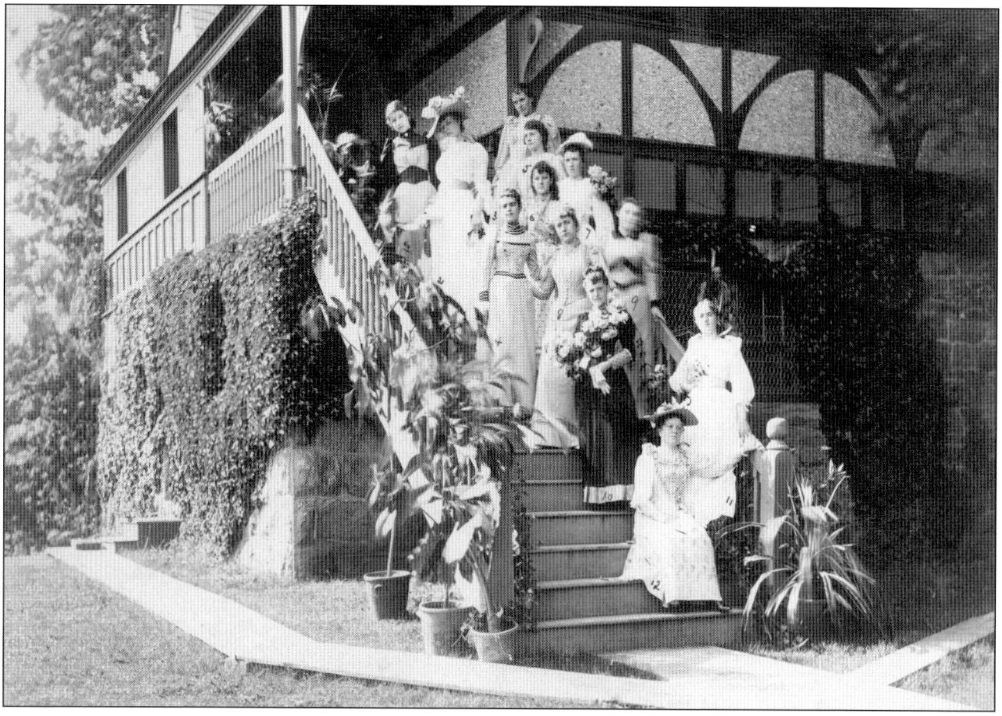

What a difference 69 years can make! Although the art students pictured above in 1892 are not at work in the art studio, they have clearly gathered for some kind of celebration on a stairway leading to the Jay Cooke mansion. Perhaps the young lady carrying a bouquet of roses has won some sort of art contest. Below, the students standing outside in their overcoats, on the other hand, are busily drawing the trees and the buildings visible from their location just beyond the duck pond. The Springhouse can be seen off to the right. (Above, the Ogontz School Archives, 1892, Penn State University, Abington College Library; below, the Ogontz School Archives, 1961, Penn State University, Abington College Library.)

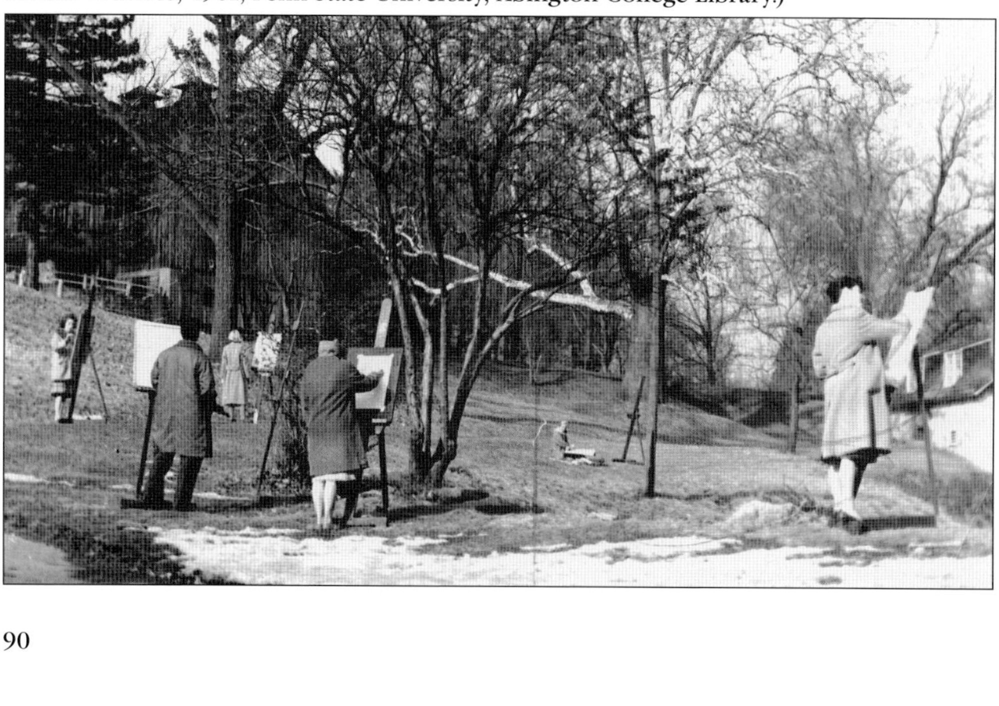

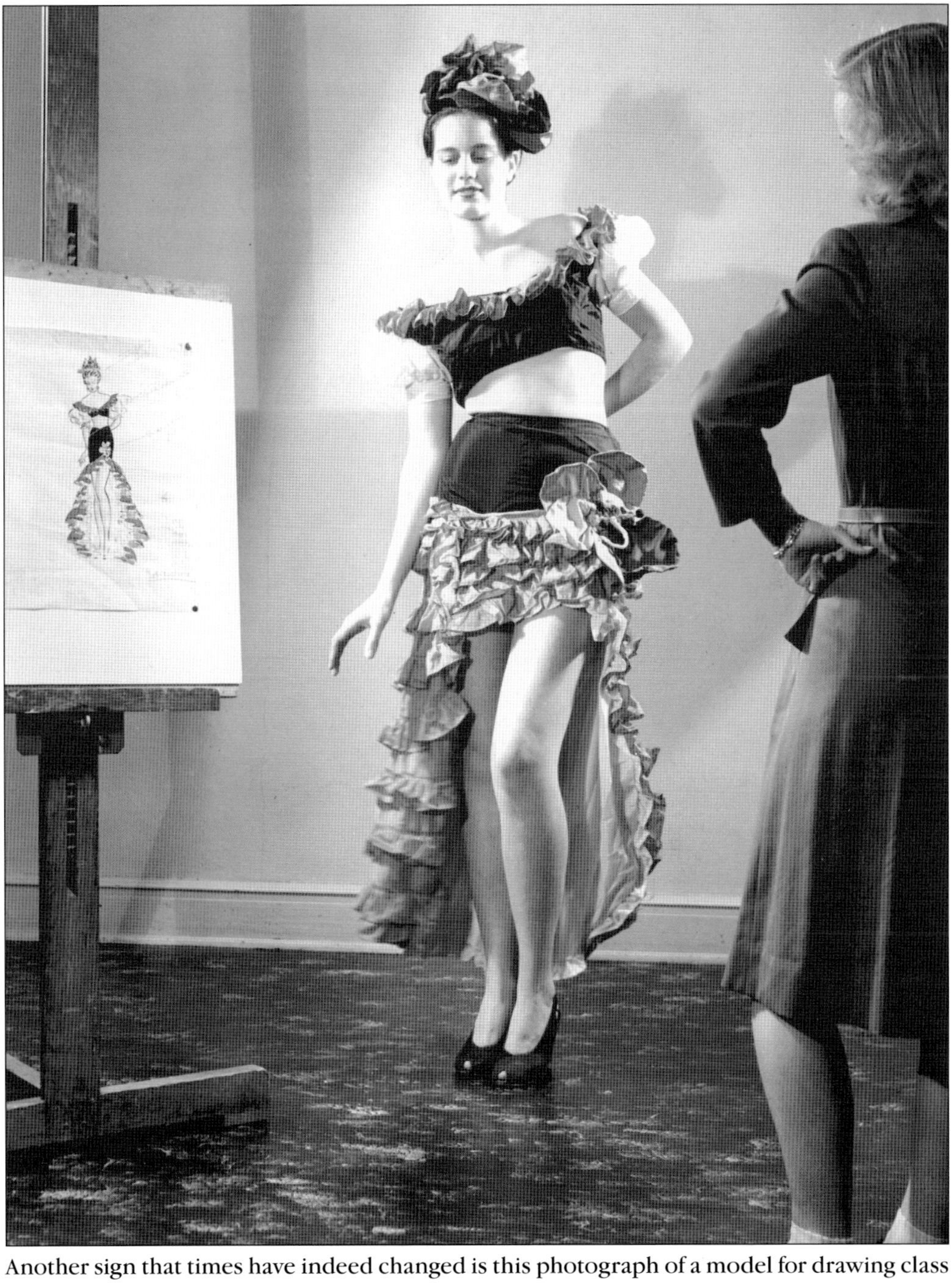

Another sign that times have indeed changed is this photograph of a model for drawing class dressed in the costume of a Spanish dancer. Although this kind of pose is hardly risqué or scandalous, it does run counter to Abby Sutherland's admonition in her *Talks with Girls*, written in 1915: "If [a girl] prefers the kind of dress which suggests the physical, which enhances the sense of sex, which scarcely covers her, she is revealing, and not through a glass darkly, a state of mind which cannot see God, because it is not pure in heart. Dress is not wholly a superficial matter. It is the outward expression of an inward state." (The Ogontz School Archives, c. 1940s, Penn State University, Abington College Library.)

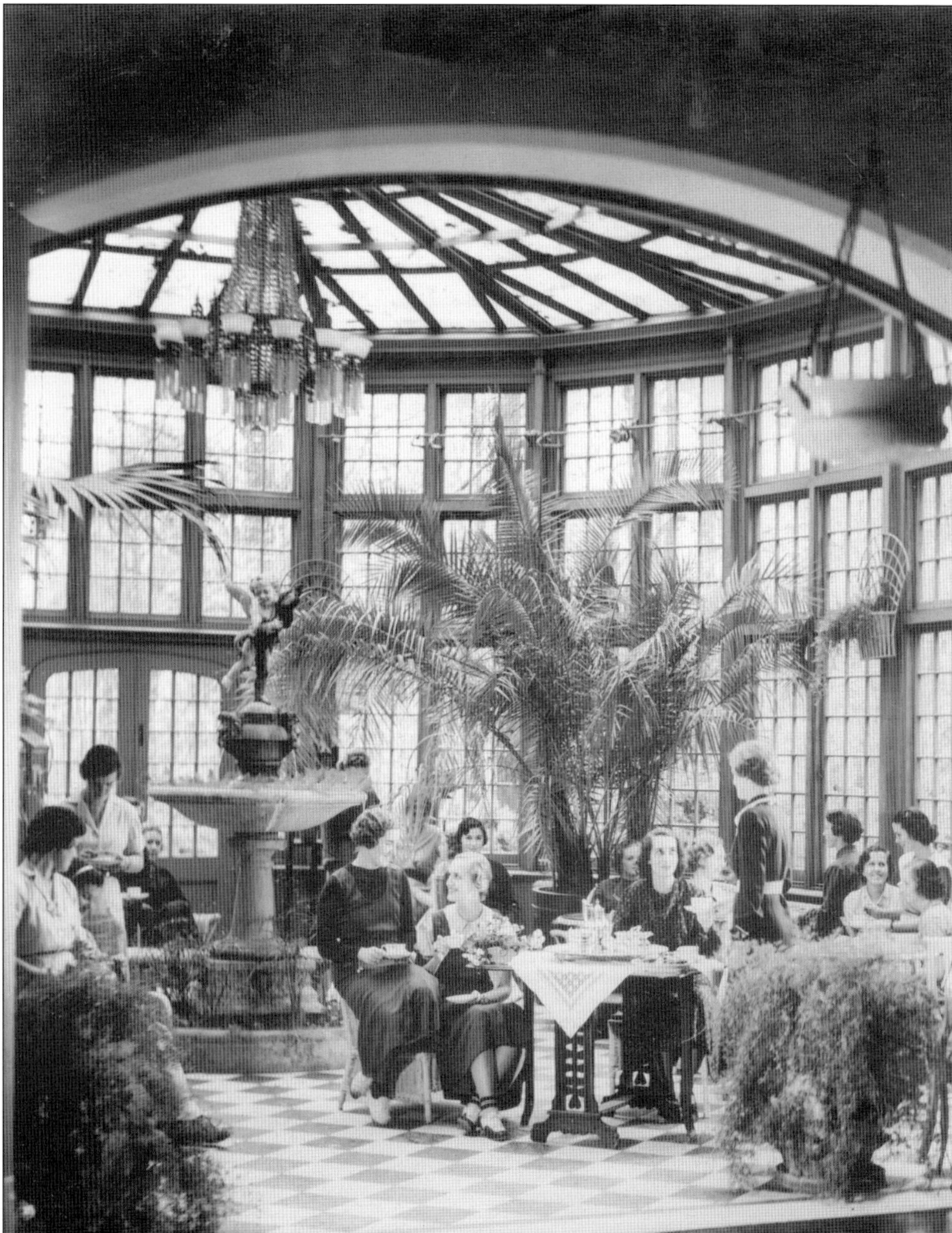

Part of the daily ritual at the Ogontz School was tea served at 3:00 p.m. for any girl so inclined in the cozy confines of the solarium. This photograph shows several girls taking full advantage of the opportunity to practice their proper "tea manners" while chatting with classmates. Perched on the arm of a wicker chair is senior Natalie Peace, who lived in nearby Meadowbrook, Abington Township. She graduated with the class of 1934. This photograph also appeared in an article on the Ogontz School published in the local *Times Chronicle* on August 16, 1979. (The Ogontz School Archives, c. 1934, Penn State University, Abington College Library.)

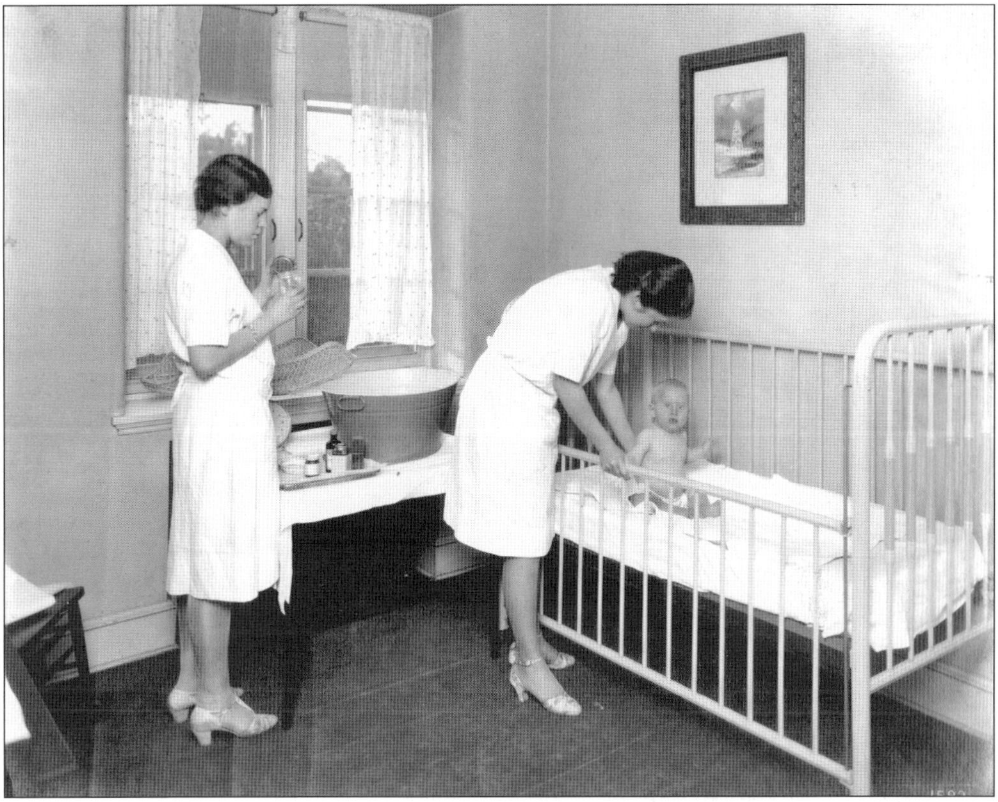

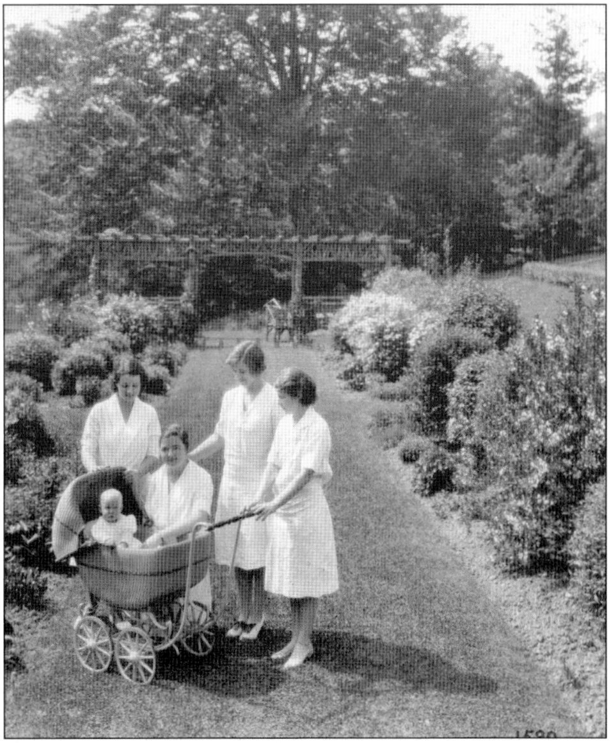

"Domestic engineering" was a unique course at the Ogontz School that gave the girls an opportunity to care for an orphan baby. According to Abby Sutherland in her book *100 Years of Ogontz*, one child, accompanied by a trained nurse, would be brought in each year to live in Lares, known informally as the home economics house. A different girl would be selected every two weeks to live in Lares and learn to take care of the baby. At the 1985 Reunion, alumna Elizabeth McFarland (class of 1940) recalls this unusual practice, "And we could go out and borrow a baby and learn how to care for it. It . . . prepared you for family responsibilities." (Both, the Ogontz School Archives, 1929, Penn State University, Abington College Library.)

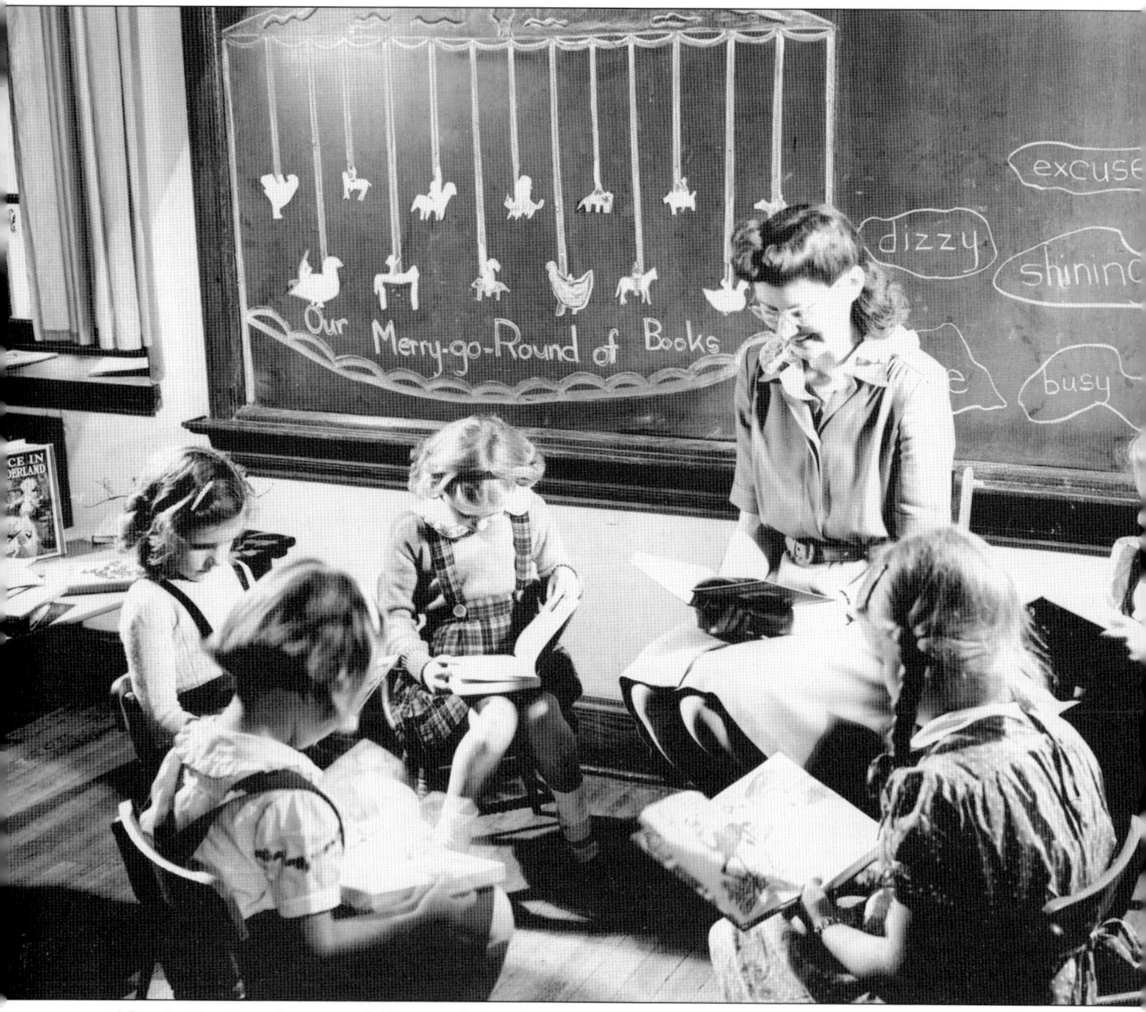

Abby Sutherland opened the Rydal School shortly after moving the Ogontz School to its new location in 1917. She thought it best for the younger girls to have their own facilities apart from the older students, so she held classes for the younger girls on a property called Shangarry adjoining the new campus. Shangarry mansion was used for primary classes until 1923, when the Horace Trumbauer firm constructed a new building on campus to serve as the elementary school. In 1925, adjacent to the schoolhouse, Rydal Hall was built as a dormitory for the girls. The photograph shows the unnamed teacher reading to her pupils. The book *Alice in Wonderland* is displayed prominently on a table, and a vocabulary drill can be seen on the blackboard. (The Ogontz School Archives, c. late 1940s, Penn State University, Abington College Library.)

Rydal School girls, armed with books, coats, and umbrellas, can be seen walking calmly up and down the stairs of what was then called Rydal Hall. The building later came to be used as the student union. Rydal School closed in 1950, when Ogontz became Penn State. (The Ogontz School Archives, c. late 1940s, Penn State University, Abington College Library.)

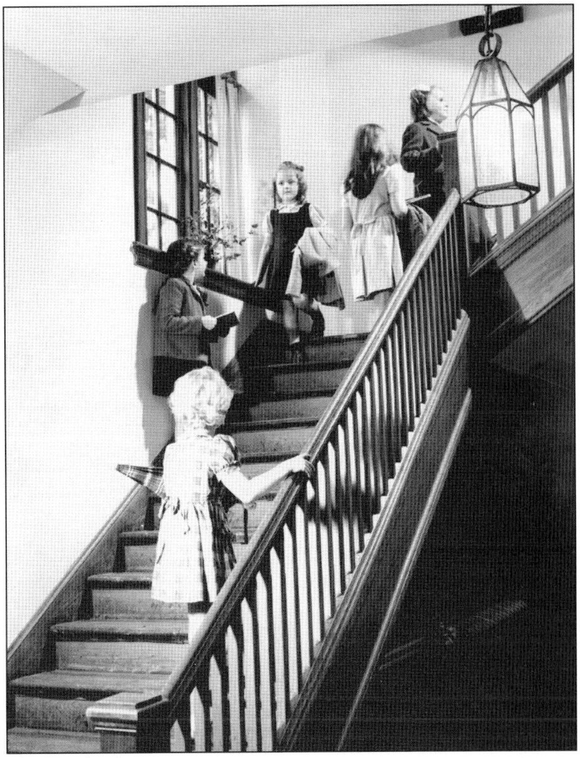

Abby Sutherland poses with nine girls from the Rydal School. They are, from left to right (first row) Betty Harbison, Edie Anne ?, Betsy ?, Dottie May Whitaker, and Martha Bishop; (second row) Barbara J. Holmes, Anne Haddock, Abby Sutherland, Jeanne ?, and Joan Dowing. (The Ogontz School Archives, 1944, Penn State University, Abington College Library.)

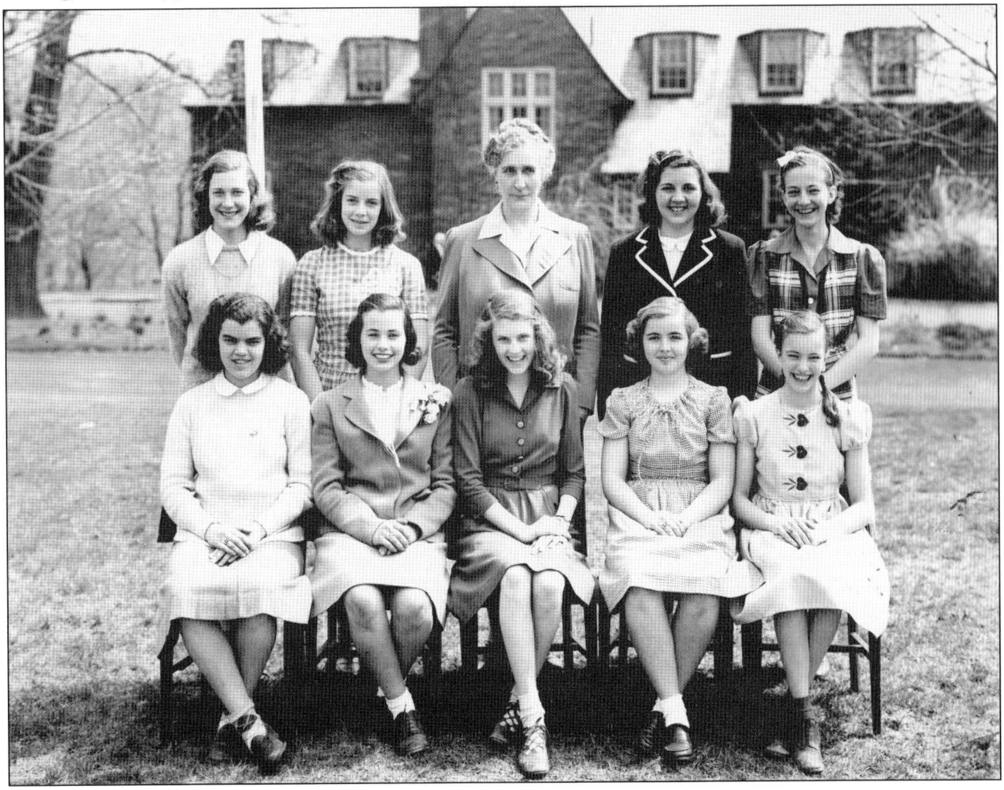

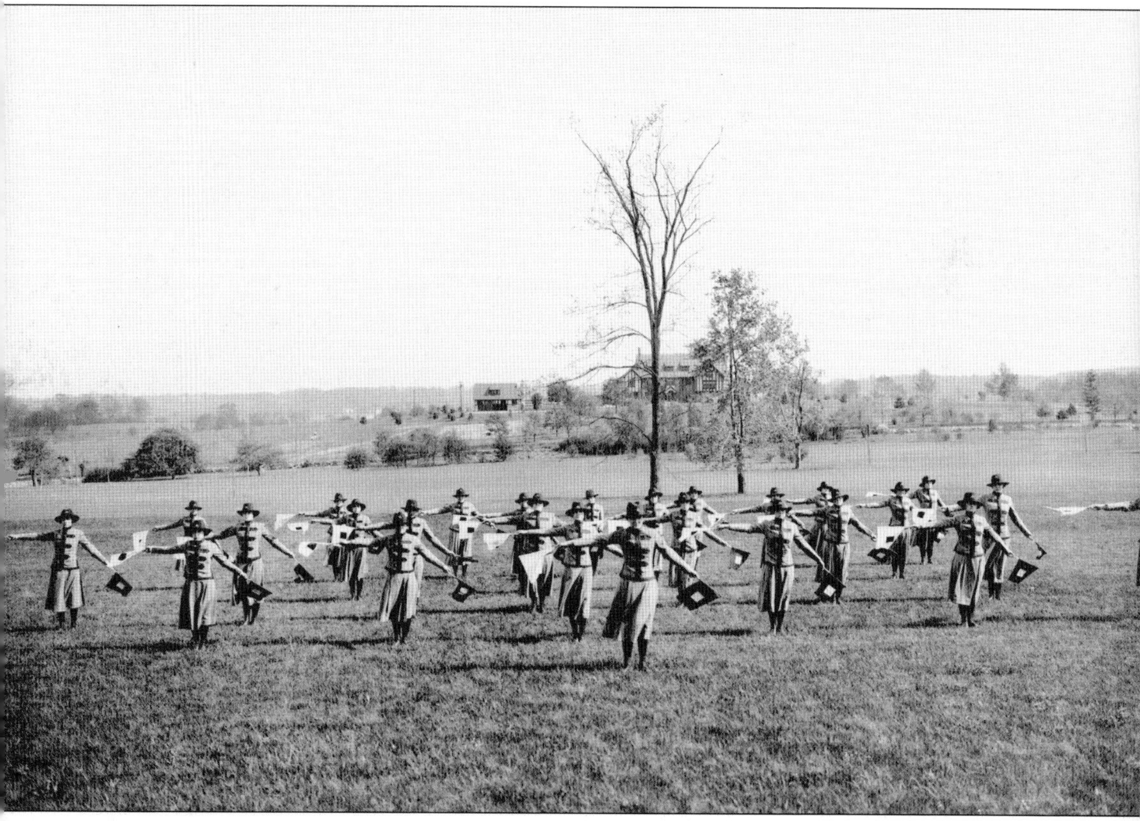

By the end of the 19th century, the Ogontz School was the oldest girls' school in the country incorporating military drills into its curriculum. As they began under Sylvia Eastman in 1886, some say the school was the first to do so. Abby Sutherland said that the drills evolved as an extension of the walks popular at the school and that they inspired attention, concentration, and a response to what she called "standards of posture, walking, consideration for others." When Amelia Earhart marched with her classmates in 1916, Sutherland said that her prized student's mind was clearly elsewhere, as "no airplane drone on the farthest horizon failed to claim her attention." At the time, Shangarry Field was still being used for drill and other outdoor activities. The girls can be seen here doing a maneuver involving signal flags. (The Ogontz School Archives, date unknown, Penn State University, Abington College Library.)

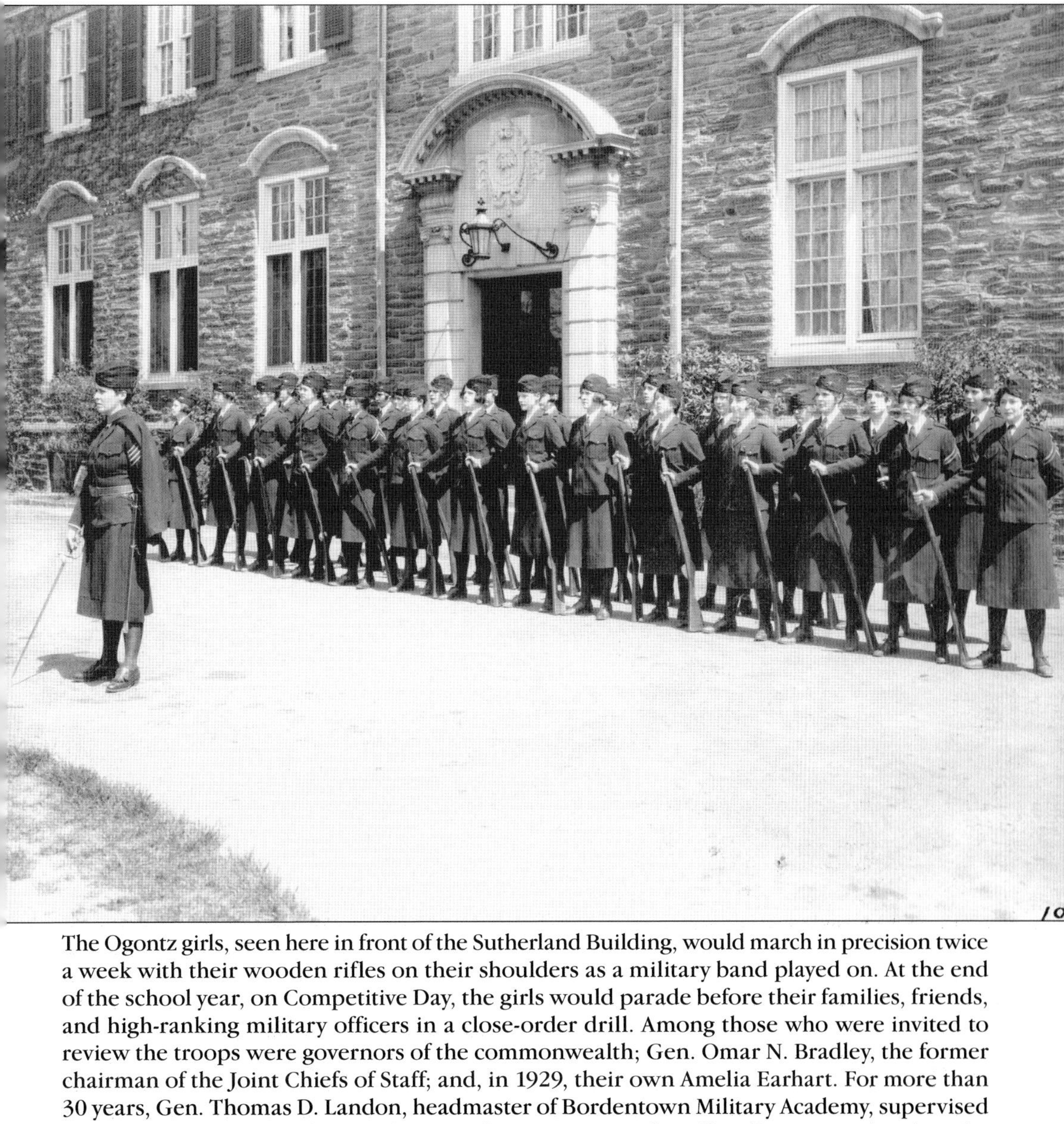

The Ogontz girls, seen here in front of the Sutherland Building, would march in precision twice a week with their wooden rifles on their shoulders as a military band played on. At the end of the school year, on Competitive Day, the girls would parade before their families, friends, and high-ranking military officers in a close-order drill. Among those who were invited to review the troops were governors of the commonwealth; Gen. Omar N. Bradley, the former chairman of the Joint Chiefs of Staff; and, in 1929, their own Amelia Earhart. For more than 30 years, Gen. Thomas D. Landon, headmaster of Bordentown Military Academy, supervised the drilling. The title of general was an honorary one—he officially was a colonel in the National Guard. The girls wore navy-blue uniforms with stripes on their sleeves signifying rank. They wore uniforms before women in the Armed Forces Auxiliary did. (The Ogontz School Archives, 1926, Penn State University, Abington College Library.)

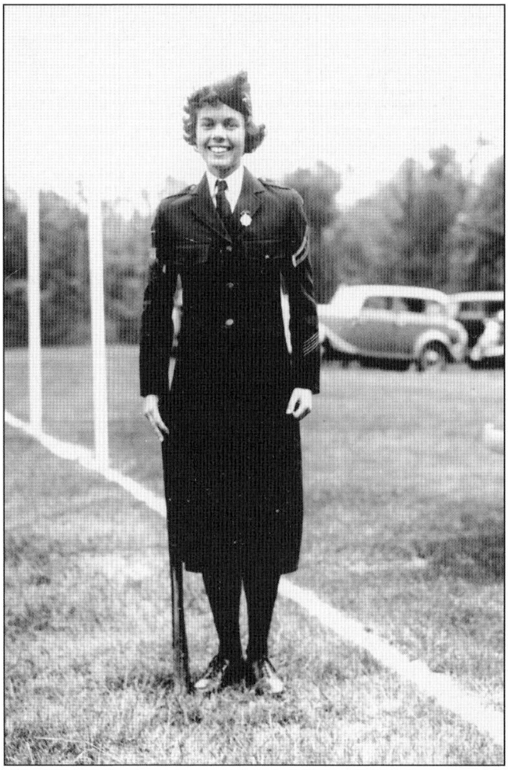

Near the end of each school year, the "old girls" and the "new girls" would gather on the drill field for the Battalion Day competitions. By a process of elimination, the girls would engage in a series of marching, rifle, and other drills to see who had earned the title of best in her class. At left, Katherine "Kitty" Cross, class of 1936, is seen in her full military regalia, wooden rifle at her side, proudly displaying her New Girl Drill Medal in 1935. In the 1944 photograph below, Pennsylvania governor Edward Martin, who, before entering public office, had served as a general in the US National Guard, presents the Old Girl Drill Medal to that year's winner, Shirley Flavelle McKee. The July 1935 issue of *Ogontz Mosaic* explained that preparing for such drills helped improve the girls' posture and taught them to act as a unit and think quickly. (Left, the Ogontz School Archives, 1935, Penn State University, Abington College Library; below, the Ogontz School Archives, 1944, Penn State University, Abington College Library.)

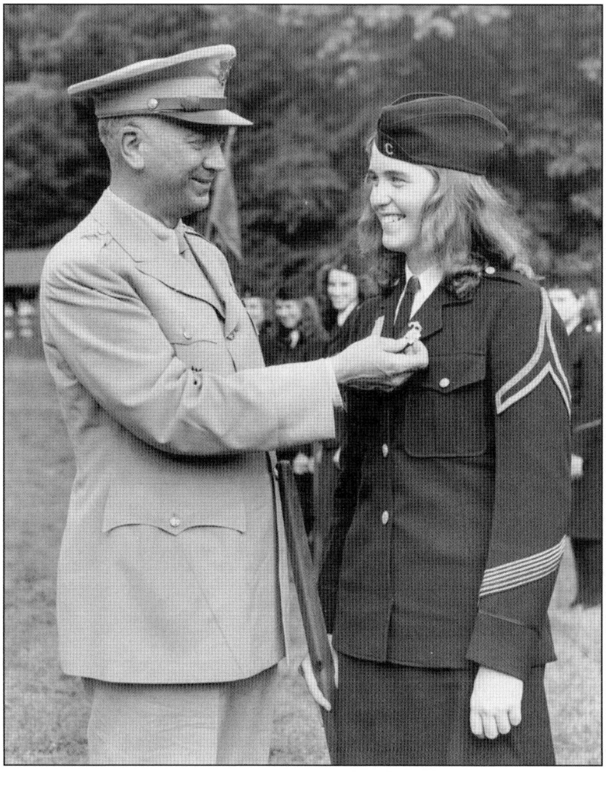

At right, change of command is conducted for the Pershing Rifles Platoon of the 5th Regiment Pershing Rifles during the 1966 Award Day ceremonies at Penn State Ogontz. Lt. Raymond H. Hanson (left), of Morrisville, Pennsylvania, presents the commander's rank shield to the 1967 commander, Glenn E. Sietken, of Willow Grove. The Pershing Rifles Platoon was the only campus military unit organized on a national level. The Reserve Officers Training Corps (ROTC) arrived on campus in 1951, bringing with it a poised and positive presence as well as an "arms room" and a very popular annual military ball. Below, the ROTC Corps of Cadets is shown passing in review at the conclusion of the 1966 Award Day ceremony on campus. (Both photographs by Sp4 Stephen E. Cohen, the Ogontz School Archives, 1966, Penn State University, Abington College Library.)

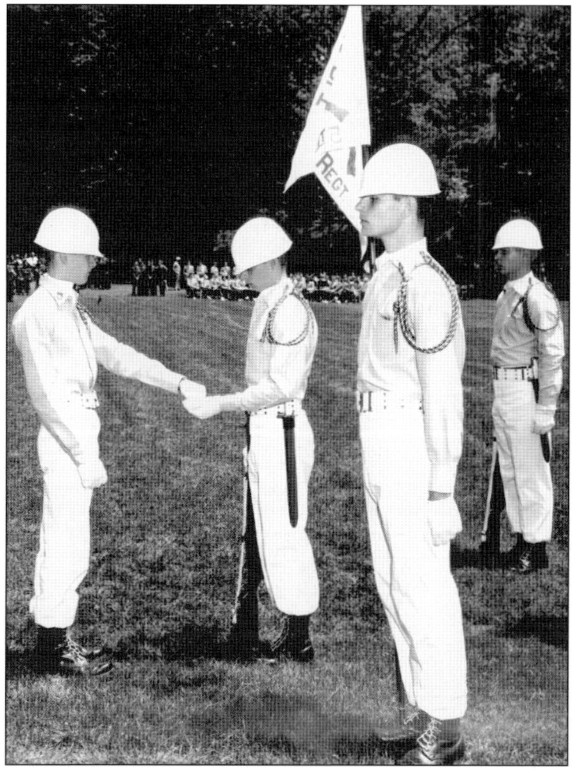

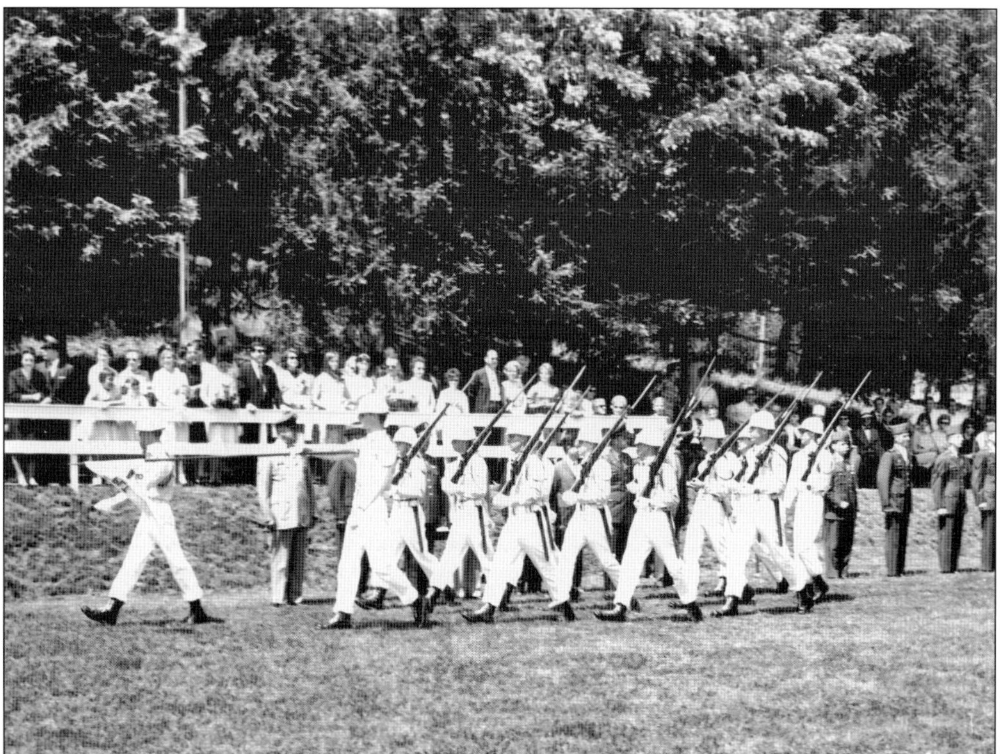

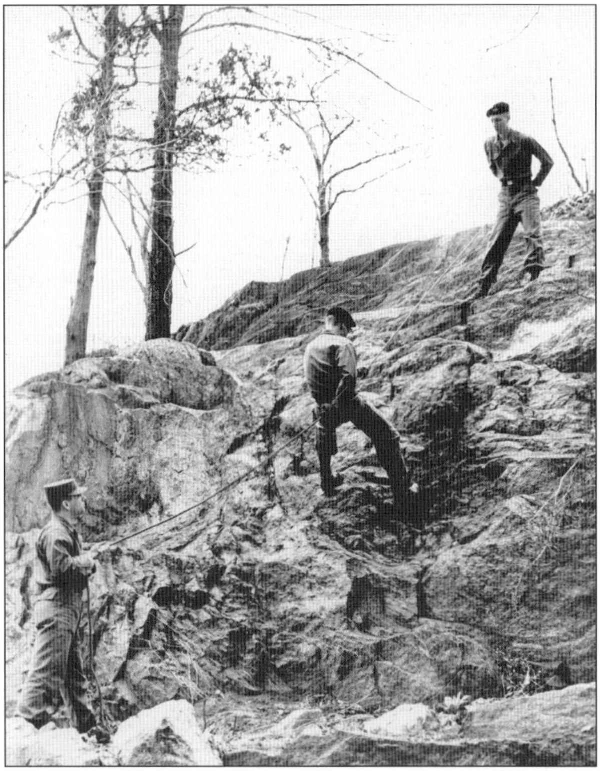

These rugged young men are members of an extracurricular club on campus called the Rangers. Formed in the mid-1960s and sponsored by the US Army, the Rangers were trained to become small military unit commanders. Their training included facets of mountain and jungle fighting as well as shock tactics employed by commando forces. (The Ogontz School Archives, 1964, Penn State University, Abington College Library.)

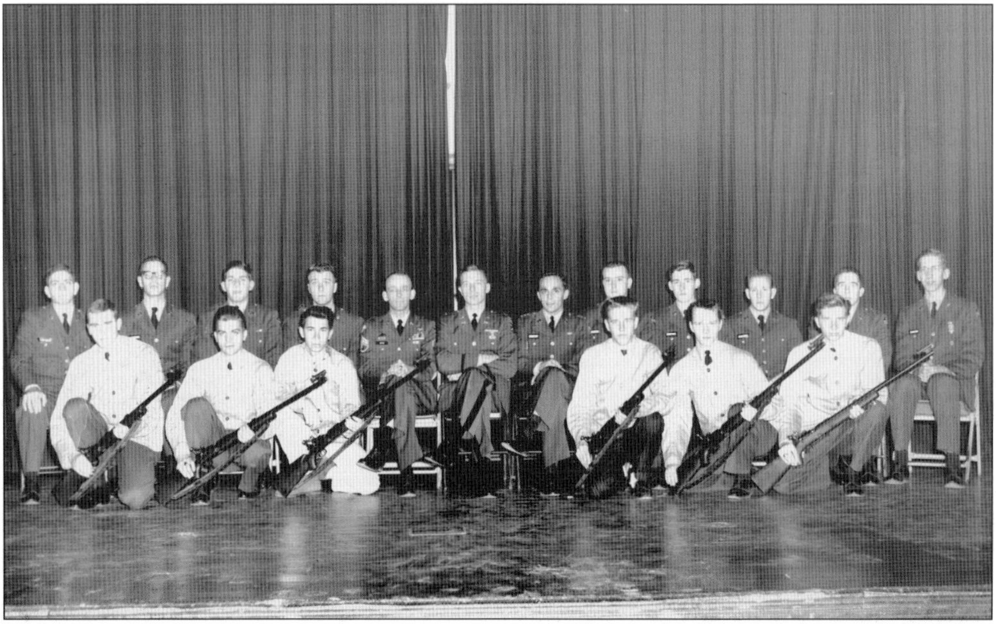

These serious-looking young men are members of the ROTC Rifle Team, a service club on campus whose purpose was to teach marksmanship. Like the Rangers, they espoused brotherly camaraderie and later served as a counterpoint to the rising tide of antiwar protest on campus. In the mid-1960s, the members would meet at the Conestoga Rod and Gun Club. (The Ogontz School Archives, 1962, Penn State University, Abington College Library.)

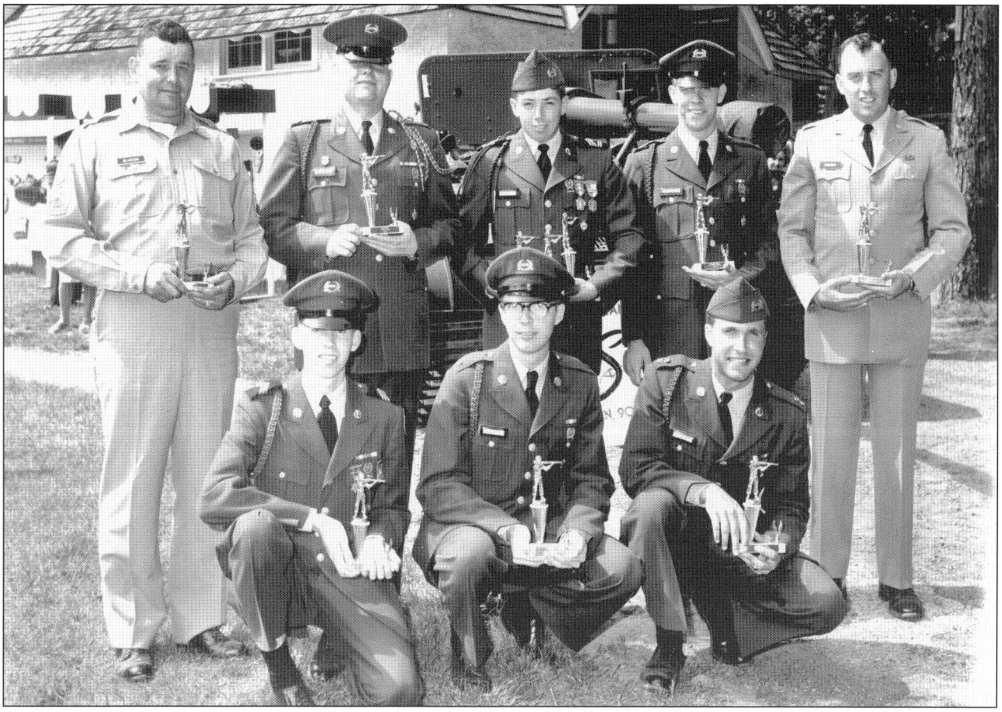

For many years, the ROTC program operated in the Springhouse, also known at the time as the Military Science Building. Pictured in front of the Military Science Building are several unidentified ROTC officers and cadets holding trophies from an unspecified competition held sometime in 1958 or 1959. (Alumni and Development Department, Penn State Abington.)

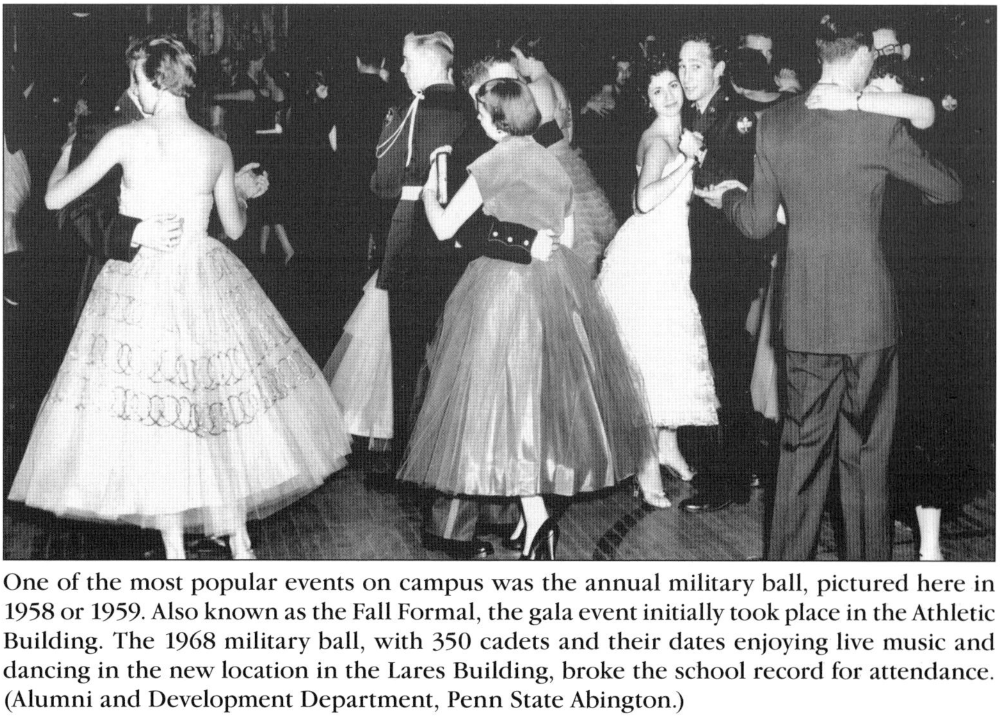

One of the most popular events on campus was the annual military ball, pictured here in 1958 or 1959. Also known as the Fall Formal, the gala event initially took place in the Athletic Building. The 1968 military ball, with 350 cadets and their dates enjoying live music and dancing in the new location in the Lares Building, broke the school record for attendance. (Alumni and Development Department, Penn State Abington.)

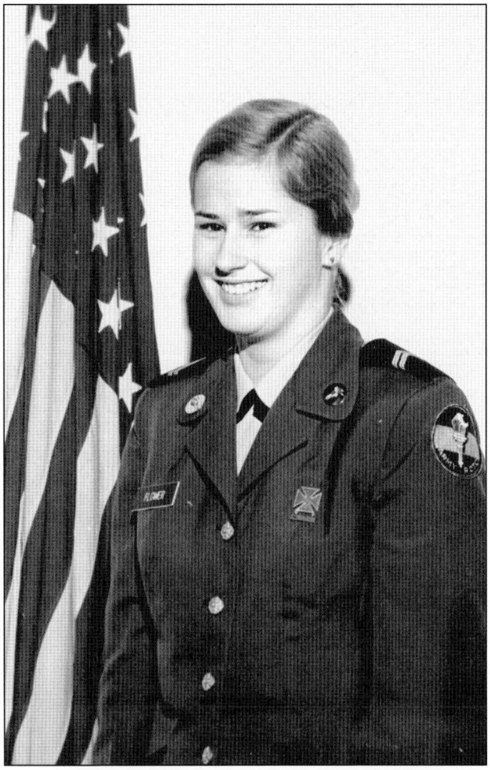

In the spring of 1973, Penn State Ogontz sophomore Elizabeth Flowers made history when she became the nation's first female Army ROTC company commander. (Both, the Ogontz School Archives, 1973, Penn State University, Abington College Library.)

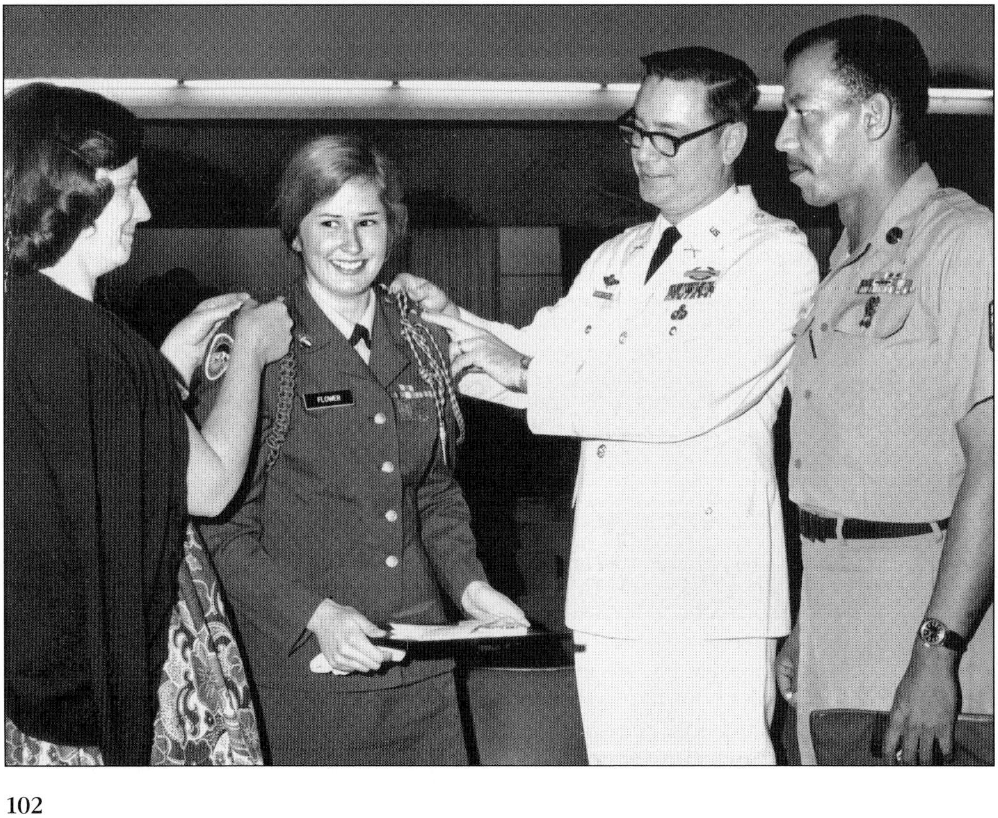

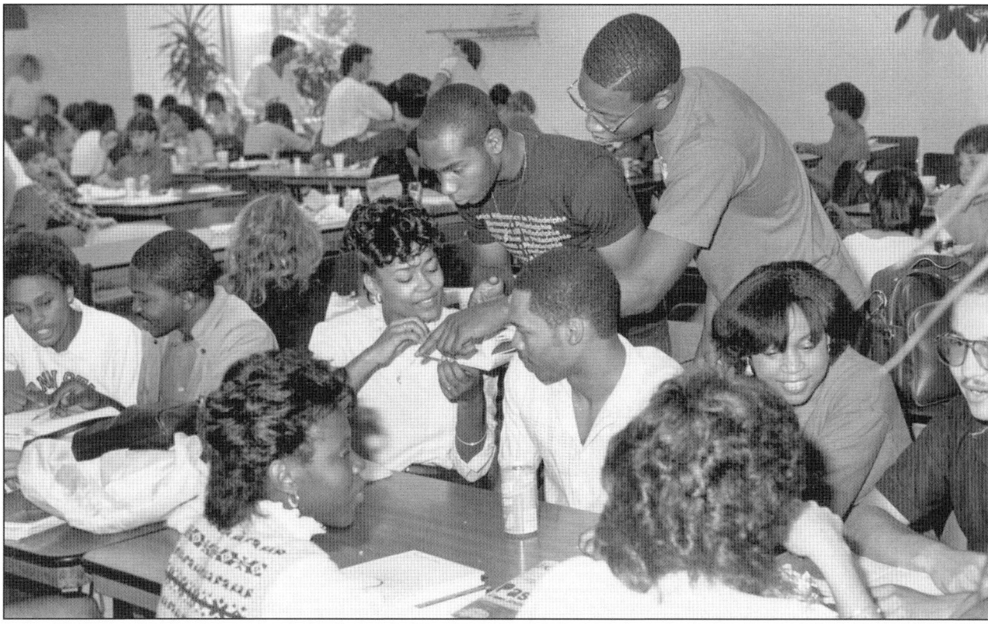

African American students contributed mightily to the social and political climate on campus in the 1960s. In 1965, CORE (Congress for Racial Equality), a new student club, sponsored a trip to join Vietnam War protests in Washington, DC. In 1968, the Afro-American Awareness Organization was founded. Students are seen here in 1968 chatting in the cafeteria. (University Relations Department, Penn State Abington.)

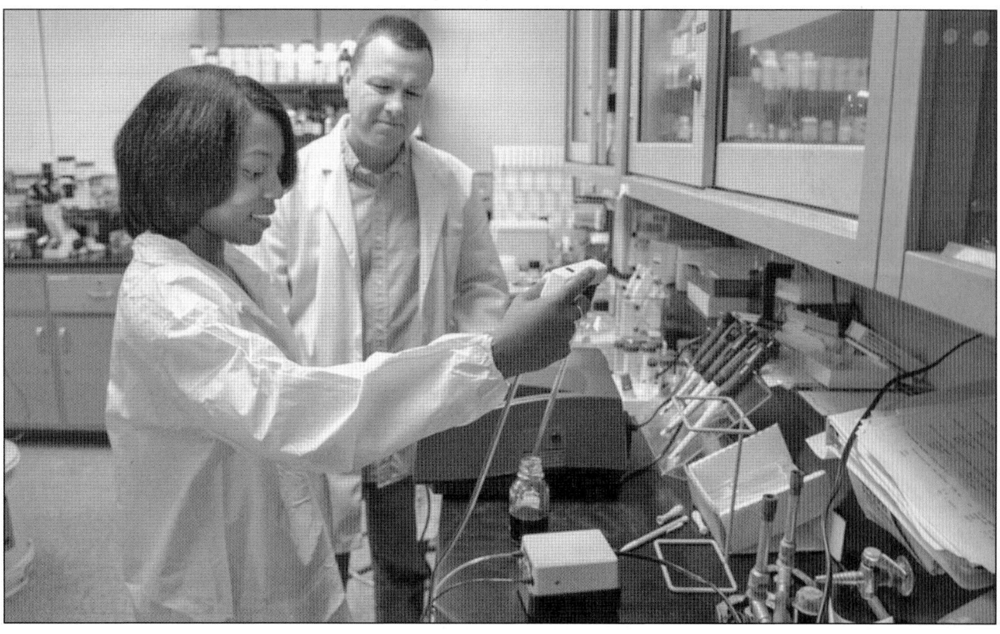

Senior lecturer in biology Dr. Thomas McGuire, working with student Ah-Lisa Hull, oversees a project in the biology lab in the Woodland Building in 2015. Dr. McGuire's current research involves the effects of the hormone human chorionic gonadotropin on breast cancer cells. He is investigating the changes in gene expression and protein production in these cells after exposure to the hormone. (University Relations Department, Penn State Abington.)

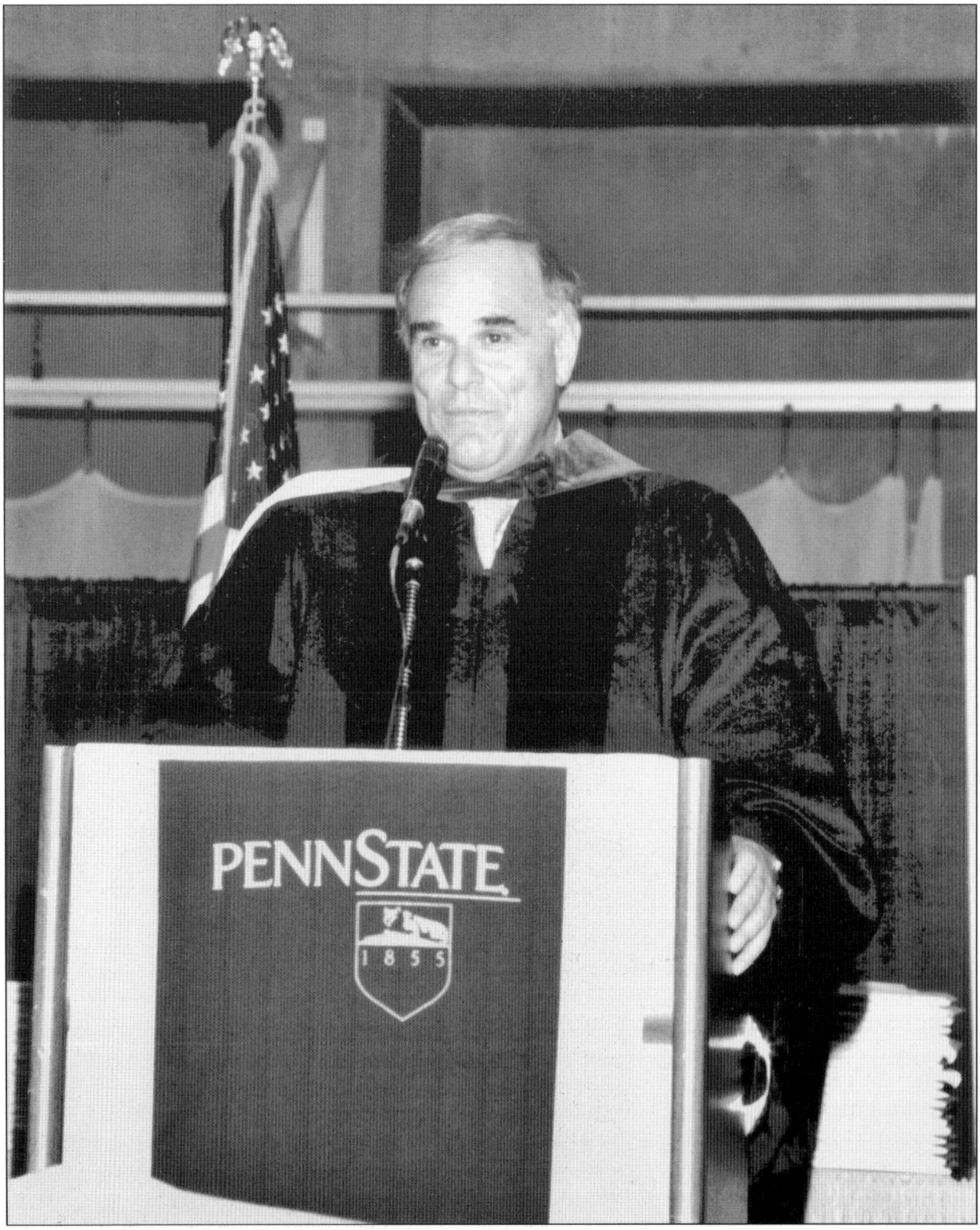

Penn State Abington was proud to welcome Ed Rendell to its 1998 commencement ceremony. The popular sitting mayor of Philadelphia (1992–2000) and former district attorney (1978–1986) was the keynote speaker. Rendell was elected to two terms as governor of Pennsylvania (2003–2011). The *New York Times* called Rendell's job as mayor "the most stunning turnaround in recent urban history." Under his leadership, Philadelphia won the bid to host the 2000 Republican National Convention. Vice Pres. Al Gore named Rendell "America's mayor" in 2000. Rendell was asked to serve as the general chair of the Democratic National Committee during the 2000 presidential election. An avid Philadelphia sports fan, Rendell often writes columns about his favorite teams and has served as a Comcast panelist after Philadelphia Eagles games. (University Relations Department, Penn State Abington.)

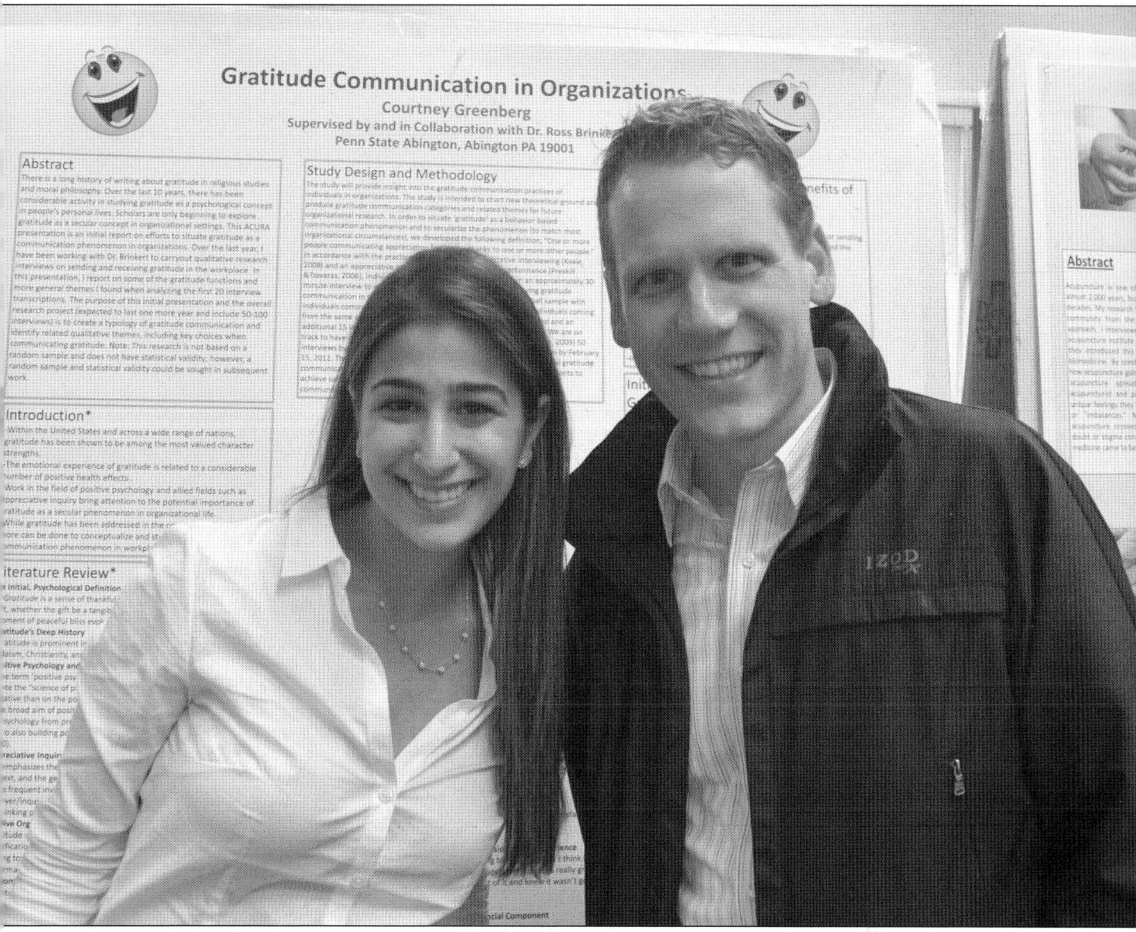

Penn State Abington student Courtney Greenberg is seen here on ACURA Poster Fair Day, April 12, 2011, with her corporate communications professor, Dr. Ross Brinkert. Greenberg collaborated with Dr. Brinkert on a special project called "Gratitude Communication in Organizations." The mission of ACURA (Abington College Undergraduate Research Activities), for which students receive academic credit, is to develop critical thinkers and creative scholars by engaging in scientific experimentation, inquiry-based research, and exploration of the arts through a yearlong research experience with a member of Penn State Abington's community of teacher-scholars. The projects for 2016 included mobile robot navigation, the implications of underemployment in the US labor market, and predicting a future security threat. ACURA is under the direction of sociology professor Dr. Beth Montemurro, who has written the book *Deserving Desire: Women's Stories of Sexual Evolution* (2014). (University Relations Department, Penn State Abington.)

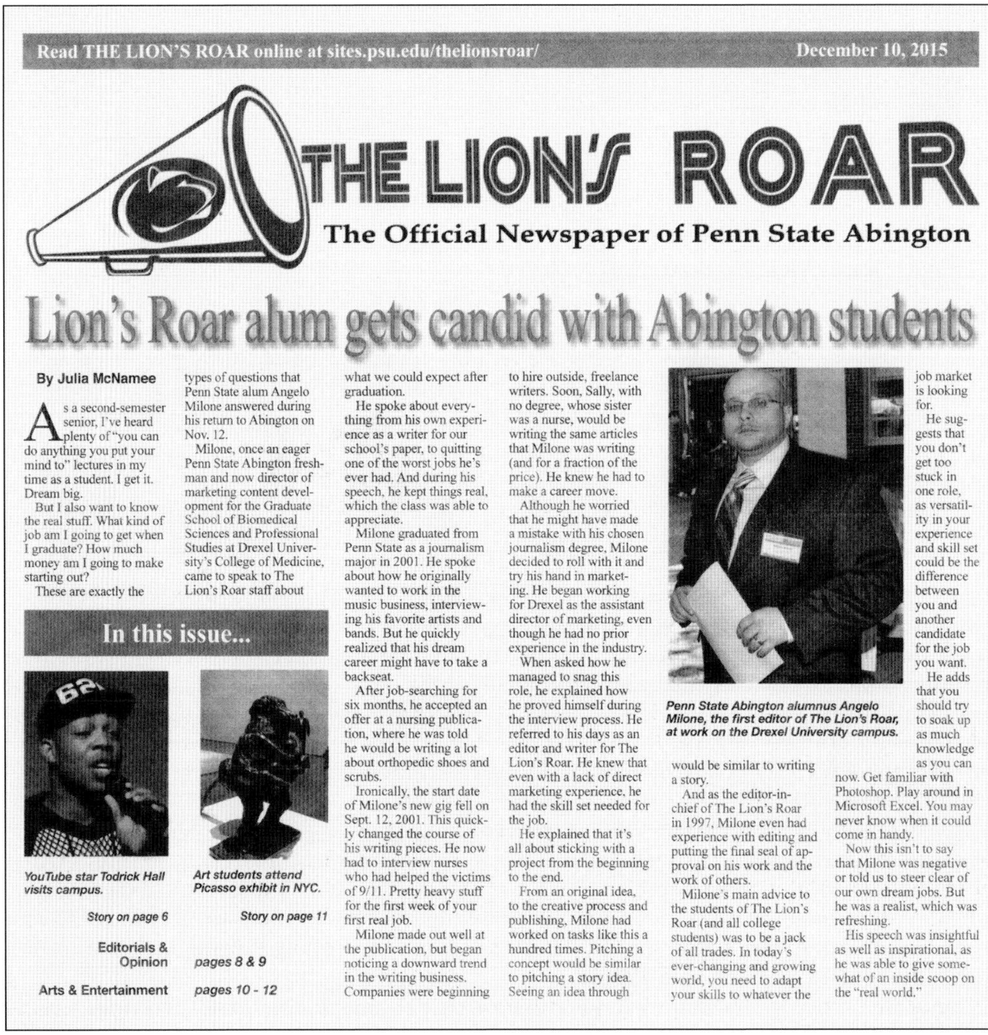

Read THE LION'S ROAR online at sites.psu.edu/thelionsroar/ December 10, 2015

THE LION'S ROAR

The Official Newspaper of Penn State Abington

Lion's Roar alum gets candid with Abington students

By Julia McNamee

As a second-semester senior, I've heard plenty of "you can do anything you put your mind to" lectures in my time as a student. I get it. Dream big.

But I also want to know the real stuff. What kind of job am I going to get when I graduate? How much money am I going to make starting out?

These are exactly the types of questions that Penn State alum Angelo Milone answered during his return to Abington on Nov. 12.

Milone, once an eager Penn State Abington freshman and now director of marketing content development for the Graduate School of Biomedical Sciences and Professional Studies at Drexel University's College of Medicine, came to speak to The Lion's Roar staff about what we could expect after graduation.

He spoke about everything from his own experience as a writer for our school's paper, to quitting one of the worst jobs he's ever had. And during his speech, he kept things real, which the class was able to appreciate.

Milone graduated from Penn State as a journalism major in 2001. He spoke about how he originally wanted to work in the music business, interviewing his favorite artists and bands. But he quickly realized that his dream career might have to take a backseat.

After job-searching for six months, he accepted an offer at a nursing publication, where he was told he would be writing a lot about orthopedic shoes and scrubs.

Ironically, the start date of Milone's new gig fell on Sept. 12, 2001. This quickly changed the course of his writing pieces. He now had to interview nurses who had helped the victims of 9/11. Pretty heavy stuff for the first week of your first real job.

Milone made out well at the publication, but began noticing a downward trend in the writing business. Companies were beginning to hire outside, freelance writers. Soon, Sally, with no degree, whose sister was a nurse, would be writing the same articles that Milone was writing (and for a fraction of the price). He knew he had to make a career move.

Although he worried that he might have made a mistake with his chosen journalism degree, Milone decided to roll with it and try his hand in marketing. He began working for Drexel as the assistant director of marketing, even though he had no prior experience in the industry.

When asked how he managed to snag this role, he explained how he proved himself during the interview process. He referred to his days as an editor and writer for The Lion's Roar. He knew that even with a lack of direct marketing experience, he had the skill set needed for the job.

He explained that it's all about sticking with a project from the beginning to the end.

From an original idea, to the creative process and publishing, Milone had worked on tasks like this a hundred times. Pitching a concept would be similar to pitching a story idea. Seeing an idea through would be similar to writing a story.

And as the editor-in-chief of The Lion's Roar in 1997, Milone even had experience with editing and putting the final seal of approval on his work and the work of others.

Milone's main advice to the students of The Lion's Roar (and all college students) was to be a jack of all trades. In today's ever-changing and growing world, you need to adapt your skills to whatever the job market is looking for.

He suggests that you don't get too stuck in one role, as versatility in your experience and skill set could be the difference between you and another candidate for the job you want.

He adds that you should try to soak up as much knowledge as you can now. Get familiar with Photoshop. Play around in Microsoft Excel. You may never know when it could come in handy.

Now this isn't to say that Milone was negative or told us to steer clear of our own dream jobs. But he was a realist, which was refreshing.

His speech was insightful as well as inspirational, as he was able to give somewhat of an inside scoop on the "real world."

Penn State Abington alumnus Angelo Milone, the first editor of The Lion's Roar, at work on the Drexel University campus.

In this issue...

YouTube star Todrick Hall visits campus.

Story on page 6

Art students attend Picasso exhibit in NYC.

Story on page 11

Editorials & Opinion — *pages 8 & 9*

Arts & Entertainment — *pages 10 - 12*

As technology advances, so has the *Lion's Roar*, the official student newspaper of Penn State Abington, which is now available online. On the *Lion's Roar*'s website and in the issue of December 10, 2015, the lead story features Penn State Abington alumnus Angelo Milone (class of 2001), the first editor of the *Lion's Roar*, who visited the members of the fall 2015 class to explain how he made his way in the professional world and how they could do the same with skills learned at the college and applied after graduation. With no prior experience in marketing, Milone became the editor of various nursing publications before becoming a director of marketing content development for Drexel University's College of Medicine. (The *Lion's Roar*.)

Six

STUDENT LIFE AND SPECIAL EVENTS

This chapter explores student life on campus outside the classroom. It provides glimpses into the living conditions of the girls at the Ogontz School—their dormitories, their physical and athletic endeavors, their preoccupation with minstrel shows and theatrical productions, and their annual May Day celebration.

It also shows changes in style as the decades unfolded at both the Ogontz School and Penn State Ogontz/Abington, both in the students' manner of dress and in the activities on campus that coincided with or reflected issues happening in their neighborhoods and around the world.

The two schools have also had their fair share of celebrated people entertaining students or speaking on campus at special events or at commencement exercises, like renowned poets William Butler Yeats and Carl Sandburg during the Abby Sutherland years; Timothy Leary, Arthur Ashe, and America's first black astronaut, Guy Bluford (an alumnus of Penn State University) in the 1980s; and *Stand and Deliver* actor Edward James Olmos and first lady Hillary Clinton in the mid-1990s.

Chancellor emerita Dr. Karen Wiley Sandler offers her perspective on the evolving changes in education and student life on campus. Penn State Ogontz, later Abington, Dr. Sandler said, has extended its welcome to students who prefer an intimate college environment and an urban lifestyle and who perhaps may not be willing or able to live away from home. However, she finds commonality between the students of the past and those who attend the college today:

> Both these institutions produced graduates who exceeded the constraints of their times and their backgrounds. Amelia Earhart, whose adventurous nature developed at the Ogontz School, illustrated how the straight road can take surprising turns even before she embraced her aviation dreams. In her first year at the Ogontz School, the young Amelia took it upon herself to campaign vigorously, and successfully, against the idea of high school sororities, calling them 'undemocratic.'
>
> Today, the graduates of Penn State Abington illustrate those surprises in their volunteerism, their commitment to helping others even when they themselves may be in constrained circumstances. . . . Many first-generation and newly immigrated students join forces with students who have come from secure middle-class backgrounds to make sure that justice is available for all. Echoing Amelia Earhart's love of democracy, these students make their own commitments to justice and equity in our world.

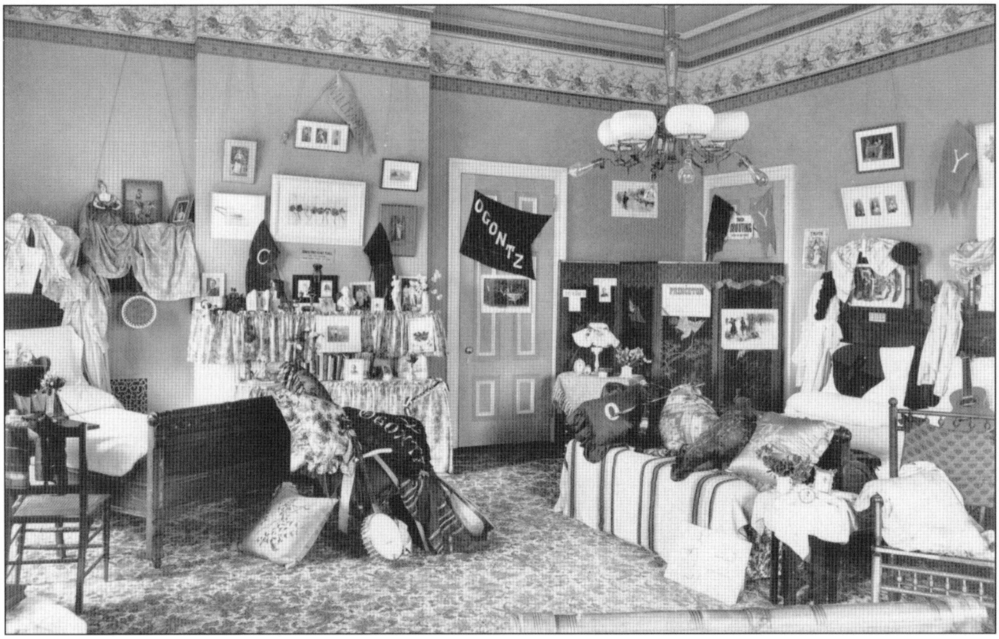

Upon close inspection, one can discern much about the fine young ladies sharing these rooms at the Ogontz School. They play several musical instruments. The banners and calendars adorning the walls of both the 1895 Acorn room above and the 1908 Apple Blossom room below—Princeton, Yale, Harvard, Andover, Cornell, Northwestern, and others—could indicate the schools and colleges attended by their family and friends. Many of the Ogontz girls' "callers" (they were not considered boyfriends or dates) took the train from Princeton once a week for their visits, on Mondays from 8:00 to 9:00 p.m. But the Ogontz banners in both photographs also reveal the school's elite standing among the top schools in the nation. The "Red Star Line Antwerpen America" poster in the photograph below shows the girls' penchant for travel, highly encouraged at the school. And teddy bears, a new craze sweeping the country, abound. (Above, the Ogontz School Archives, 1895, Penn State University, Abington College Library; below, the Ogontz School Archives, 1908, Penn State University, Abington College Library.)

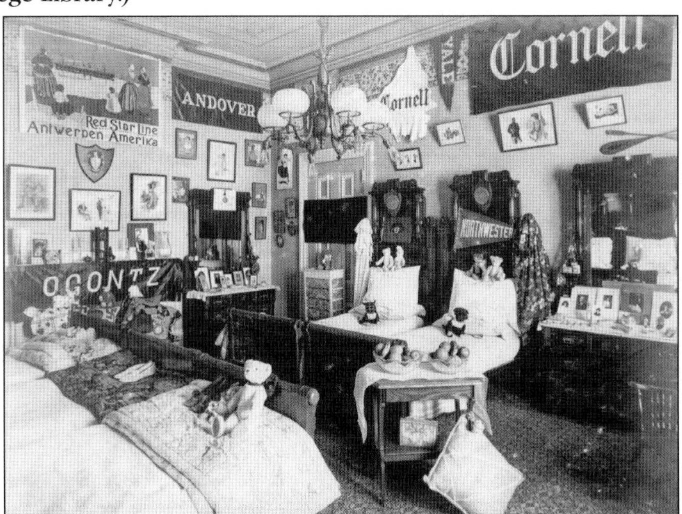

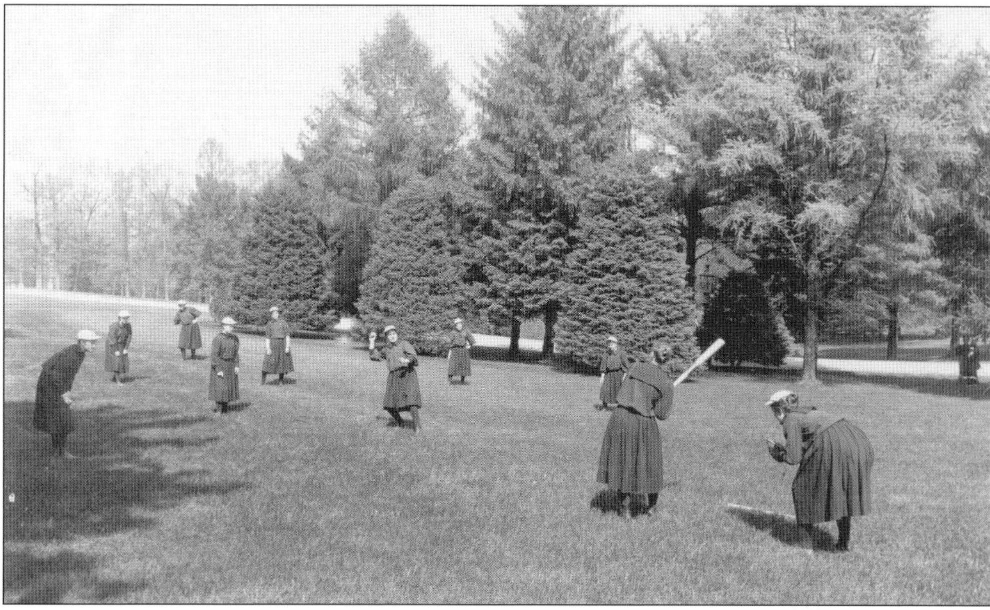

The Ogontz School's vaunted physical culture was a critical part of the girls' regimen. All the school's principals expected the girls to participate in a variety of gymnastics or other sports. Walking was the preferred exercise. Even dancing was considered exercise. The girls, as one can see here, would engage in baseball on the beautiful grounds of the Cooke mansion, but they also played basketball, hockey, golf, tennis, and more. Field Day at the end of each school year was an occasion the girls eagerly anticipated. At Field Day, prizes would be awarded to the winners of various competitions, including gymnastics, 50-yard dash, baseball throw, discus throw, archery, 100-yard dash, shot put, potato race, and others. The girls were highly competitive but valued good sportsmanship even more. (Both, the Ogontz School Archives, 1895, Penn State University, Abington College Library.)

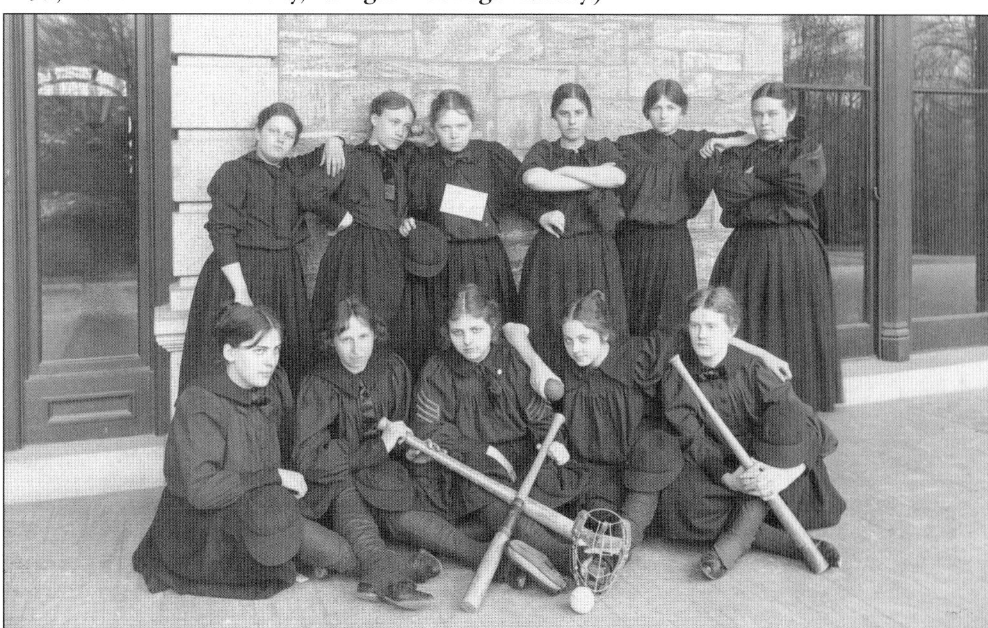

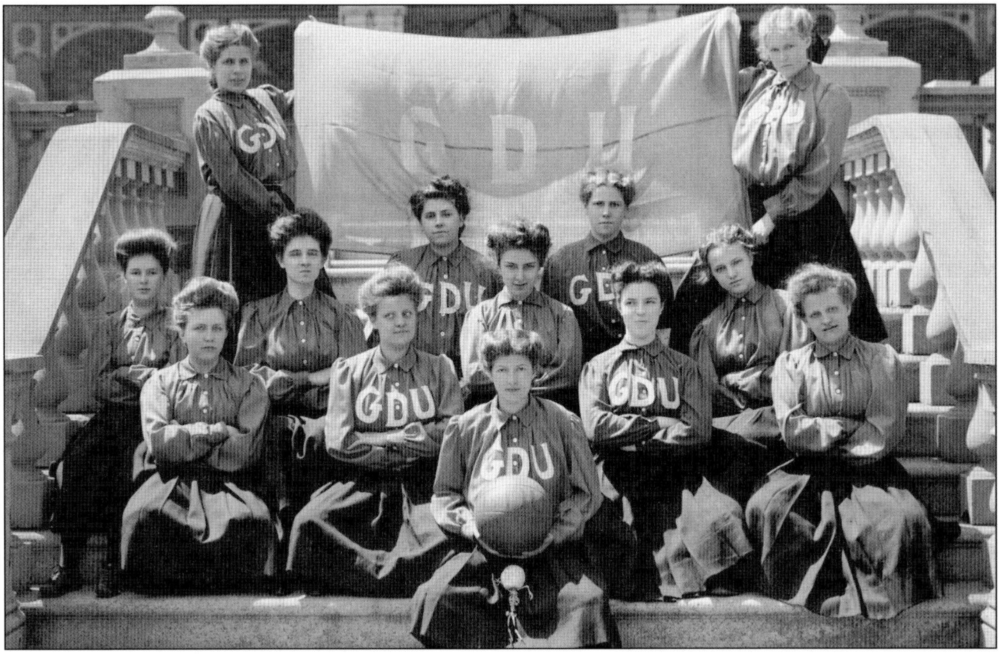

Posed on a set of steps leading into the mansion are two of the Ogontz School's 1905 athletic teams, basketball in the photograph above and field hockey below. If the letters on their blouses seem puzzling, Ogontz student Dorothy Wurts (class of 1938) tried to clarify it in the Athletics column in the December 1937 *Ogontz Mosaic*. She explained that every student was a member of the Athletic Association, divided into two teams, the Orange and the Green. The winning team at the end of the school year won the Color Cup. "These teams," she wrote, "are known as the 'GDU,' the 'TWT,' the 'CBB,' and the 'OBBN,' all of unknown significance." So the mystery remains, as does the specific relationship between the so-called "alphabet teams," as the Oranges and Greens. In effect, Wurts was describing intramurals. It appears that the varsity basketball and field hockey teams, who could compete against other schools, were chosen from various players on the Oranges and Greens. Other sports available at the time were baseball, track, golf, tennis, and swimming. (Both, the Ogontz School Archives, 1905, Penn State University, Abington College Library.)

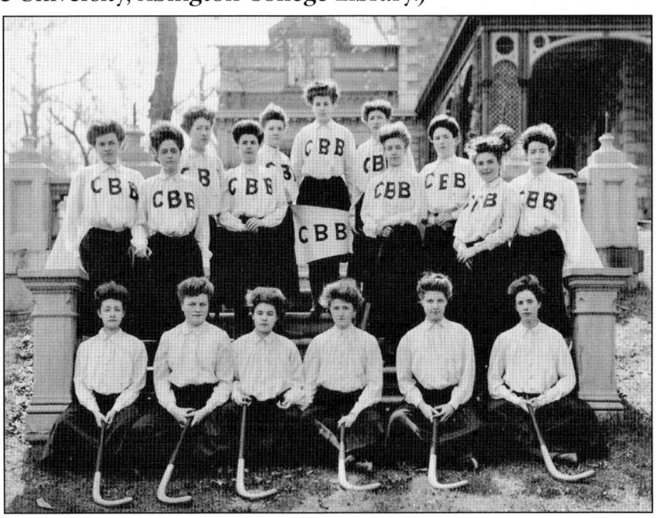

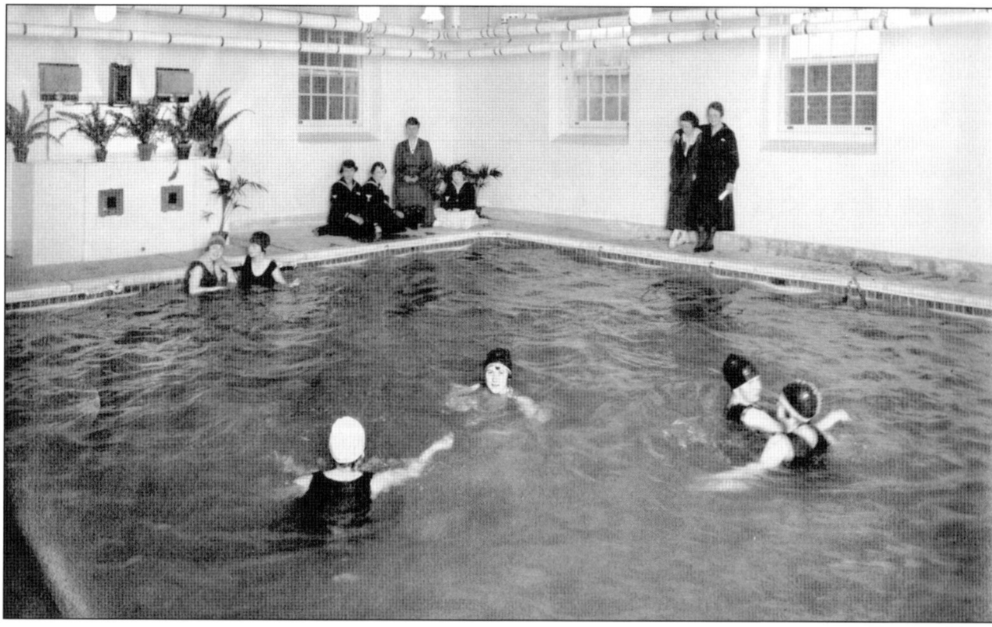

Abby Sutherland did not like the swimming pool at the old school. It was a 20-foot-by-20-foot pit resembling, she said, the ruins of an English castle. One of her requirements for the new school in Rydal was met when she had a modern swimming pool installed on the ground floor of the Sutherland Building. In the 1920s, it was reputed to be one of the finest in the Philadelphia area. (The Ogontz School Archives, date unknown, Penn State University, Abington College Library.)

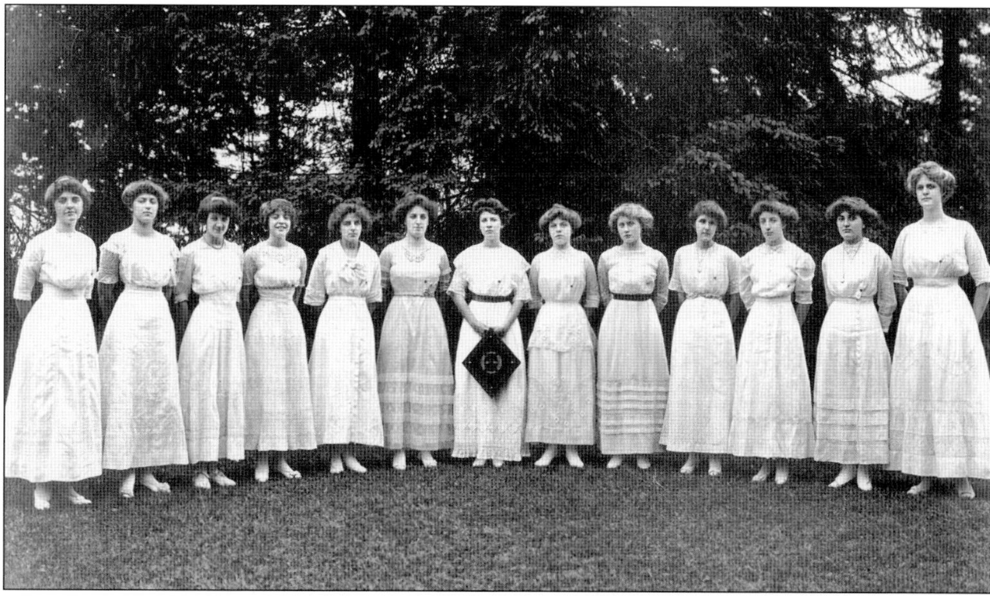

There were four sororities at the Ogontz School: Alpha Phi, Omega Delta, Sigma Theta, and Theta Chi. Posed here on the school grounds are the sisters of Theta Chi. Amelia Earhart's campaign to make the sororities more inclusive, and their failure to do so, led Abby Sutherland to disband them in 1917. (The Ogontz School Archives, c. early 1900s, Penn State University, Abington College Library.)

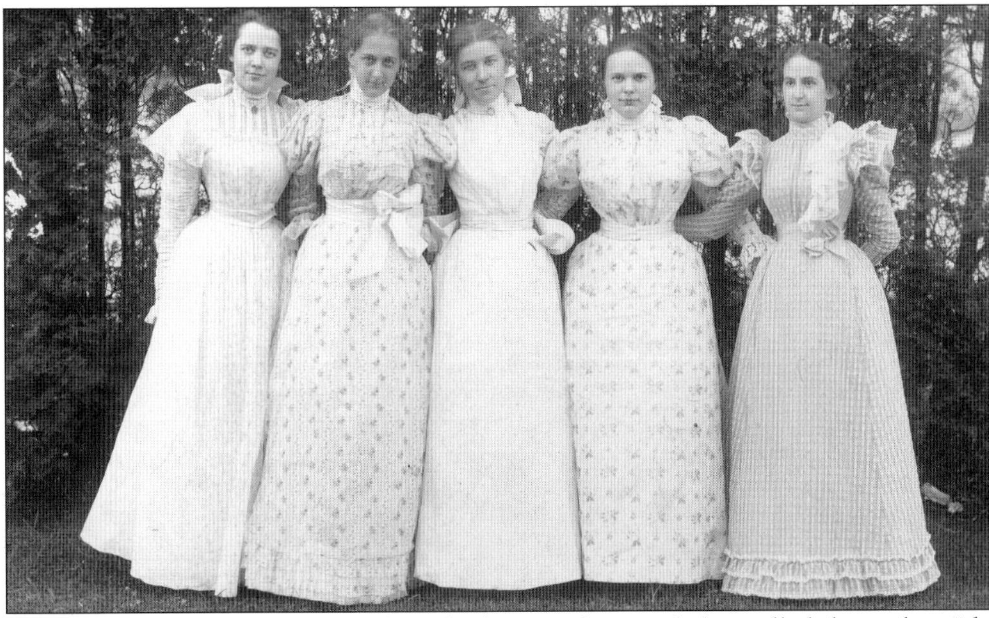

Roommates in the Thistle room, these high-spirited young ladies called themselves "the Thistles." The top floor of the Jay Cooke mansion contained a spacious amusement room, outfitted with a stage and plenty of space for bunting, posters, and other decorations for the endless stream of shows the girls mounted, including the popular annual minstrel show. Other theatrical presentations took place in the conservatory, like the one pictured below in the early 1900s. Wearing costumes with heart designs are (in no order) Bertha Dobbins, Charlotte Herbert, Marie Wright, Margaret Kendrick Reid, Carrie Cass, Harriet Balken, Lucille Dutton, Clara Harmer, Helen Pierce, Helen Ayres, Florence Cunningham, Eloise Holden, Louise Hamilton, Nancy Carey, Helen Harrison, Mable Talbott, Virginia Parks, Lillyan Cary, Anna Wright, and Bernice Jones. (Both, the Ogontz School Archives, early 1900s, Penn State University, Abington College Library.)

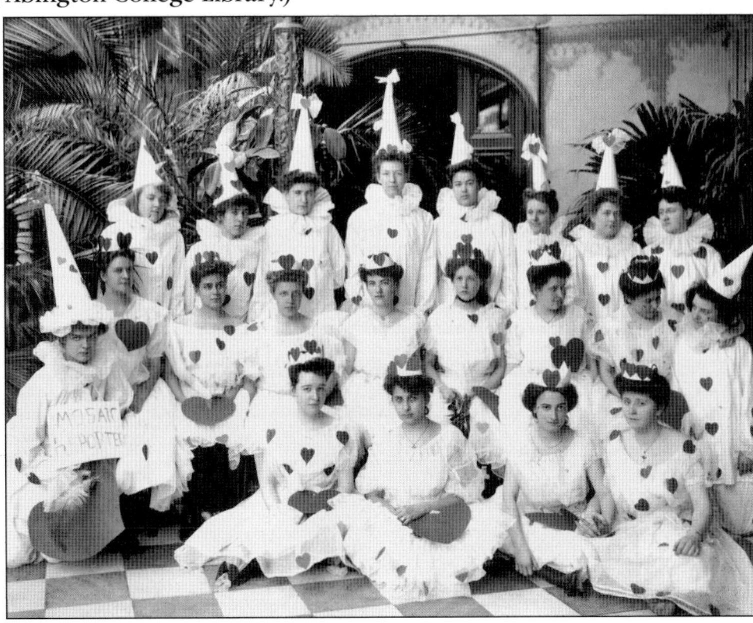

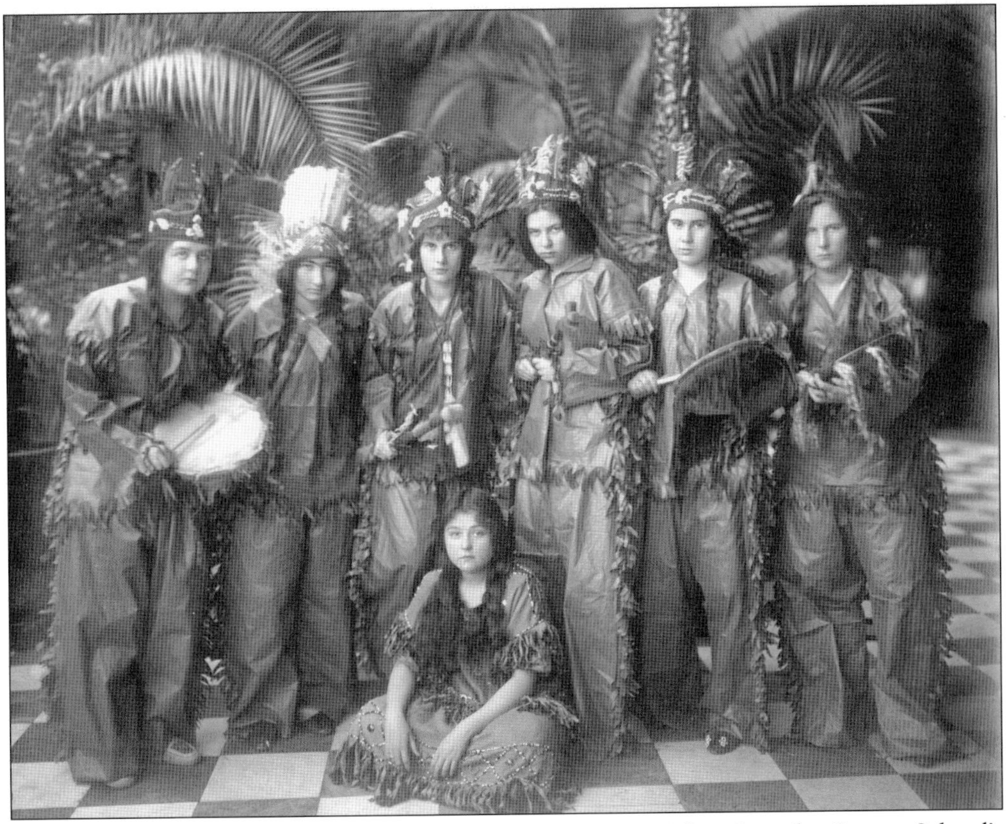

At a time when racial sensitivity was not yet a common consideration, the Ogontz School's annual minstrel show featured girls dressed as sheiks, cowboys, Indians (no doubt in homage to the school's namesake, Chief Ogontz), sad little women in bonnets and shawls, and fierce-looking men carrying pistols and sporting long black mustaches. (The Ogontz School Archives, early 1900s, Penn State University, Abington College Library.)

The Ogontz girls loved to dress up. If it were not elaborately staged tableaux of their favorite authors' works—William Shakespeare, Robert Burns, or Robert Browning—they might dress in togas to stage an ancient Greek festival or a Roman pageant such as this along the driveway of the old Ogontz School. (The Ogontz School Archives, 1911, Penn State University, Abington College Library.)

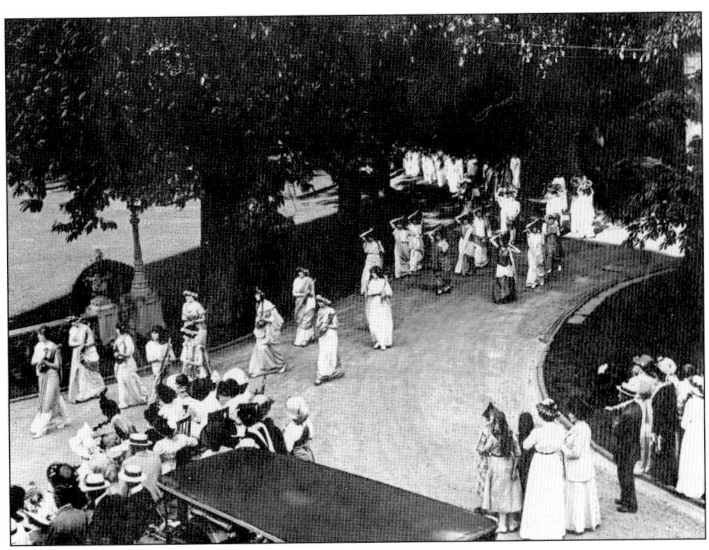

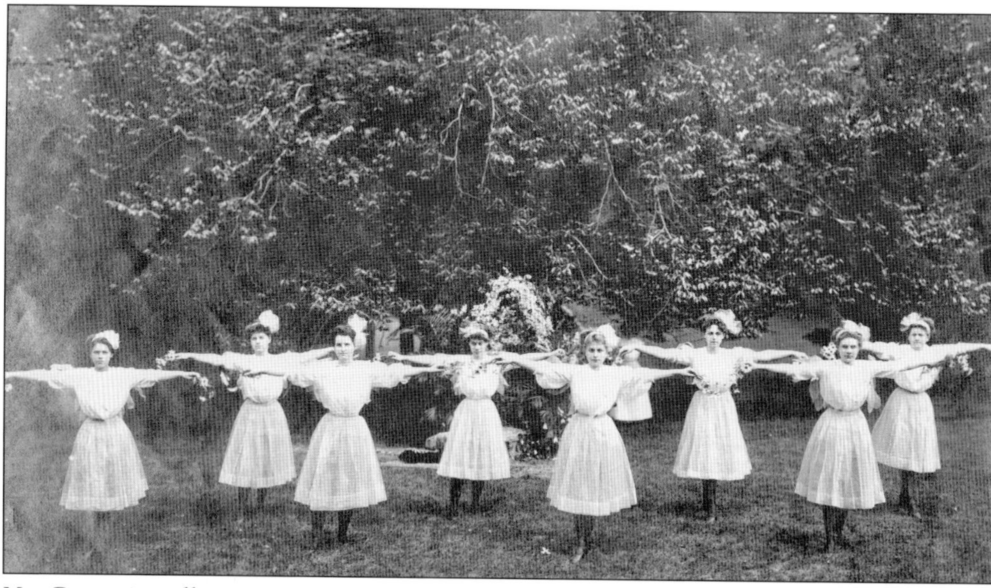

May Day, originally a pagan rite of spring that welcomed the blossoming of that season, was one of the most anticipated events of the year at the Ogontz School. The girls would spend weeks preparing the posters and decorations, rehearsing the dances, creating the costumes, and selecting the May Queen and her attendants. Pictured here is a beautifully synchronized dance of the fairies, performed at the first May Day celebration at the new school in 1917. (The Ogontz School Archives, 1917, Penn State University, Abington College Library.)

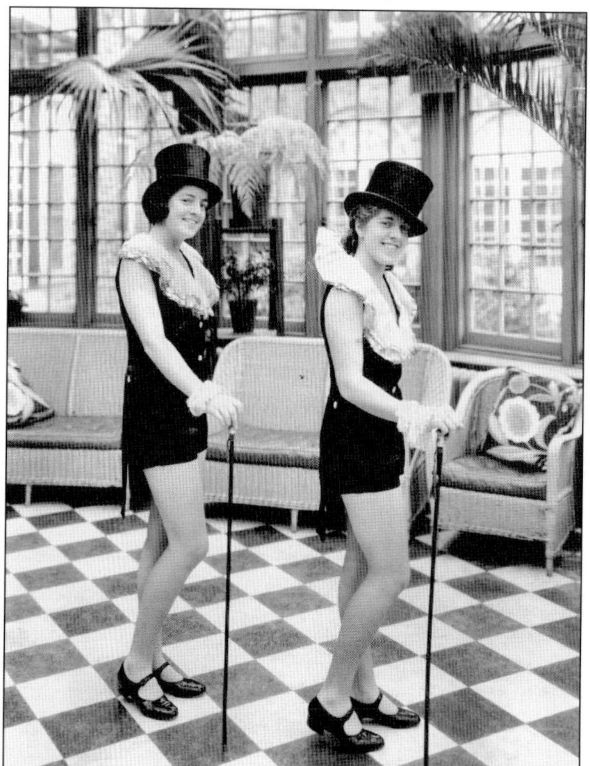

By the 1920s and 1930s, the girls had added tap dancing to their repertoire of entertainments. An article in the November 1931 issue of the *Ogontz Mosaic* reported on a series of so-called "stunts" (including tap dancing) performed by the undergraduates for the seniors, "who by their applause, proved themselves to be immensely gratified." (The Ogontz School Archives, 1931, Penn State University, Abington College Library.)

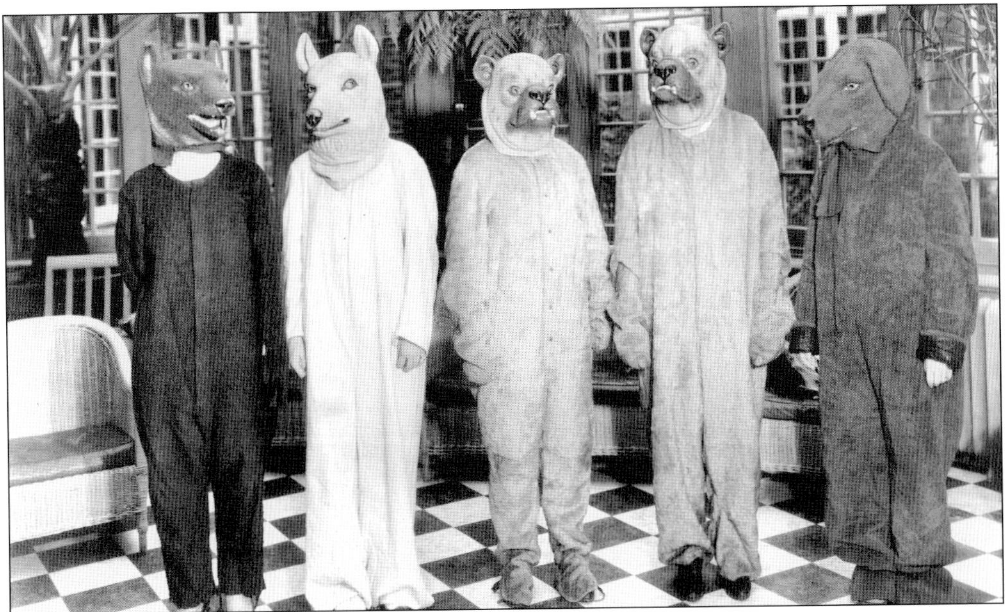

A quintet of students is dressed in animal costumes. Students' imaginations were boundless. In one of their variety shows, the floor of the solarium was overrun with Mickey Mouse clones. Another found them dressed as fruits and vegetables—carrots, asparagus, and tomatoes on the run—creating a smorgasbord of laughter for the Ogontz School community. (The Ogontz School Archives, 1931, Penn State University, Abington College Library.)

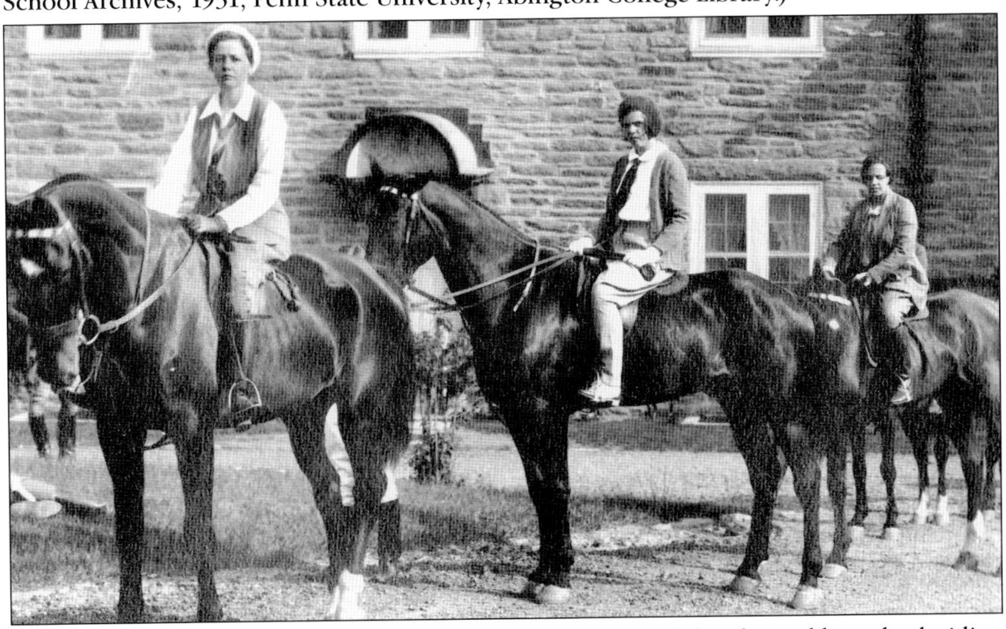

The girls at the Ogontz School in Elkins Park and later in Rydal embraced horseback riding wholeheartedly. Some owned their own horses, while others rented them from a neighboring hunt club. Some were skilled enough to ride after hounds with the best riders. A horse show was always a main feature at the closing activities in June. Pictured here are girls riding their horses in front of the Sutherland Building. (The Ogontz School Archives, c. 1930s, Penn State University, Abington College Library.)

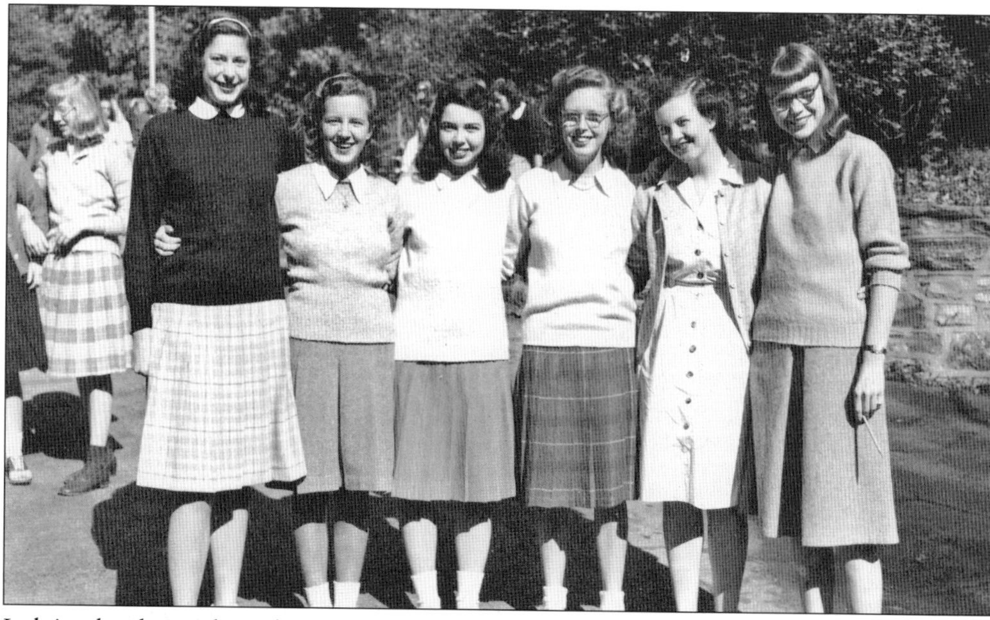

Judging by their A-line skirts, cardigan sweaters, penny loafers, white socks, and casual hairstyles, these Ogontz School girls have fully embraced the 1940s. From left to right are Joan Wilson, Pat Smith, Mary Dowell, Barb Weir, Kitty McConnell, and Madeleine Chew. (The Ogontz School Archives, c. 1940s, Penn State University, Abington College Library.)

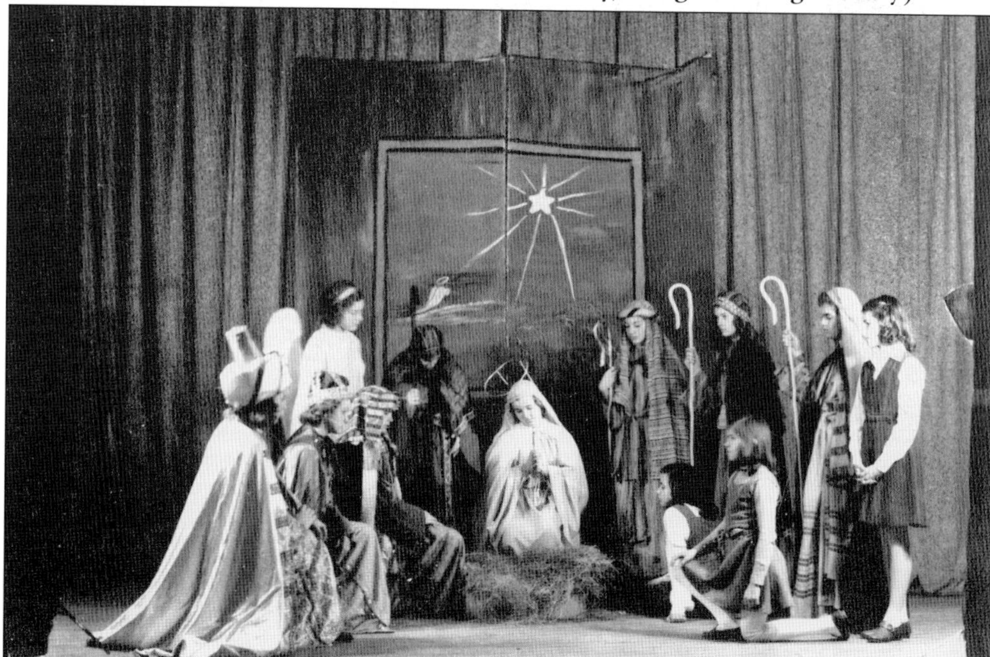

Students from the Rydal School are seen reenacting a Nativity scene. It is described in an article in the March 1944 *Ogontz Mosaic* as a traditional Junior Candlelight and Vesper Service based on a similar service in Bavaria. The pageant included Christmas carols, Bible readings, and a performance by the School Chorus and Glee Club. (The Ogontz School Archives, 1943, Penn State University, Abington College Library.)

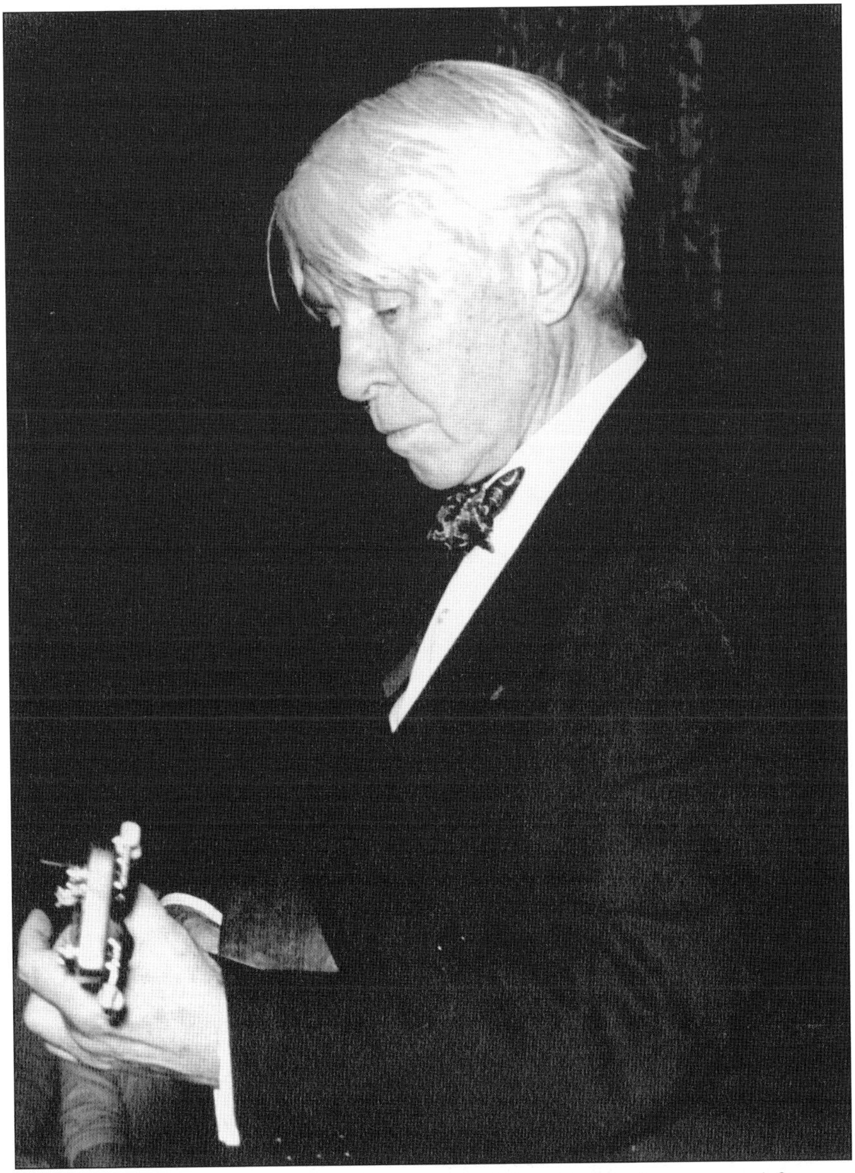

On alternating Wednesday evenings, the Ogontz School invited renowned figures on the cultural landscape to entertain the girls in the solarium. Among these guests were famed Indian poet Rabindranath Tagore, actor Maurice Evans, soprano Queena Mario (a former Ogontz student), Irish poet William Butler Yeats, and American poets Vachel Lindsay and Carl Sandburg, pictured here during his visit on May 2, 1941. A personal friend of Abby Sutherland, he visited the campus several times. On this occasion, accompanying himself on guitar, Sandburg performed three new original dramatic works, called "Mr. Lincoln and His Gloves," "Mr. Baudelaire and His Green Hair," "Mr. Longfellow and His Boy," and an allegorical anecdote called "Elephants Are Different to Different People," which he said "represented all the easy tolerance that once existed in the world and has gone." According to an article in the June 1941 *Ogontz Mosaic*, all but two of these works received their first public presentations before being reprised shortly thereafter at the Library of Congress. (The Ogontz School Archives, 1941, Penn State University, Abington College Library.)

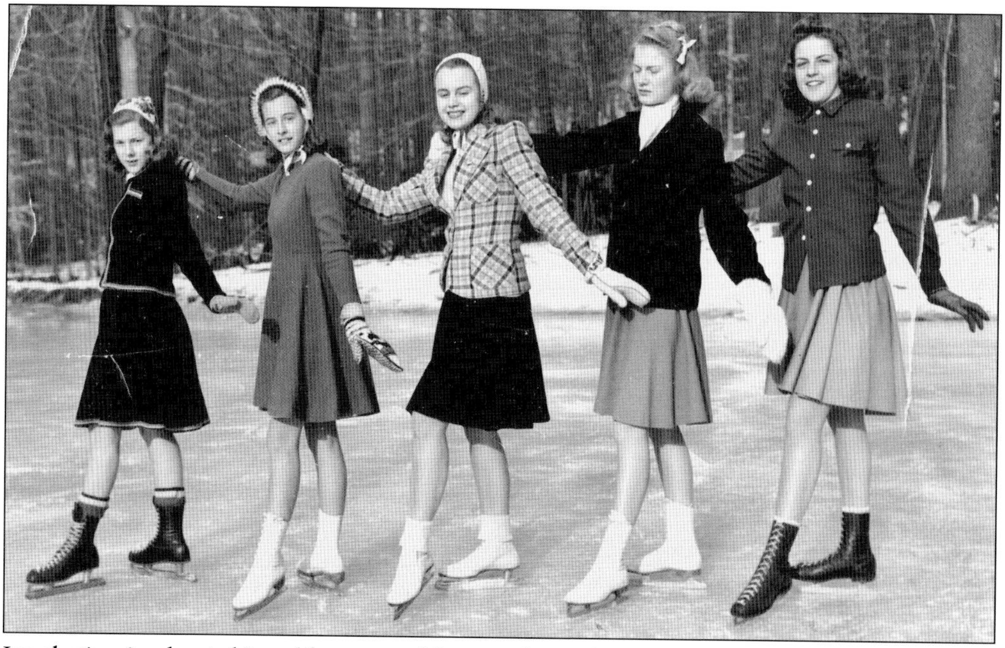

Ice-skating in short skirts, blazers, and long jackets, these girls from the Rydal School are enjoying a pastime that carried over from the old days at the Jay Cooke estate. The 1942 Ogontz School catalog specifies four hours a week of required exercise, including (each girl's choice of) field hockey, basketball, riding, tennis, archery, golf, badminton, and skating. (The Ogontz School Archives, mid-1940s, Penn State University, Abington College Library.)

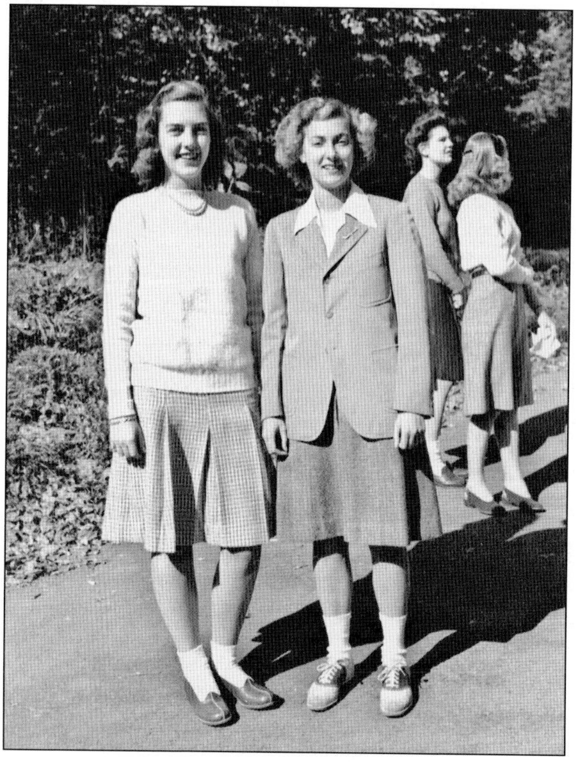

Mary Steele (left), class of 1947, and an unnamed friend walk the campus in blazer jackets, cardigans, knee-length skirts, saddle shoes, and bobby socks, the height of casual fashion in the late 1940s. Steele was a member of the varsity field hockey team. (The Ogontz School Archives, 1947, Penn State University, Abington College Library.)

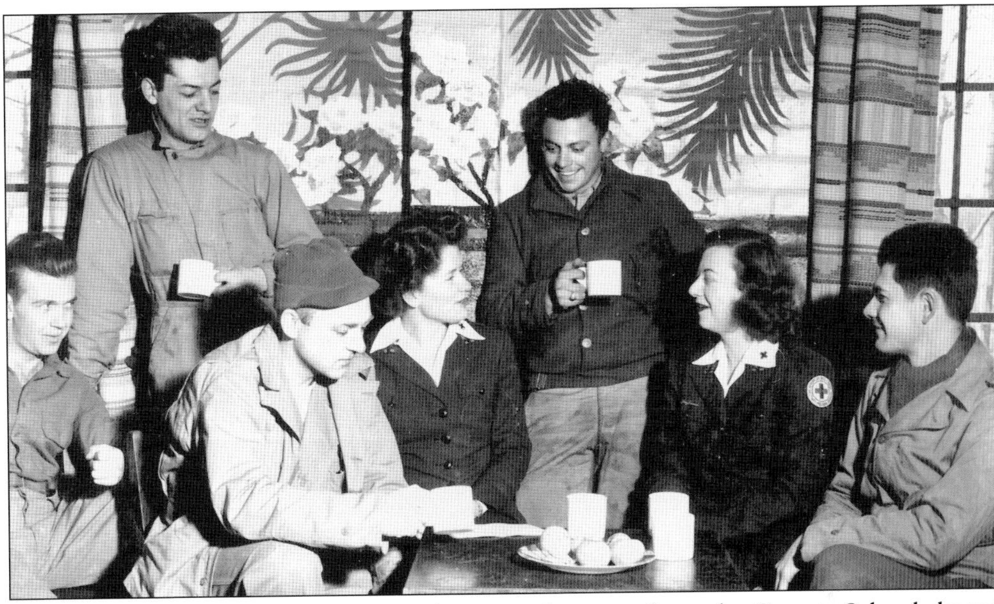

At the beginning of World War II, Red Cross volunteers from the Ogontz School shared pleasantries with GIs who were visiting the campus. It was the sight of wartime amputees at a hospital in Toronto in 1917 that induced Amelia Earhart to forego her final semester at the Ogontz School to serve wounded soldiers as a nurse's aide. (The Ogontz School Archives, early 1940s, Penn State University, Abington College Library.)

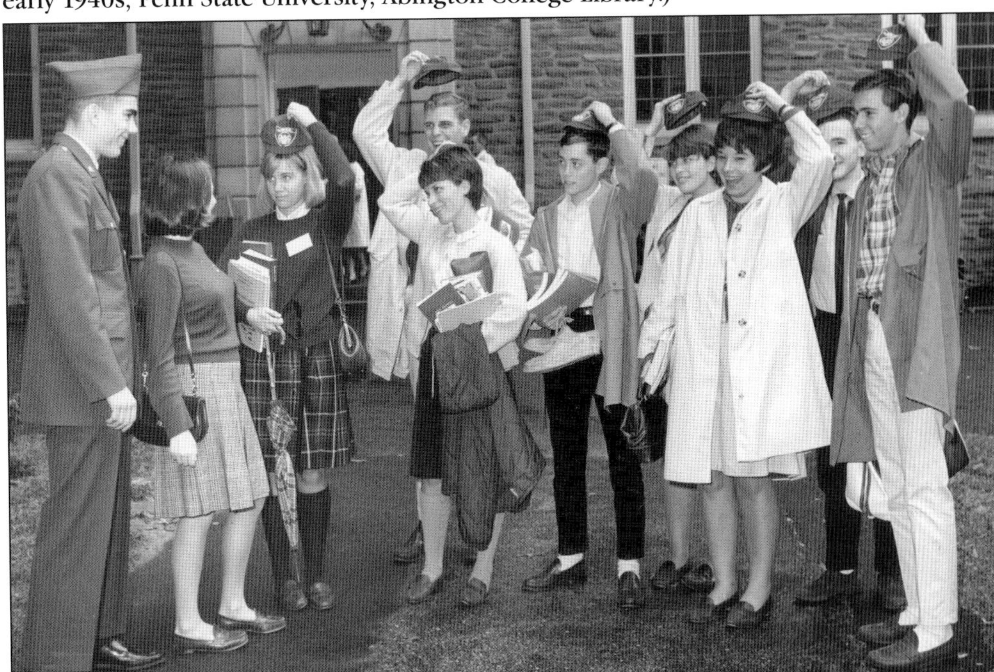

In 1959, the same year that Penn State Ogontz broke a national record by squeezing 51 male students into a Volkswagen, freshmen are seen observing newly initiated campus rituals, including wearing "dinks" and name tags and chanting school regulations, songs, and cheers on demand. (The Ogontz School Archives, 1959, Penn State University, Abington College Library.)

Ogontz Center News

Vol. 1 No. 1

FALL IS BUSTIN' OUT ALL OVER

We've been tripping over carpenters, electricians, plasterers, painters, ladders, boards, tool-boxes, saw-horses, typewriters cluttering the second floor of Sutherland Hall.

The Physics and Electrical Engineering labs have risen from the Sutherland catacombs to 222 and 224. Room 223, formerly an office, is now the supply room for these labs. The Biology lab has expanded itself out of the Science Building (where there is now another classroom) into 232-4 Sutherland. Classes are going on in these three labs, although they are still unpainted and lack new work benches, wiring for direct or indirect current, and a special wiring unit for heavy-duty motors and electronics work. And rooms 204 and 205, being battered into a lecture hall seating 100 people, will be ready October 8, three weeks after we jammed the hall, every hour on the hour, hoping no teacher would show up, then sadly trooping over to the well-ventilated Log Cabin.

Alterations in Hillcrest have moved a staff family from the first to the second floor, and have given them a new kitchen. The first floor has been converted into one large classroom, a music studio, and a faculty office. The day classes began, at first no one could find 101 Hillcrest, and then two classes reported at the same hour. The two handsome upstairs cats, since meowndering into Speech 200, have been attending pretty regularly; but according to the instructor, Mrs. Lowell Boorse, "Neither has given any speeches yet."

New painting and lighting brighten the men's locker room and the swimming pool, and the once dark and lonely path around the playing field toward the Student Union is now well lighted. Trees have been cleared for the new parking lot, and the grading and grass planting on the buffer strips have been done. The trees and shrub

(Cont'd on P.5)

ORIENTATION WEEK

Sweet, motherly D-Day!

After furiously filling out dozens of cards, forms, and other immortal documents, I was told to run down to the dining room to work out my schedule, but unfortunately 200 students were ahead of me. Finally admitted to heaven, in the form of the dining room, I found most of my sections filled, and I ran from table to table signing up for anything being sold. I wondered if I shouldn't surrender and go looking for a good job.

Then physicals, book-buying, club-joining, campus-mapping, car-pooling, finding out the truth about R.O.T.C.!

And now classes--when do we sleep?

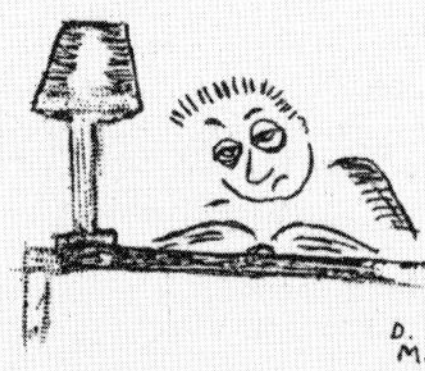

FOOTBALL

Sports writers agree that Penn State has good ends. Four wingmen have letters; three others are experienced. Starters will be Paul North and Jack Farls, from last year's team, backed up by Ron Markiewicz and Les Walters. But Romeo Panozzo and Jim Caldwell are pushing hard for a position.

The Blue and White expect to lean heavily on quarterback Milt Plum's passes to the ends. Captain Sam Valentine is left guard.

(Cont'd on P. 4)

Here is the first page of the first issue of the *Ogontz Center News*, one of the many incarnations of the campus newspaper following the heady, steady stream of *Ogontz Mosaics*. The *Mosaic* was generally published six times a year from its inception in 1884 until its robust final issue of 60 pages in July 1950. Although the first student paper published at Penn State Ogontz in 1950 was a glossy affair called the *Penn Statement*, the *Ogontz Center News* was a mimeographed weekly paper available at convenient locations on campus every Friday. The paper professes, in the 1964 edition of "Ogontz Campus Life: A Student Handbook," that "[f]reedom of the press is not only an ideal, but a practice at Ogontz." Like the front page of its campus counterpart the *Lion's Roar* nearly 41 years later (1997), the lead story reports on campus changes and renovations, including the new physics and electrical engineering labs that "have risen from the Sutherland catacombs to [rooms] 222 and 224." (The Ogontz School Archives, September 28, 1956, Penn State University, Abington College Library.)

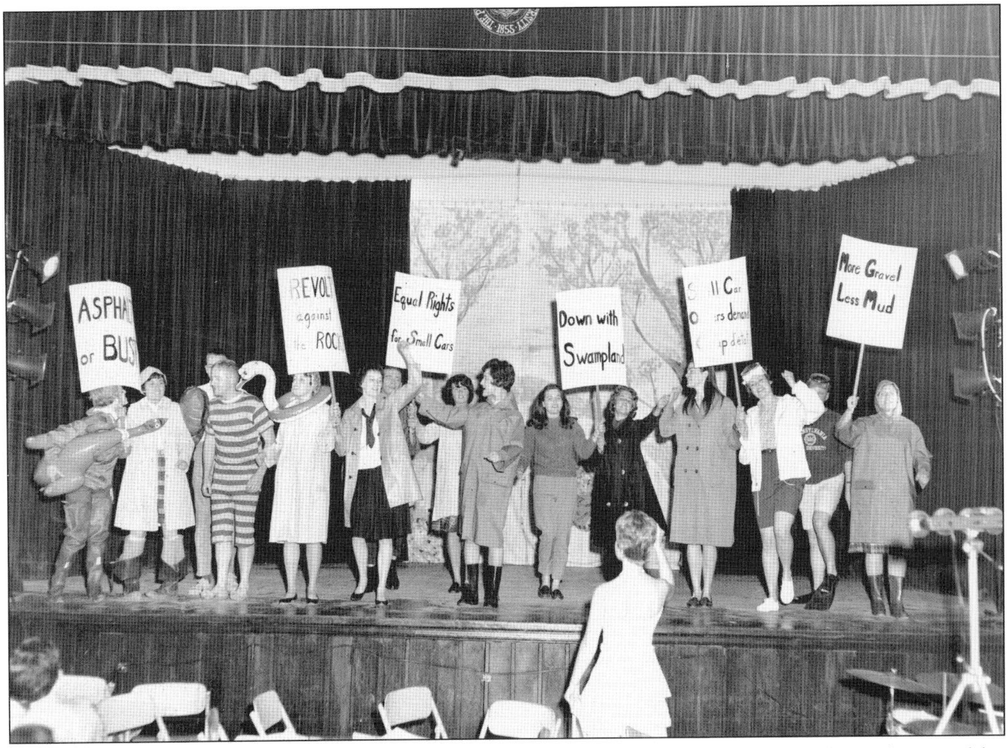

Freedom of speech was clearly afoot in this scene from a student/faculty show directed by drama teacher Marian Herbert. Judging by the placards brandished by the cast, it is clear that the issue of parking has not yet been resolved. (The Ogontz School Archives, 1963, Penn State University, Abington College Library.)

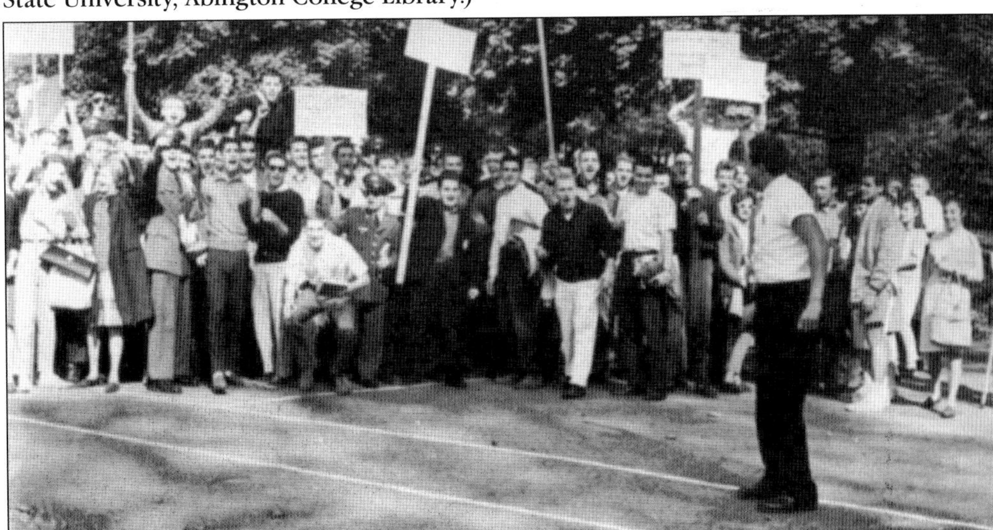

Although the signs cannot be easily read, this Penn State Ogontz rally sometime in the 1960s might not be related to parking. In 1969, four hundred Ogontz students, faculty, and staff participated in the national antiwar moratorium, a one-day boycott that featured speakers, folksingers, and poetry readings. (The Ogontz School Archives, 1960s, Penn State University, Abington College Library.)

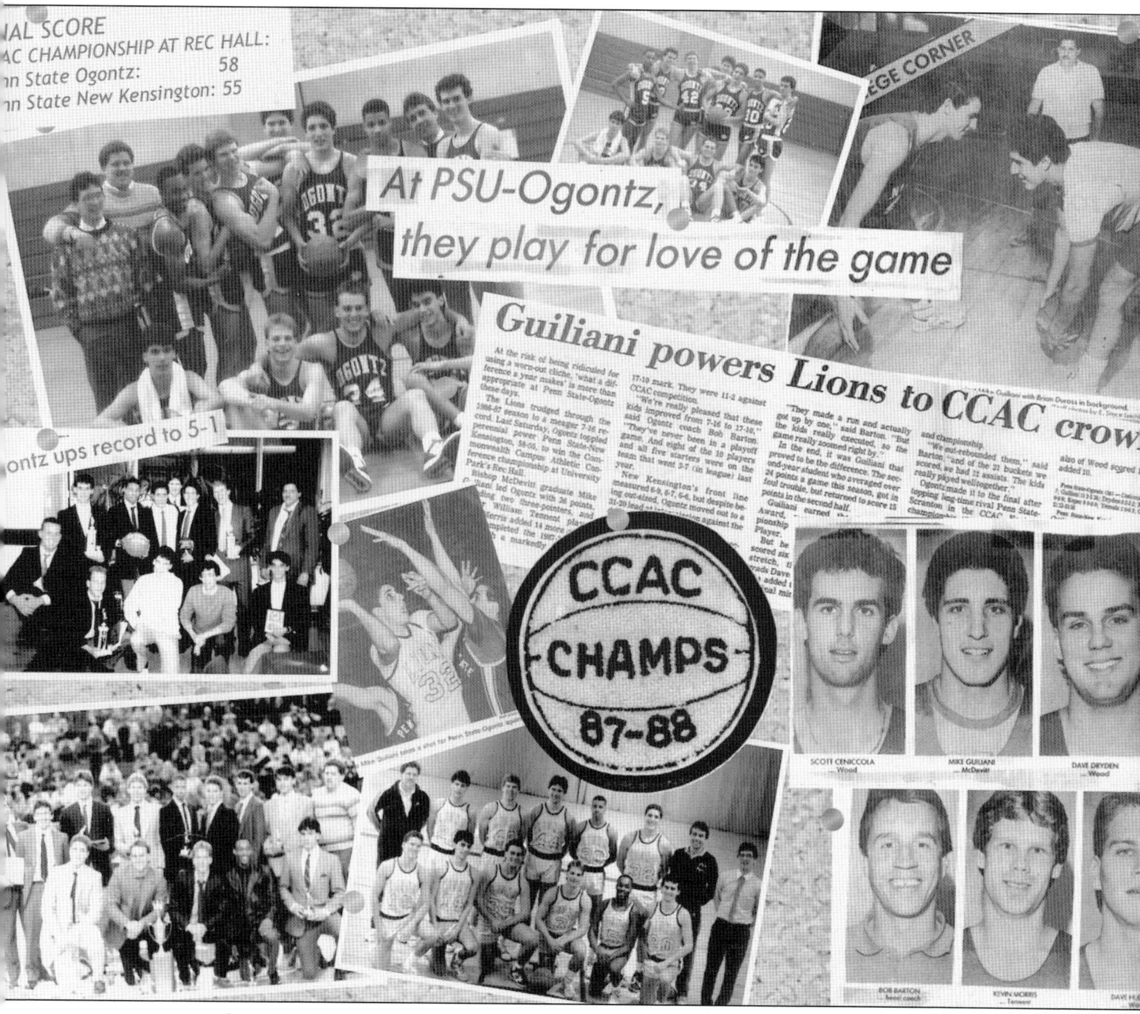

One year after the Ogontz Lions suffered through a disastrous 7-16 record, the 1987–1988 squad roared back to life, defeating perennial hoops power Penn State–New Kensington 58-55 to win the CCAC (Commonwealth Campus Athletic Conference) championship in a hard-fought game at University Park's Rec Hall. Bishop McDevitt graduate Mike Giuliani led the Lions with 26 points. Head coach Bob Barton said "the kids really executed, so the game really zoomed right by." Framed in the Hillcrest Building, this collage is a testament to the college's pride in its varsity men's basketball team. (The Ogontz School Archives, 1988, Penn State University, Abington College Library.)

In the thick of the presidential campaign of 1996, first lady Hillary Clinton paid the campus a visit. Although her appearance was billed as a talk on education, the placards below the stage and the backdrop promoting her husband, Pres. Bill Clinton, and Vice Pres. Al Gore were clear signs that this was politics as usual. Still, the first lady appeared to be enjoying the adulation of the crowd, much as she did during the heated presidential campaign of 2016, as she sought the Democratic nomination for president. Onstage with Clinton (below, second from left) was Joe Hoeffel, a former member of the Pennsylvania House of Representatives who was seeking election to the US House of Representatives for the 13th District, representing eastern Montgomery County and Northeast Philadelphia. For the record, the Clinton/Gore ticket won that election, whereas Hoeffel had to wait until 1999 to take his seat in the US House. A crowd of more than 2,000 cheered Clinton as she promoted her husband's education agenda and urged the audience to participate in the political process. (Both, the Ogontz School Archives, 1996, Penn State University, Abington College Library.)

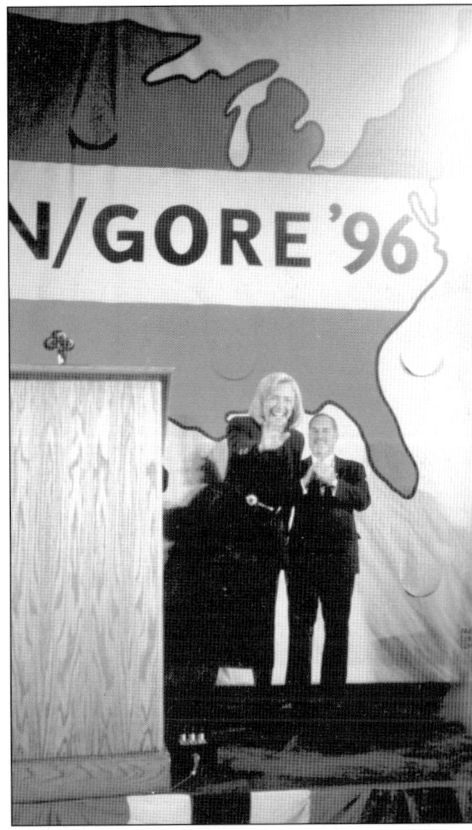

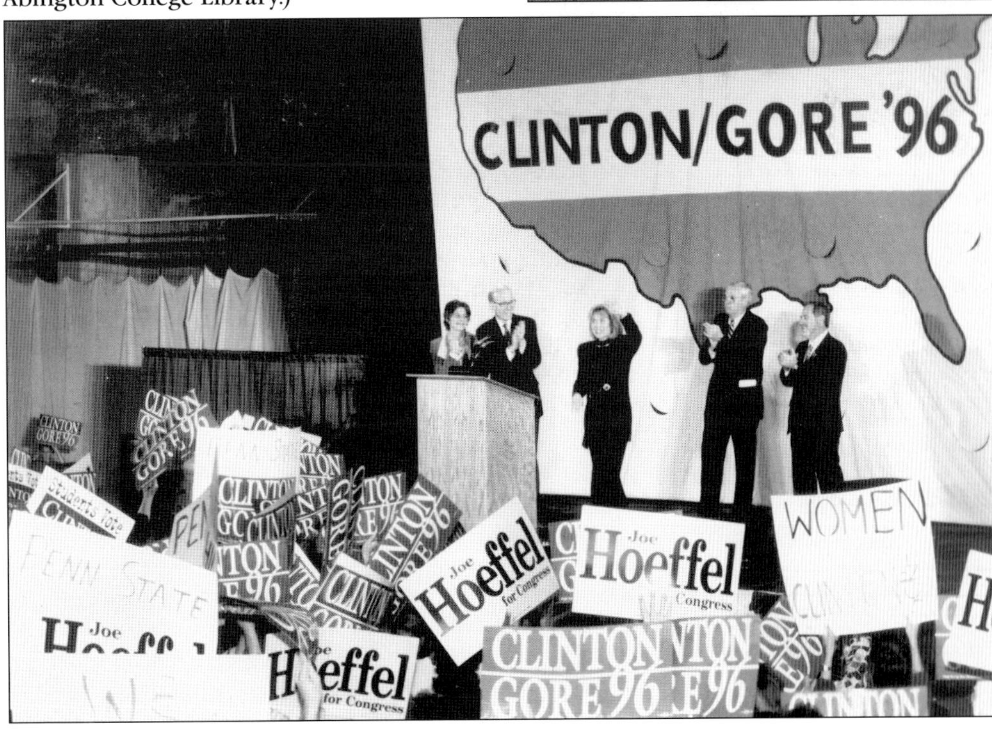

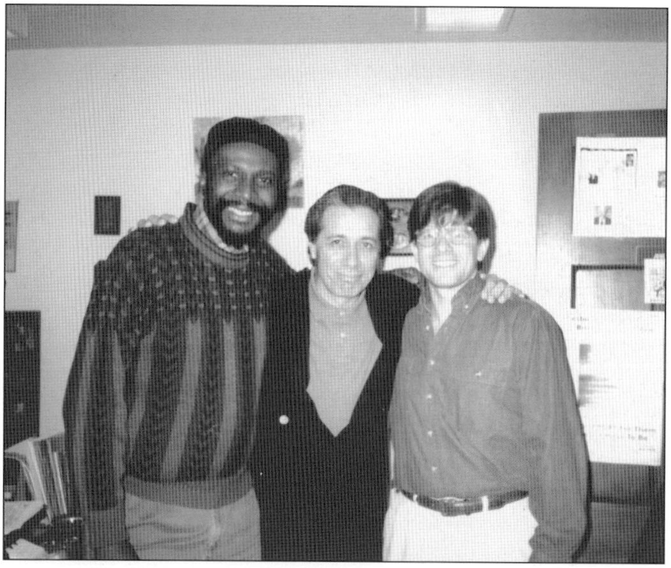

Actor Edward James Olmos (center, with Morris Jenkins [left] and Bill Geary) visited Penn State Abington in September 1997 to stress the importance of education and being an activist for good causes. His message is that "we all have a choice about where life takes us." Olmos received an Academy Award nomination for Best Actor for his role in *Stand and Deliver* (1988). (The Ogontz School Archives, 1997, Penn State University, Abington College Library.)

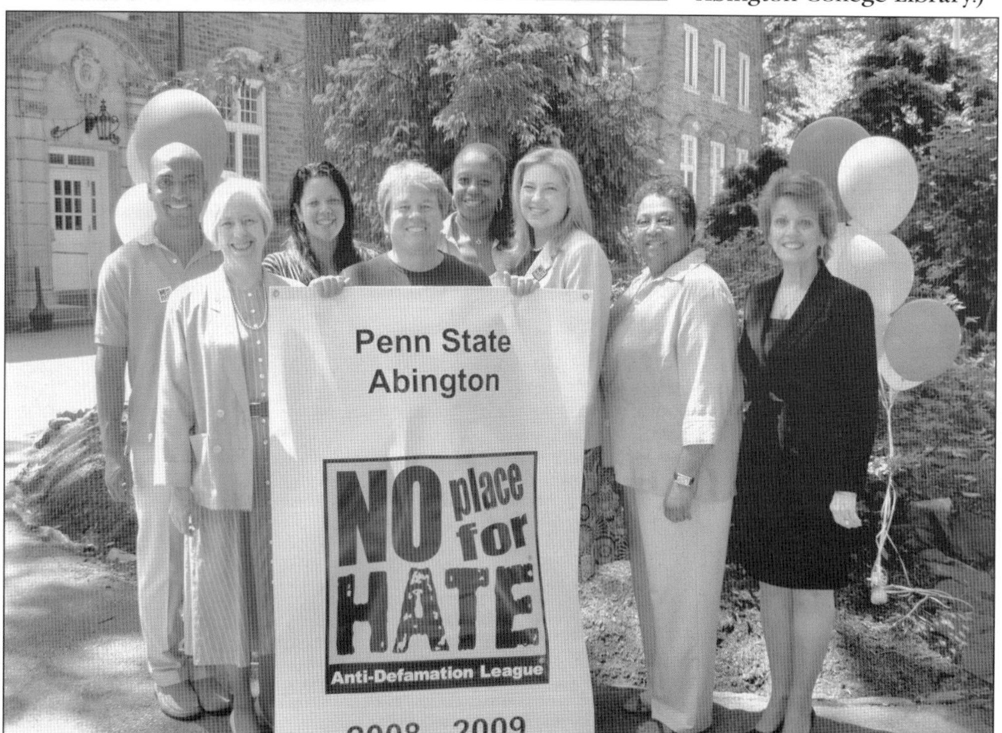

Standing behind a banner proclaiming that Penn State Abington is a No Place for Hate college—it was the first in the country to be so designated by the Anti-Defamation League—are, from left to right, director of intercultural affairs José Rodriguez, chancellor emerita Dr. Karen Wiley Sandler, assistant director of student life Tracy Reed, former athletic director Karen Weaver, director of admissions Latanya Moore, Anti-Defamation League representative Lisa Stewart, former EOP (Educational Opportunity Program) officer Yvonne Love, and Career Development Center director Carol DeBunda. (University Relations Department, 2009, Penn State Abington.)

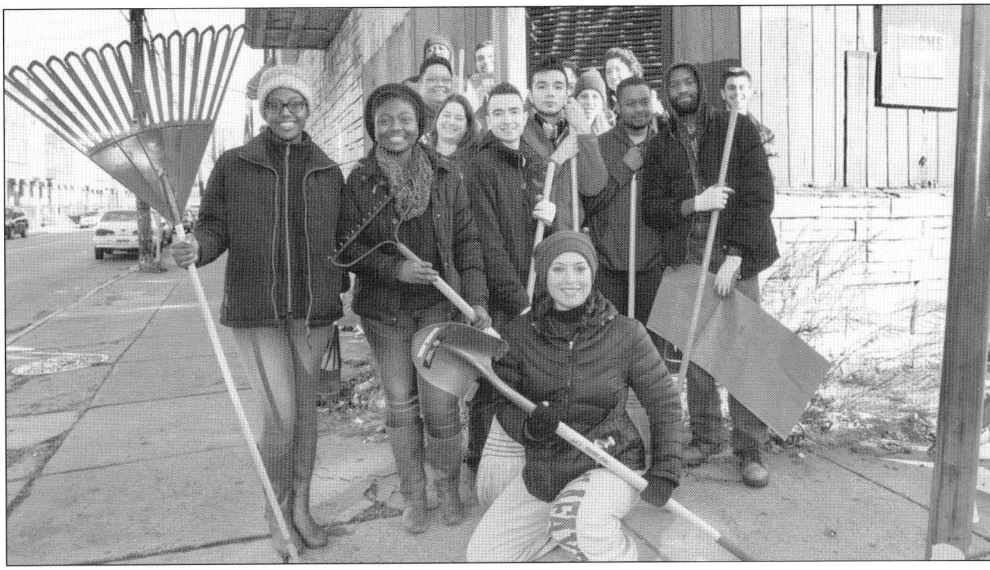

Volunteerism is the norm for students at Penn State Abington, who take pride in their ethic of service as they work toward making a difference in challenged communities. So it was during the Martin Luther King Jr. Day of Service in January 2015, when more than a dozen students joined 200 volunteers at a neighborhood cleanup in North Philadelphia. (University Relations Department, Penn State Abington.)

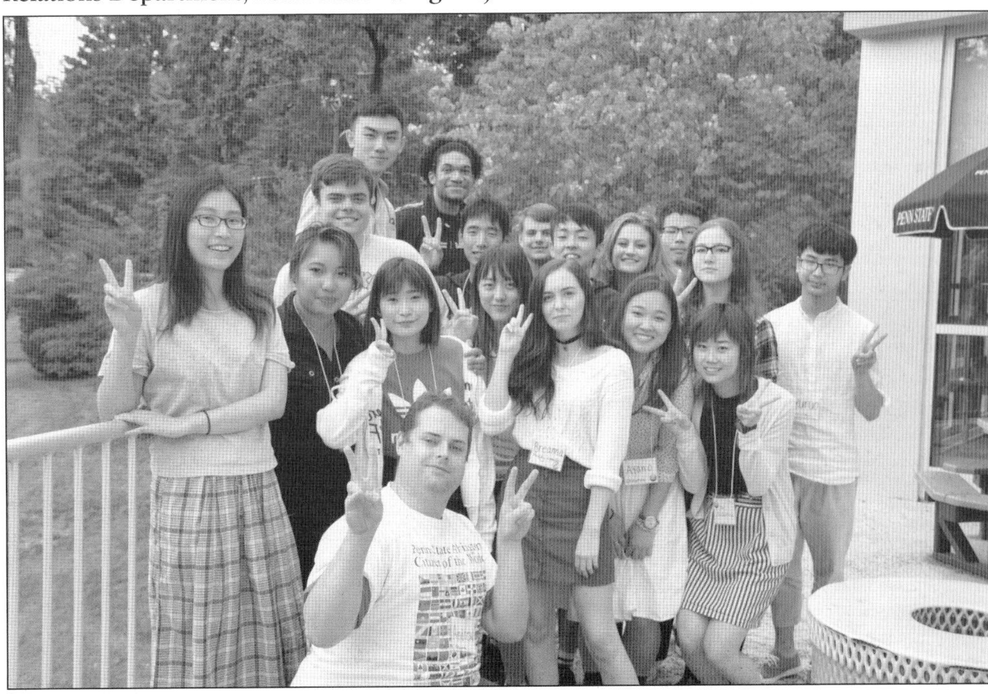

Penn State Abington's Global Buddies join Japanese students from Seinan Gakuin University in a gesture of peace in 2015. The Japanese students, who visited the college for a two-week intensive academic program, said they were most impressed with the level of interaction between the professors and students at Penn State Abington, a college with an acclaimed Global Studies program. (University Relations Department, Penn State Abington.)

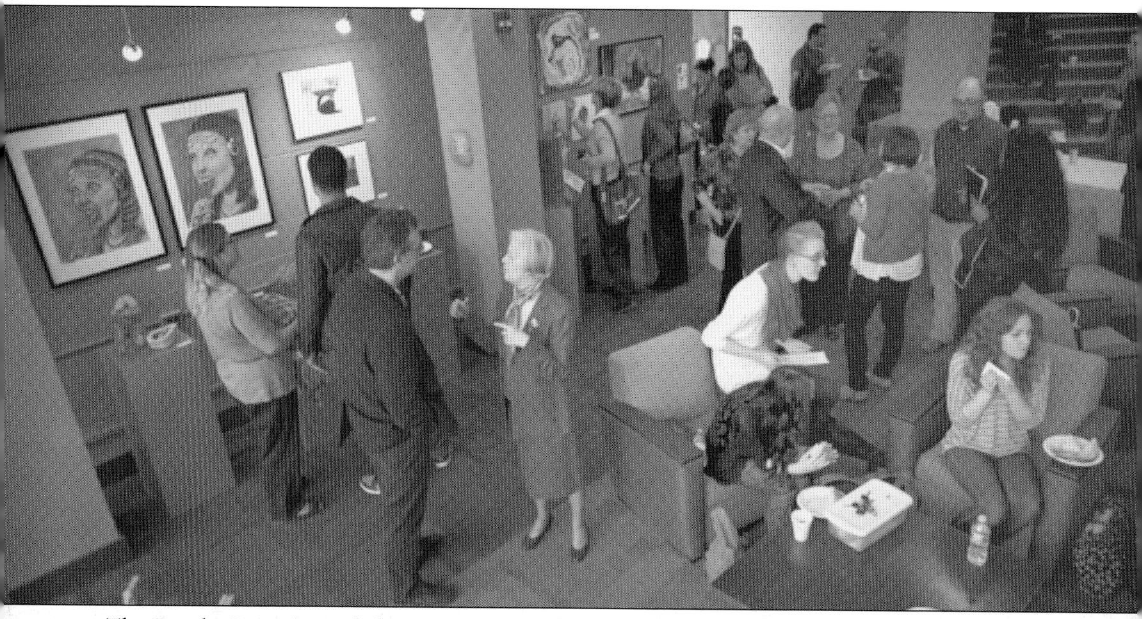

The Bertha Lear Art Exhibition, pictured in 2015, features sculptures, paintings, drawings, ceramics, photography, printmaking, and new media work by student artists of Penn State Abington. Founded by alumnus Robert Lear (a 1967 graduate in business) and his wife in memory of his mother, whose passion was art, the Bertha Lear Art Exhibition Program Endowment supports this annual program, by which students have the opportunity to share their works of art with the community and compete for a recognition award. (University Relations Department, Penn State Abington.)

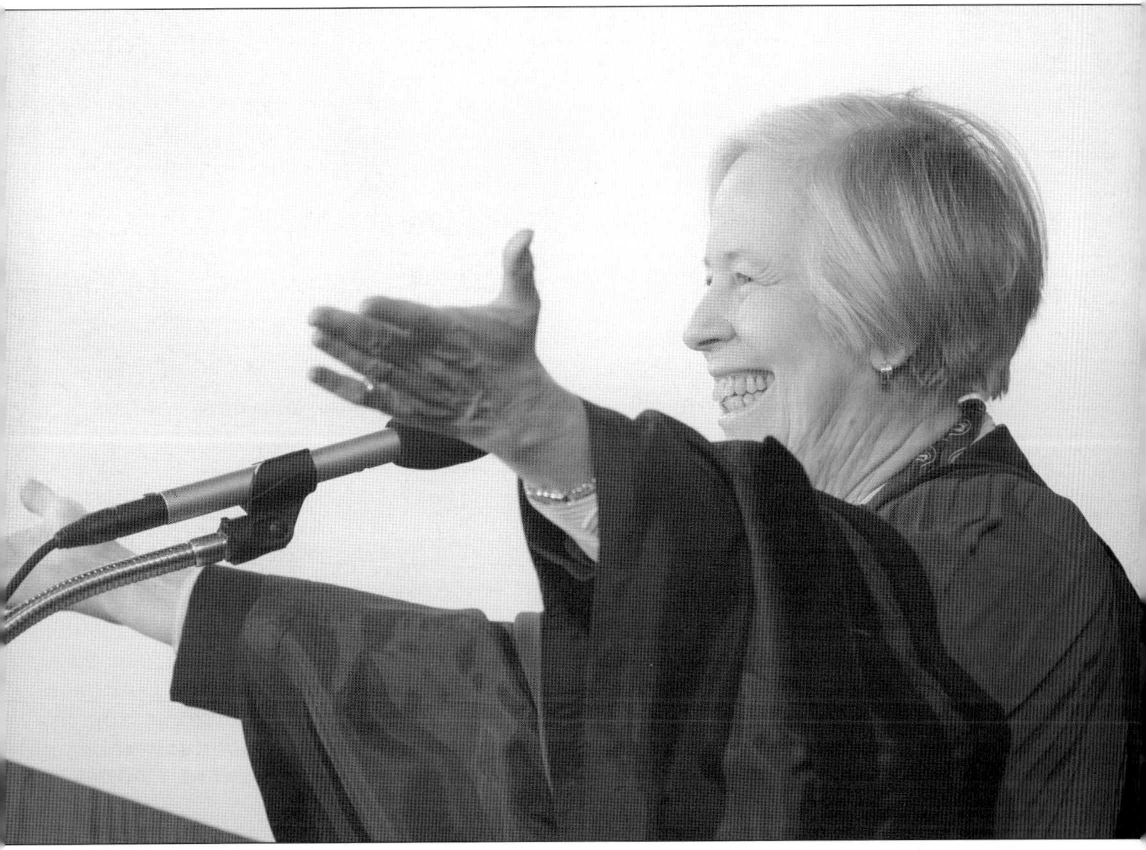

The sincere exuberance on her face says it all, as chancellor emerita Dr. Karen Wiley Sandler greets and congratulates the graduating class of 2014. Dr. Judith Newman, a longtime member of the Penn State Abington faculty, feels she speaks for many at the close-knit college when she says, "I love Dr. Sandler's personal leadership style. She has taken us through some difficult times and held us up. There's a resilience here that I love. Under her leadership, Penn State Abington has become an attractive four-year degree-granting global institution close to Philadelphia that is remarkably diverse and goes out of its way to assist students who have special needs," and balances Penn State University's emphasis on public research with a passion for teaching. Dr. Sandler retired at the end of the 2015–2016 academic year. She had served Penn State Abington for nearly a quarter of a century since she was hired as the college's first female chief executive officer in 1994. (Photograph by Dan Johnson, University Relations Department, Penn State Abington.)